THE
BUSINESS
OF
CHANGING
THE WORLD

THE BUSINESS OF CHANGING THE WORLD

HOW BILLIONAIRES, TECH DISRUPTERS,
AND SOCIAL ENTREPRENEURS ARE TRANSFORMING
THE GLOBAL AID INDUSTRY

RAJ KUMAR

COFOUNDER OF **devex**

BEACON PRESS, BOSTON

Beacon Press
Boston, Massachusetts
www.beacon.org

Beacon Press books
are published under the auspices of
the Unitarian Universalist Association of Congregations.

22 21 20 19   8 7 6 5 4 3 2 1

This book is printed on acid-free paper that meets the uncoated paper
ANSI/NISO specifications for permanence as revised in 1992.

Text design and composition by Kim Arney

Library of Congress Cataloging-in-Publication Data
Names: Kumar, Raj, author.
Title: The business of changing the world : how billionaires,
tech disruptors, and social entrepreneurs are transforming
the global aid industry / Raj Kumar.
Description: Boston : Beacon Press, [2019] | Includes bibliographical
references and index.
Identifiers: LCCN 2018045841 (print) | LCCN 2018051388 (ebook) |
ISBN 9780807059708 (ebook) | ISBN 9780807059579 (hardcover : alk. paper)
Subjects: LCSH: Philanthropists. | Humanitarianism. | Economic assistance. |
International relief. | Social entrepreneurship.
Classification: LCC HV25 (ebook) | LCC HV25 .K86 2019 (print) |
DDC 361.7/4—dc23
LC record available at https://lccn.loc.gov/2018045841

For Dr. A. H. Somjee, my uncle born fifty years before me to the day, who opened my eyes to global development and still does.

For my father Mohan Kumar, who supported some nontraditional career choices and made it possible for me to launch Devex.

For aid workers and development professionals everywhere. And for kids living in extreme poverty—may theirs be the last generation.

CONTENTS

PROLOGUE

An Enduring Gift

AS A KID IN INDIA, long before I began covering the global aid industry, I saw a lot of poverty. I remember one childhood experience when I was seven and my sister, Sona, was nine. We were on the beach in Kanyakumari, the windblown southern tip of the country. Two girls about our age were spying us from a distance. This was not unusual. American kids with an Indian father and a Jewish American mother, we had light skin that in those days made us a marvel in many parts of the country. This time those two young girls conferred and then, smiling broadly, suddenly ran up to us. From the way they were dressed, it was obvious to us even then that they were extremely poor.

The older one pulled something from beneath a tattered sari fold: it was an orange. A gift. For these sisters, girls who may not have had a proper meal that day or even that week, this orange was clearly a prized possession. Something moved them to want to cross a divide, to share what little they had with two advantaged children with clean clothes and shoes and full bellies. Once they deposited it in our hands, they merrily skipped off.

This made an impression on us—an experience from 1982 that's still fresh for Sona and me—but it took until adulthood to understand why. We had seen so much destitution when we would visit India—mothers pressing their naked babies against car windows in traffic to beg for money, thousands of people defecating along the train tracks—but this was different.

Here was a moment in time, frozen like a transparent image so we could look through it from both sides and see what our own lives could have been like had we been born to different circumstances. It was a chance to see the humanity in all people, no matter their hardships, and a gut-wrenching realization that no one should be forced to live in such severe poverty.

■ ■ ■ ■ ■

It was August 1999, I was twenty-three years old, and I didn't know what to do with my life. So I did what other privileged young people do in those circumstances—I went to graduate school.

It's not that I needed a career. I already had one and was doing well at it. Starting as a volunteer in the White House press office while I was still an undergraduate student at Georgetown University's School of Foreign Service, I had bounced around working on campaigns ultimately landing as political director at a consulting firm in Manhattan. Penn Schoen & Berland was a Democratic powerhouse with clients such as Bill and Hillary Clinton and Michael Bloomberg. But I was restless.

With some Georgetown friends, I helped to start a financial media dot-com called SmartPortfolio. We ended up selling it to TheStreet .com, a much larger competitor. Nonetheless, I knew deep down that sharing stock tips with investors and campaign advice with wealthy candidates, while intellectually challenging and interesting, wasn't what I really wanted to do with my life.

I left the dot-com and political campaigning, hoping a master's degree in public policy from Harvard's Kennedy School would help me find my way to a career that had something to do with making things better for poor people in poor countries. What would that be? I had no idea.

Right from the start, that question consumed me. My wife, Maria Teresa Kumar, whom I met standing in line to register for classes on the very first day, reminds me that I would walk around with a yellow legal pad for jotting down ideas. I took a course taught by Brian Atwood, who had just left the Clinton administration, where he headed the US Agency for International Development (USAID), and began to get a slightly clearer picture of the fuzzy foreign aid and charity landscape. I would pester my best friend and roommate, Kami Dar, who was working at a major USAID contractor, with questions about how the aid industry really worked.

It turns out not understanding the aid industry was an advantage. I asked people doing global development work a lot of basic questions and was surprised by things that seemed natural to them.

For one thing, I learned that those working in the aid industry didn't see themselves as working in an industry at all. They were dedicated to a specific issue, such as health or education, or they worked inside the bubble of a particular institution—for example, UNICEF or Catholic Relief Services. They were doing important work but were disconnected from what was happening outside their own orbits.

For another, I found that there was no independent media outlet for aid industry professionals, as there was for professionals in law or finance or education or politics. Nor was there an easy way to get connected to the industry—to know who was doing what, to research employers or find funding opportunities, to feel a part of a community of mission-driven professionals. When I asked about finding a job in global development, the university career center pointed me to a slim newsprint publication, and classmates suggested I go to Washington and attend cocktail parties to network.

I was just a newcomer, but suddenly it became clear to me: here was one of the world's most consequential industries, stuck in the dark ages.

By 2000, Kami and I—soon joined by Jason McNaboe and Alan Robbins, two lifelong friends, with support from Brian Atwood as the chairman of our advisory board—had hit upon the outlines of an idea. We would try to knit together this global industry by building an online community.

Almost immediately our online startup, Devex, took up all my time, as fledgling companies do. When I should have been doing homework, I was emailing with potential investors and punching up our business plan. With the lure of internet-era stock options, I somehow was able to convince two professionals in their fifties, both experienced managers of thousands of employees, to take over as our CEO and COO, respectively. I can still remember one of them feigning composure when he visited our office and realized it was my apartment. Not surprisingly, the arrangement didn't work out.

I now faced a decision: stick with school or plunge into the business. I told Joe Nye, who was then dean of the Kennedy School and already famous for having coined the term "soft power," all about Devex, and he—surprisingly to me—urged me to drop out and pursue it. Hadn't I come to the school for the very purpose of finding my own way into a global development career? Harvard wasn't going anywhere, and I would be welcome back at any time. As I told my shocked parents, who was I to question the wisdom of the dean?

From the start, we considered Devex a business with a social mission. We tried to say "social enterprise," but no one had any idea what we meant in those days. That's a big reason why nearly all the investors I met, and literally every single venture capital firm I spoke to, gave us a flat "no." If it weren't for friends and family, we would never have gotten off the ground.

We moved Devex operations to Washington, DC, the epicenter of the aid industry and home to USAID, the World Bank, and some of the biggest international nonprofits in the world. With little money to spare, four of us were sleeping in a two-bedroom apartment, and four more joined us during the day to work there. We were true believers who expected immediate success, but it actually took quite a while to get traction. It would be several more years before we had an office that wasn't my apartment.

Some who had been working in global development for decades thought we were a fad. Some questioned the need for a marketplace for talent and funding in our industry. Others told me they got all the aid industry news they needed from the occasional coverage in the *Washington Post* or the *Economist*, or, more often, from their personal network of friends and contacts.

Our motto from day one was "Do Good. Do It Well." By this we mean that it's not enough to try to do good, as the $200 billion aid industry certainly does. Instead, we need to make the aid industry more efficient and effective. To get there, our journalism highlights what works, but also calls out what doesn't. We help professionals, especially from developing countries, get jobs on aid projects in their own countries. We match up organizations with funding opportunities and maintain the largest database of grants, tenders, and other funding information. We try to make sense of an important but complicated industry.

What started in the proverbial college dorm room in 2000 had morphed, by 2007, into a full-fledged media platform—the *Washington Post* compared us that year to a "Bloomberg-style platform for the aid industry." Today Devex has around 150 full-time staff around the world, with an audience of more than a million aid-industry professionals. We are invited to moderate sessions in Davos, help recruit aid workers for the World Food Programme, and advise Fortune 100 corporate foundations how to be more effective. Our news has been cited in congressional testimony, used to inform deliberations in the European Parliament, and included in briefing books for prime ministers and corporate CEOs. Everywhere I travel, from Ethiopia to Myanmar to Colombia, I meet aid workers who say they found their job, funded their NGO, or get their news from Devex. We've become a kind of connective tissue for the aid industry.

For me personally, my role as president and editor in chief of Devex involves getting to know an array of remarkable people—from global leaders to courageous professionals working on the front lines of aid initiatives. I've been a fly on the wall in some of the most rarefied meetings with finance ministers and billionaire philanthropists, and shared my own views before audiences around the world. Still, I can't shake the image of those girls and their gift. I can't help but wonder what more this world of aid in which I'm now so enmeshed can do for the hundreds of millions of people still living in extreme poverty.

In this book, I try to distill an often-complex field filled with acronyms and jargon into a clearer picture of how the aid industry actually operates, and where it's headed. I share what I've seen up close: that seventy years after the Marshall Plan and the birth of institutions like UNICEF, the World Bank, and Oxfam, the aid industry is at a pivotal moment. Billionaire philanthropists, technology disruptors, and social entrepreneurs are revolutionizing this industry in ways that have implications for all of us.

Our members and readers at Devex are professionals working on global development, global health, humanitarian aid, and sustainability. It's only natural that I would have them in mind as I wrote this book. But the aid industry is rapidly expanding, and I made a special effort to write for corporate executives, investors, and entrepreneurs who may not be aid industry insiders but need to understand where they fit in. Public policy and foreign policy enthusiasts will find much of what this book tackles relevant and, I hope, new.

This is also a book designed for students. I often thought of myself as a graduate student as I wrote this book, and how much I could have benefited from going beyond the theory to really understanding in plain terms how the aid industry actually works.

Finally, every one of us—taxpayers, voters, donors—has a stake in how this story turns out. We are witnessing the end of aid as we know it. What comes next is up to us.

INTRODUCTION
The End of Charity

AT HARVARD'S KENNEDY SCHOOL IN 2000, the year we started Devex there, the atmosphere was heady. The internet had arrived and was turning the world upside down. That year two Harvard Business School professors, Michael E. Porter and Jan W. Rivkin, published a paper entitled "Industry Transformation," in which they argued that the internet was transforming businesses in many sectors in a revolutionary way.[1] Indeed, five of the ten most valuable companies in the world today were formed during the internet revolution.

At the same time, on the other side of the Atlantic in West Africa, a ten-year-old girl named Jaha Dukureh was grappling with the fact that she had already been promised to a much older man in New York. At one week old she had undergone a ceremonial brutality common in her country, the Gambia: her labia and clitoris were cut off in what is known nowadays as female genital mutilation, or FGM. Two hundred million women and girls in the world today have undergone this horror, which, among other things, increases the chances of death during childbirth. Now, she was soon to join the four hundred million women aged twenty to forty-nine alive today who were forced to marry while still girls, which meant, among other things, she wouldn't get an education.[2]

This internet era we saw budding in 2000 ultimately brought the decoding of the human genome, the development of artificial intelligence we can speak to in our homes, and such prosperity that well over two thousand people around the world are billionaires in US dollars.[3] And yet, today 10 percent of all people on earth are still living in "absolute" or "extreme" poverty.[4] Those adjectives are arbitrary but important. They're an attempt to describe people who are so destitute their day-to-day survival is in doubt. Some economists refer to people in these circumstances as the "ultrapoor."

In the country of Dukureh's youth, the Gambia, half the people live in extreme poverty.[5] In mine, India, it's one-quarter of the people. Where there is extreme poverty, it's not simply about not having enough income. Economists might measure poverty in dollars and cents, but it's actually the sum of many interconnected deprivations too awful to put a price on. Not having enough to eat is one, sure, but another aspect of poverty is the girl with no say in when and whom she marries, how many children she has, or whether or not she gets an education. These injustices don't just make people poor, they keep people poor.

An entire industry dedicated to ending that kind of poverty has been growing for well over half a century. The names are famous: UNICEF, World Bank, Save the Children, Bono, Bill and Melinda Gates, Malala. The industry writ large is enormous: each year more than $200 billion is dedicated to aid for the poorest people and countries.[6]

Initially, the booming aid industry had been slower to adapt than other industries had been. This is probably because the transformational triggers that Porter and Rivkin identified—disruptive new technologies, "a change in what customers need or want," and new regulations—were not in place.[7] Today, they are. The new aid industry has the kind of ambitions we usually associate with Silicon Valley disruptors like Uber, Facebook, and Tesla. A confluence of related technology trends—increased internet connectivity, biometric identification, and mobile banking—is making it possible to reach the world's poor directly and get real-time results about what's working and what isn't. Aid recipients are adopting the expectations of customers while donors expect results, not just feel-good information about how much money was spent on a school or how much medicine was distributed.

We are on the precipice of a new global aid industry, one that is undergoing massive transformation in three fundamental ways. First, there is a shift away from the dominance of a few big foreign aid agencies and established philanthropies into an era of more open competition. There are new players, including hard-charging billionaire philanthropists;

for-profit businesses and investors aiming to make money and do good; "pure" social enterprises, "buy one, give one" companies; online crowd-funding sites; and many small startup initiatives working throughout the world. And there are new partnerships, some with major corporations, pension funds, and ordinary investors. The aid industry—formerly a closed club of mainly expat professionals—is fast becoming a global industry in which startups and social entrepreneurs challenge the power and influence of foreign aid agencies in Washington, London, and Brussels.

Second, there is a shift from a wholesale model to a retail model of aid. The wholesale mind-set envisioned aid projects as the main "unit of activity." These often large-scale, multiyear projects are designed to reach entire populations over a set period of time within a particular budget. They are structured around identifying a problem that a population is facing, designing a solution, and implementing that solution through a cascade of contractors, subcontractors, grantees, and independent consultants—perhaps checking in at the midpoint and end of the project to monitor its actual effectiveness. Today's technology and connectivity make it possible to do something very different. Now the individual in need, not the project, is becoming the main unit of activity. The aid industry today is increasingly targeting funds and tailoring programs to specific individuals and communities. These programs are set up like a retail business would be. They're designed to react and iterate based on customer feedback. This is part of a major shift toward seeing aid recipients as "customers" of aid instead of nameless, voiceless "beneficiaries."

Third, this growing focus on figuring out and rewarding what works is unleashing creative new approaches to solving the world's biggest problems, including deeply rooted injustices like child marriage that are so linked to extreme poverty. These go well beyond the economic analysis typically associated with aid projects to include behavioral science, human-centered design, and systems thinking. Delivering results for the world's poorest people now entails a new way of understanding poverty, hunger, disease, lack of education, and other societal ills—and what to do about them.

There is another, harder to pin down, shift going on—in attitude. The global aid industry has long operated with an underlying assumption that the most important thing is to have good intentions. This is, after all, a kind of charity. The World Bank lobby has a sign that says, in jumbo font, "Our Dream Is a World Free of Poverty." USAID's bags of grain delivered to hungry refugees say, "From the American People."

For as long as people have been giving money and help to strangers, after all, they have felt driven by the intention to do good and, often, to take credit for it. Even the word "charity" derives from the Greek word *agape*, which refers to unconditional love for one's fellow human beings.

The concept of charity, in other words, has been largely about the *giver*. It's "our" dream and it's "from" us. It's a sign of "our" love: the good people who make a sacrifice to help others. When it's all about the sacrifice, not surprisingly the amount we give somehow equates with how much love we have for those in need and, ultimately, suggests how good we are. I attended Catholic school growing up, and I recall that when a local priest named Monsignor Cassidy visited my eighth-grade theology class he made this very point. True charity, he said, is about "giving from your want." In other words, giving so much it hurts.

This attitude is being turned on its head. In the new aid industry, giving is increasingly being evaluated not by the goodness of the intentions or the amount of money given but rather by results. Are fewer children stunted? Have more families become self-sustaining? How much good has actually been accomplished and for what cost?

Taken together, these changes are transforming the aid industry from an "old aid" model to a very different "new aid" approach.

Old aid said: give things away for free. *New aid* says: where it makes sense, give things away for free but do so in a targeted manner. Limit the time duration. Pay attention to market dynamics and the broader systems at play. Work to get local economies going on their own and to get people back to work.

Old aid said: come in from outside with the Big Idea. *New aid* says: ask local people what's holding them back. Listen to them. Then provide support for their own ideas, which are usually smaller, more incremental, and more realistic.

Old aid said: development is a project with a budget and a timeline. *New aid* says: development is a process. Build a business model that is self-sustaining, long-term, and can adapt based on shifting circumstances.

Old aid said: help the victim. *New aid* says: support the most powerful force for changing a person's life—him- or herself.

In 2015, the General Assembly of the United Nations endorsed the Sustainable Development Goals, a list of seventeen ambitious targets for the world, to be reached by the year 2030. At the top of the list, which was signed by 193 countries including the United States, is ending extreme poverty.[8] Other goals include eliminating hunger, radically improving human health, and reducing inequality and discrimination.

To some, these goals may sound quixotic, hyperbolic, unachievable. Really, in just a decade or so we're going to eradicate several diseases and end extreme poverty? These are, after all, challenges human beings have faced since the advent of our species. If we follow the approach of the traditional aid industry, the cynics may well be right. Just writing bigger checks for larger aid projects won't yield the kind of results humans have been waiting millennia to achieve. Even so, the new aid industry has largely taken these goals to heart and is working to eradicate specific diseases, dramatically improve nutrition, transform education and healthcare systems, and make extreme poverty a thing of the past. Could we possibly achieve these goals?

Consider the powerful new technologies and the tremendous wealth created in our time. Entire industries are being transformed before our eyes in what the World Economic Forum has termed the Fourth Industrial Revolution. Even the way we live day-to-day is changing. The aspiration to drive your own car is diminishing in favor of the convenience of on-demand transportation, which explains why Uber and Tesla are each worth as much as General Motors.[9] More than half of all Americans now get their news from Facebook, a new reality with concerning implications. And something as basic as going to the store is changing as e-commerce infiltrates everyday life. Amazon, with a market capitalization above a trillion dollars, is now more valuable than the next twenty-one American retailers combined, including such massive companies as Walmart, Target, Home Depot, and Costco.[10]

Ready or not, a similarly radical transformation is coming to the aid industry. As I will detail in this book, there's a tidal wave of new actors shaking up the way aid work is done.

Jaha Dukureh ultimately was forced to cross the ocean and marry at fifteen. But she escaped and argued her way into a New York City public high school, even without a parent to consent. Later she settled in Georgia, where she got a college degree, remarried, started a family, and founded a small nongovernmental organization (NGO) called Safe Hands for Girls. It's not exactly well-resourced or well-known. In one example she shared with me, Dukureh went back to the Gambia and borrowed a car. She drove around the country, attending all of the Gambian president's speeches and appearances until finally he agreed to meet with her. In 2015, her campaigning led the president to outlaw FGM.

How quickly the aid industry transforms and whether it leads to achieving the global goals will be up to grassroots leaders like Dukureh. It will also be up to aid industry professionals, voters and taxpayers who fund foreign aid, ordinary givers and billionaire philanthropists, corporate and nonprofit leaders, and, ultimately, all people affected by global poverty, pandemics, climate change, and human rights infringements. In other words, it's going to be up to you.

A CLOSED CLUB

From the colonial era, through the post–World War II period that brought the Marshall Plan and the creation of Cold War institutions like the World Bank, and all the way up until about the year 2000, what we now call the aid industry was a kind of monopoly. In technical terms, it was a *monopsony*—an entity that dominates a marketplace because it is the major *buyer* of certain goods and services.

In the days before social-impact investors and billionaire philanthropists began flooding the market, there were just a few major players in the aid industry. In the United States it was the government—more specifically, the foreign aid agency known as the US Agency for International Development (USAID). Established in 1961 by President John F. Kennedy, USAID's mission was to grant federal resources to help out other countries during humanitarian crises and to develop their economies, health systems, and agricultural sectors. (Pronunciation tip: insiders still refer to it as "yüs-aid"; newbies sound out the letters more, as in "you-s-aid.")

In the United Kingdom, the monopsony player was the Department for International Development (DFID), the UK's equivalent of USAID. Travel to the capitals of most rich countries and you will find an equivalent agency, each with its own acronym but essentially the same function.

Yes, there were other "buyers" involved, such as the Ford and Rockefeller foundations. They had money to spend, but they were drops in the ocean compared to the funds controlled by entities like USAID and the World Bank. Today the combined annual giving of these two famous philanthropies equals just 2 percent of USAID's yearly budget.[11]

The monopsony accomplished a lot of good but also created distortions in the aid industry. When there are just a few dominant entities dispensing all the money (technically an *oligopsony*), everyone who wants funding for a project has to conform to what the few funders want. There is no sense of healthy competition for ideas and approaches that comes from a more vibrant market. Imagine a world in which there are plenty of architects but only one person hiring them to build all the houses—pretty soon the buildings might all start to look the same. That's what was happening in the aid industry.

There were lots of nonprofit and for-profit organizations involved in executing aid initiatives. These included NGOs, which are typically nonprofit groups with skills in implementing charitable programs, such as CARE, Catholic Relief Services, and Oxfam. NGOs, along with consulting firms, engineering companies, and university based research and consulting groups were paid by DFID, USAID, EuropeAid, and similar foreign aid agencies to work in developing countries, but there wasn't much diversity in what they were paid to do. The customer is always right—especially when it's the dominant buyer in a monopsony—and these buyers usually had a definitive idea of the big problem they were addressing and the best solution for it. They even had a clear idea of the kind of person who should be hired to do the work, and sometimes even had a specific individual in mind.

Over time, many NGOs and companies structured their internal departments to mimic those at USAID or DFID or whatever organization was funding their projects. They sought to hire people who had knowledge of how the foreign aid agencies worked, their complex procurement rules, and their lingo. There was a great deal of pressure to match their work to the vagaries of government contracting.

Development work, for example, was organized into "projects," each with a set budget and schedule. Money not spent by the deadline would be forfeited. There was little wiggle room to redefine the problem or adapt solutions based on changing circumstances or knowledge gained on the ground.

Because these were government contracts, there were rules—sometimes written, sometimes not—that gave advantages to entities based in the donor country. As a result, most DFID contracts were awarded to British companies that engaged British citizens to do the work. And the same situation existed for the other wealthy donor countries, including France, Germany, Japan, the United States, and others.

The market structure was top down. The aid agencies with the money called the shots. This worked relatively well when newly independent countries—like the seventeen countries that shed colonial status in Africa in 1960—had few trained and experienced people running their governments and fewer local entities with expertise to manage development projects. But as governments of these countries steadily advanced, tens of thousands of their citizens earned graduate degrees and developed professional expertise. Domestic nonprofits and companies became more and more capable of implementing aid projects in their own countries. The big foreign aid agencies and the international organizations they hired to do the work, however, did not necessarily adjust their approach to the changes taking place in the countries they meant to help.

What had begun with the best of intentions in the post–World War II era and had done so much good—from the Green Revolution to humanitarian and health aid that's saved millions of lives—was becoming sclerotic. For all the real successes the industry could point to, the top-down market was leading to some serious failures too.

A prime example of the dangers of a monopolistic aid industry was the provision of American rice to feed impoverished Haitians starting in the 1990s. Rice is an important part of the Haitian diet, and the country once had a major domestic rice industry, accounting for 47 percent of its rice consumption in 1988.[12] But with free US rice flooding the market, two decades later Haiti was producing only 15 percent of its rice consumption.[13]

The gutting of this essential industry—and the impoverishment of thousands of farmers whose livelihoods depended on it—came about as the result of good intentions. Haiti is a poor country, and the United States wanted to help the hungry. The US also wanted to further some of its own economic interests, namely supporting American farmers, American agribusinesses, and American shippers.

Much of the damage was done during Bill Clinton's presidency. After honeymooning in Haiti with Hillary in 1975, Bill Clinton developed a strong personal connection to the island that he has maintained to this day. This was a case of good intentions obscuring a focus on results, and Clinton ultimately acknowledged the folly of the policy. Admirably, in 2010 he appeared before the US Congress to apologize for its harmful effects. "It may have been good for some of my farmers in Arkansas, but it has not worked," he said. "It was a mistake."[14]

Despite this lesson, similar policies continue under presidents of both parties. The US food aid program totals $2.8 billion per year, the largest such program in the world.[15] But what's known as the "cargo preference rule" requires that only US-flagged ships transport the food. The use of an old fleet of US vessels specifically for this purpose means shipping costs that are 46 percent higher than they would be if shipped at international competitive rates, and shipping times that can be up to fourteen weeks longer.[16] The net result is that 1.8 million fewer people get fed each year than might receive food if faster, cheaper vessels were used.[17]

In addition, because of rules that allow for monetization, or the practice of US NGOs taking American-made food donations and selling them in poor countries for cash, local markets are often undermined, as they were in Haiti.

What's more, the benefits that accrue to US producers are minuscule. US food aid accounts for less than 0.3 percent of the US agricultural market.[18] It is almost meaningless to American farmers. Yet, by one estimate, between forty thousand to fifty thousand children's lives could be saved if we stopped requiring the food to be "Made in the USA," stopped allowing it to be sold locally, and stopped requiring US vessels to ship it.[19]

A more practical, results-oriented approach would prioritize saving lives and creating sustainable domestic agricultural markets. Organizers may ship in food only at specific times of greatest necessity, such as at the very beginning of a crisis, and only when local sources of food are not available. They may provide local people with money or vouchers to buy food locally during a crisis. They may even buy food aid in the local market in order to help jump-start the domestic agricultural industry.

These are the kinds of ideas that could take hold and win out in a competitive market, but in one dominated by a single buyer, an ineffective and sometimes counterproductive approach like US food aid policy can continue for decades.

A POLITICAL INDUSTRY

When taxpayer funded foreign aid is so dominant, politics can become an important factor in how the aid industry operates. As we've seen, aid is not just about helping impoverished people overseas but also about domestic interests. The result is an industry attuned to avoiding political risks and obsessed with securing political support from voters and those in office. Sometimes that means using cumbersome contracting mechanisms that cut down the chances of corruption even if they're hugely expensive to implement. Other times it means tying foreign aid to an important domestic constituency like farmers or American businesses.

Making a case to taxpayers that all this charitable activity really adds to their family's security and economic opportunity is an essential tenet of how the aid industry functions. One of the few highly successful aid programs to come out of US involvement in Afghanistan, for example, was killed because of a minor error that connected to that broader narrative. The program funded the Afghan Ministry of Public Health to provide care to 90 percent of Afghanis at the remarkably low annual cost of just $4.50 per person. The results were stunning, especially in those difficult circumstances: life expectancy rose from forty-two to sixty-two years from 2004 to 2010, the biggest improvement in the world during that period.[20]

Nonetheless, the project was called into question and ultimately suspended because US auditors distrusted the Afghan ministry's accounting systems. They didn't allege corruption and the project's results were clearly exceptional, but nonetheless it was stopped. Accounting for every penny was more important than saving lives. This sentiment of mistrust is perhaps best captured by the late US senator Jesse Helms, who famously alleged that aid was going down "foreign rat holes."

Throughout the twentieth century, the aid industry was a tool of statecraft, and thus a point of debate for elected officials. Some of the aid was even still connected to colonial-era obligations and alliances. During the Cold War, aid was a standard part of the foreign policy approaches of both the United States and the Soviet Union, and led to obscene situations with money intended for supposedly charitable purposes landing in the hands of brutal and kleptocratic leaders.

One famous case is that of Mobuto Sese Seko, who led the Democratic Republic of Congo (he renamed it at the time Zaire) for thirty-two years. His government was a major foreign aid recipient until 1990, when members of Congress, led by an early Devex advisory board member—the late congressman Stephen Solarz of Brooklyn—defied the George H. W. Bush administration and turned off the spigot. He told the *New York Times* that year that fears about an aid cutoff ushering in instability were misplaced: "What jeopardizes the prospects of regional stability is the existence of a kleptocracy in Zaire that has driven the standard of living lower than it was at the time of independence three decades ago."[21]

Fortunately, the aid industry has evolved a lot since that era. Much of the change took place after the year 2000. The Cold War, which had driven so much foreign aid decision-making, had ended. Globalization made other people's problems seem closer to home. It began to be apparent that the approach to aid was due for some revision.

In the US, George W. Bush deviated from the Republican script and pushed for far more foreign aid spending, targeted to specific issues like AIDS and malaria. His government pioneered new models of aid in an effort to address the problems of government contracting and monopsony. One such model was the Millennium Challenge Corporation, which is still around and seeks to reward countries for making smart governance decisions with big grants that the recipient countries get to direct. At USAID, the Bush administration created new mechanisms for partnering with major corporations to achieve development results, something that was expanded upon by the Obama administration.

US foreign aid has more than tripled in the past two decades, and, globally, foreign aid has more than doubled since that time. There are now more governments with major aid agencies, including those of China, South Korea, Australia, and Turkey. With the birth of these new entities and mechanisms all around the world, there are more ways to channel government money to address big challenges than ever before.

Even with all this change and advancement, much about the aid industry remains the same. Most USAID funding still goes to a small group of American NGOs and contractors, and the same is true of funding from the British, French, Germans, Japanese, Australians, and so on. Preference is still given to NGOs and aid contractors from the donor country. Most major aid projects and organizations are still led by Americans and Europeans. The old model of rigidly designed "projects" still persists.

There's some truth to what aid critics in academia, the media, and beyond say about what ails the aid industry. Too much energy has been directed at pleasing taxpayers and politicians instead of serving the world's poorest people. It's true there are some insincere aid ministers seeking higher office, prime ministers and presidents chasing reelection and legacy, and bureaucratic warriors cautiously working their way to the top at UN agencies and multilateral banks, taking on more prestige, responsibility, and compensation along the way. But this view obscures a bigger picture.

ONE FOR YOU, TWO FOR ME

Critics of the aid industry have another, related complaint: they argue that it wastes money and indulges in profligate ways, often to the benefit of the richest countries and to the aid workers themselves. The aid industry, after all, provides employment for many thousands of experts and professionals. These people often earn first-world salaries and some even live first-class lifestyles. I've personally sat awkwardly through lavish buffets at annual meetings of the Asian and African development banks while discussing global hunger.

It's true that expat aid workers often live far more luxurious lives than those of the people they are trying to serve. Because the cost of living can be so low and domestic services so inexpensive in poor countries, aid workers may even enjoy some luxuries and amenities they would not be able to afford back home.

This natural desire of critics to point out hypocrisy, to scoff at signs of selfishness among do-gooders, only makes sense when the underlying objective of the aid industry is to display good intentions. If results are what really matter, the focus should shift from how much better aid workers live than the people they are helping, to what they are actually getting done for those people.

After all, aid workers are professionals who have jobs to do. They would hardly be as productive if they lived in the same substandard conditions that many people struggle with in these countries—without regular electricity and internet.

Nonetheless, taxpayers and donors can be sensitive about the perception that aid workers are living too well. For example, Oxfam maintains a guest house in Nairobi for its aid workers based there that is available to workers from other organizations who might be passing through. It's actually cheaper than local accommodations, and certainly more convenient, but there was a problem: the house had a swimming pool. Oxfam worried that supporters back home in the UK would get the wrong idea, and it eventually closed the pool. This shows how perversely people cling to the idea of good intentions as the underlying objective of aid. Keeping the pool would have probably led to better results for Kenya. Not only did it make for happier aid workers, Oxfam might have opened it for local community use.[22]

In 2010, Australia's tabloid media reported on what they called the "megasalaries" of Australia's foreign aid worker consultants. In a piece titled "Millions in Foreign Aid Blown on Executives," the *Daily Telegraph* highlighted the cases of specific consultants it said were overpaid.[23] But these "briefcase advisors" were experts in technical areas, and their fees were pretty much in line with market rates.[24]

The media and the public remain fascinated with the salaries paid and perquisites offered in institutions dedicated to ending global poverty, especially in those that receive public funds. In fact, a 2018 deal struck with the Trump administration to infuse more capital into the World Bank contained the provision that salaries there couldn't go up more than inflation—a requirement that appeals to those who see well-compensated aid industry professionals as hypocrites.[25]

But it's complicated. Seth Berkley is CEO of the Vaccine Alliance (also known as GAVI), the world's main vehicle for ensuring vaccines get to children in the poorest and most marginalized circumstances. Set up by the Gates Foundation in 2000, this alliance now includes nearly every major government and representatives of the private sector, such as pharmaceutical companies. Having immunized seven hundred million children since its inception, it's one of the biggest success stories in the aid industry.

England's *Mail on Sunday*, however, ran a sensational story in 2016 headlined "The Fattest Charity Fat Cat of Them All." It featured an unflattering photo of Berkley and claimed that he had earned a total of more than £2 million in the preceding four years. Berkley actually received far less (his base compensation was £220,000, not £623,370, as the piece reported).[26] GAVI tried to correct the story, to no avail.[27] Meanwhile, GAVI earned the UK government's highest rating for aid effectiveness in its annual review of multilateral organizations.[28]

All of this can be hard for some to stomach. Would you support taxpayer dollars going to an aid agency whose CEO earns, say, half a million dollars a year? What about to an NGO that puts on training programs for its staff at nice resorts? Or an organization that, like Oxfam did briefly, maintains a swimming pool for its workers?

In this new era of aid, this all misses the point. This is a mission-driven industry, so there of course must be limits—the aid industry can't adopt the winner-takes-all ethos of Wall Street, for example. But, except for rare cases of truly obscene compensation, what a nonprofit CEO is paid doesn't necessarily have anything to do with what really matters—the cost-effectiveness of the results the agency is achieving. If a nonprofit is the most cost effective in the world at saving the lives of kids in poor countries, why should we care if executives there earn big salaries or staff eat out on the company credit card? In fact, why don't more people get that angry when a program designed to help people in desperate and urgent need fails to do so?

Sometimes bad results correlate with insensitive spending, this is true. The era of the aid industry as it exists today has largely been shaped by this narrative and is, as a result, more focused on avoiding risks and displaying generosity than achieving results. People in the aid industry live in fear of a bad newspaper headline and rightly so: much mainstream journalism about foreign aid is aimed at poking holes in positive stories, finding the examples of corruption or waste that feed into readers' existing worldviews about places like Africa.[29] That one negative headline can sink a project or end a grant.

THE COLONIAL MIND-SET

It's important to acknowledge that the aid industry only exists because nearly all of the world's wealth resides in countries of European ancestry and Japan. That reality is not an accident but a direct result of colonial history, and vestiges of it remain even in the aid industry mind-set and language.

At the World Bank, the standard terminology for traveling to a borrowing country is "going on mission," something I can imagine an officer of the British East India Company saying. The top USAID official in a recipient country is given the official title "mission director," while the person in charge of a USAID project is officially known as a "chief of party." They sound a bit like the commander of a NASA shuttle launch and the head of an expeditionary group exploring the Serengeti, respectively, but the terms are still used today.

We use phrases like working in "the field" or being "on the ground" to indicate our presence in places like Haiti or Senegal. Recipients of aid are called "beneficiaries," and even enormous economies such as those of the BRICS nations (Brazil, Russia, India, China, and South Africa) are routinely referred to as "developing countries" and placed in the same category as the poorest countries in the world.

Then there's the word "local," which is used to describe national organizations, some of them quite large. It's meant as the antonym of "international." An expat, for example, can be an "international hire," while a citizen of the country where the work is happening is a "local hire." (According to an opinion article in the *Guardian*, the term "expat" is itself pernicious, in that it seems to apply only to people from rich countries who go overseas, and typically conjures up a white person. Everyone else is just an "immigrant.")[30]

The term "appropriate technologies" is often used in the context of global health. It has intellectual underpinnings that date to Mahatma Gandhi, who promoted the use of the spinning wheel to make cloth in India over the purchase of machine-made yarn. It is often used as a euphemism for spending less on medical devices or drugs for poor people, avoiding more advanced and costly technology. And "capacity building"—a similarly pragmatic bit of development lingo that essentially means training or expanding the capabilities of people or institutions—hints pejoratively at the idea that "locals" don't have capacity and need to be trained by Western experts.

Even the term "aid" itself is antiquated. It suggests saviors from above, when the reality of global development is empowered people lifting themselves out of poverty. Perhaps as this transformation takes hold, even the term "aid industry"—which already rubs many who do this work the wrong way—will be replaced by something like "impact industry."

We'd like to think that colonialism is long gone, but it didn't die so many years ago. Indonesia, for example, became independent just several decades ago, in 1949, after Sukarno fought off Dutch colonial rule in the aftermath of World War II.

I recall visiting a prominent and highly credible Dutch nonprofit known as the Royal Tropical Institute in Amsterdam some years ago and being surprised by the museum collection in its grand headquarters building—colonial artifacts like giant masks from Indonesia and the other former Dutch colonies that seemed from another era and out of tune with its current work. Then I learned that the organization had grown out of the Colonial Museum, founded in 1864, and the institute itself was known as the Colonial Institute when it was founded in 1910. Not that it takes away from the good work it does today, but even its current nomenclature—"royal" and "tropical"—points to a worldview of the last century.

▪ ▪ ▪ ▪ ▪

Aid critics make a lot of valid points, including that the aid industry has a deep connection to colonialism, but there's one essential question: does aid actually work?[31] Considering the political and historical motivations that have distorted the aid industry away from a results orientation, the overall picture is quite good. A study conducted by the World Bank that looks at detailed aid data across sixty countries over two decades conclusively shows that aid benefits the poorest segments of society by increasing well-being through income growth.[32] Another study by the United Nations University looked at forty years of data to conclude that foreign aid positively contributed to economic growth and to several indicators of human progress, including reduced poverty.[33]

We know that aid can work under the right circumstances, and there are many individual initiatives like GAVI that have been successful, some wildly so. However, though there is a strong foundation to build on, achieving something as monumental as the end of extreme poverty and the other global goals by 2030 seems unlikely to happen on our current trajectory.

The sad reality is that the world is unjust and unequal, and the aid industry itself reflects that. This has been an industry too tied up in knots from trying to showcase good intentions while not getting on the wrong side of politics or appearing hypocritical. But that's changing fast. There's a transformation underway forcing us to ask fundamental questions about why we do this work and how we can reach seemingly impossible goals, like the end of extreme poverty.

THE BILLIONAIRE EFFECT

Disruptors with Deep Pockets

CARI TUNA NEVER EXPECTED, or even wanted, to be a billionaire, which is perhaps why she doesn't behave like one. And while few people have heard of her or her husband, this young couple is on track to donate more each year than the Ford Foundation.

Tuna was raised in Indiana. In high school she founded a chapter of Amnesty International. She went to Yale, where she studied political science and reported for the *Yale Daily News*. She wrote dozens of articles about campus issues: the results of the sailing team races, the rising use of hookahs, the highlights of a seminar on stem cell research, a peek into Sex Week. When she graduated, she landed a job at the San Francisco bureau of the *Wall Street Journal*.

In 2009 a coworker arranged a blind date for Tuna with a guy named Dustin Moskovitz. The two hit it off. He had been raised in Florida, attended Harvard, majoring in economics, but took a year off in 2004 to move to California and start a business with his roommate, Mark Zuckerberg.[1]

Tuna knew that Moskovitz was a cofounder of Facebook who by that time had left the company to start a new venture, Asana, a developer of mobile productivity apps. They got along well, but it was only after a few dates that Tuna realized Moskovitz was going to be supremely wealthy, thanks to his stake in Facebook.

Indeed, just two years later, in 2011, *Forbes* declared that Moskovitz, age twenty-seven, was the youngest-ever self-made billionaire. Although they hadn't married, Moskovitz and Tuna were by then soul mates and life partners. She decided to quit the *Journal* and devote her time and energy to philanthropy. Together, they founded Good Ventures, whose mission is "to help humanity thrive."

This relatively unknown couple and their cutting-edge foundation represent the future of global philanthropy: wealthy, committed, and personally engaged donors with a results-oriented, Silicon Valley-style approach. Moskovitz and Tuna also pick up on the unprepossessing style of another billionaire philanthropist, Warren Buffett, the understated Oracle of Omaha, Nebraska. The Moskovitz-Tuna net worth hovers around $12 billion, but they are known for living simply. They share a single used car. They bike or bus to work when they can. They fly coach when they travel, which is often. They live in a two-bedroom apartment in Silicon Valley, and their unflashy hobbies include taking walks together and practicing yoga.

Good Ventures is similarly low profile. The foundation does not have its own full-time staff but rather outsources its management to the Open Philanthropy Project, a group dedicated to finding the most effective aid opportunities in order to do as much "good" as possible. It funds the project (internally known as OpenPhil) in the hopes of advising its own giving as well as that of other major donors. Good Ventures also funds the work of GiveWell, a website offering advice to individuals about how to make the most cost-effective donations. All three organizations are under one roof, and some of the people working there have titles at each outfit.

This group is noteworthy in its approach to giving because it has not committed to a single moonshot goal like, say, curing Alzheimer's or ending child marriage. Rather, it seeks to support many initiatives, chosen according to three criteria. For a cause to be selected, it must demonstrate "importance," meaning it must be significant in helping humanity thrive. It must also show "neglectedness," which means the area must be underfunded or underrecognized by other funding sources. And, finally, it must have "tractability"—it must be something that can be solved through grantmaking.

In 2016, Good Ventures awarded $126 million in grants. Precisely half that amount ($63 million) went to global health and development initiatives identified as the most cost-effective by GiveWell.[2] The rest funded initiatives in a handful of focus areas based on the work of Open-Phil: US criminal justice reform, farm animal welfare, biosecurity and pandemic preparedness, and potential risks posed by advanced artificial intelligence.

Tuna, Moskovitz, and their collaborators call themselves "effective altruists"—people who want to maximize the good they can do. They are zealots for good, analyzing every detail and squeezing out every insight to ensure they are doing the most good possible. One of the core arguments of effective altruism is prioritizing helping others now rather than waiting to bequeath money after death. So this young couple has made an unusual commitment: they have publicly declared their intention to give away nearly all their wealth in their lifetimes.

In 2017, their giving rose to $314 million, about one-and-a-half times what the Rockefeller Foundation donated.[3] And, at this rate, this little- known couple may within a decade give away annually as much as the Ford Foundation—the largest foundation of the last century. The two, with around $12 billion, have the same wealth as does Ford's endowment. Their investments are almost certainly more growth oriented, while Ford is naturally more conservative in the management of its portfolio. Moskovitz-Tuna are giving just over half of what Ford does today, which means their total wealth will grow faster than Ford's. And unlike Ford, theirs is not a perpetual endowment, so they can spend both their income and all their wealth. As a result, this couple could represent in this era what storied philanthropic forces like the Rockefeller and Ford Foundations represented in the last.

THE NEW PHILANTHROPIST CLASS

Of the many factors that have contributed to the transformation of philanthropy into the new aid industry, none has had a greater impact than the emergence of billionaire philanthropists like Dustin Moskovitz and Cari Tuna, Bill and Melinda Gates, George Soros, Michael Bloomberg, and many others, including many outside the United States who are not household names.

The Carlos Slim Foundation, for example, was founded by Carlos Slim, a Mexican business magnate who ranks in the top ten of the world's richest people, in part, his critics say, due to monopolistic control of the telecom sector. The Slim Foundation funds major initiatives around health and education in Latin America. There's Aliko Dangote, the wealthiest man in Africa, with a net worth of $11 billion.[4] Although his foundation is comparatively small, giving away perhaps tens of millions per year and so far endowed with a reported $1.2 billion, he is emerging as a major player because he has strong connections in Africa and has a crisp focus on saving children's lives through better nutrition and health.

It's hard to overstate the impact of these billionaires and their foundations so far, and it's even harder to overstate the impact they will have in the coming years. In 1987, *Forbes* published its first list of the world's billionaires. *Forbes* found 140 billionaires in the world at that time, including forty-four in the United States, and one in India.[5] Thirty years later, *Forbes* calculated there are 2,043 billionaires in the world—565 in the US and 101 in India—and, collectively, they are worth $7.6 trillion.[6]

With a global economy that benefits the wealthiest among us, billionaire assets are growing fast, up over 300 percent since the Great Recession of 2008.[7] In 2017 alone, the top five hundred richest people in the world saw their wealth grow by a trillion dollars.[8] Those five hundred people could donate that entire amount and not in any material way negatively impact their financial security or lifestyle. Even by giving away a trillion dollars, they would still not be living up to Monsignor Cassidy's exhortation to "give from their want."

Sadly, most of the world's wealthiest people have not yet taken to the approach of Bill and Melinda Gates, who have donated over $35 billion and still have assets of approximately $90 billion, let alone shown the kind of philanthropic inclinations of Moskovitz and Tuna. Even so, making the decision to donate large amounts of money to a cause for social good is rapidly becoming the modish thing to do. It's a sign of the times: with this much wealth in the world today, buying another private island or mega-yacht doesn't really move the needle on social status. What really brings attention, fame, respect, admiration, and a positive legacy is taking on one of the world's big problems, such as the need to conquer extreme poverty or eradicate a disease.

One of the most illustrious and persistent of the billionaire class of philanthropists is former New York City mayor Michael Bloomberg, who gives through Bloomberg Philanthropies, the Bloomberg Family

Foundation, and his business, Bloomberg LP. With a net worth of over $50 billion—four times the Moskovitz-Tuna "endowment"—and a public commitment to give away over half of his wealth during his life or upon his death, Bloomberg has the money, political clout, and business orientation to move the needle on the limited number of significant but narrowly focused issues he has chosen.

He has given away some 10 percent of his wealth since 2000, making him, by at least one measure, the third most prolific charitable giver after Warren Buffett and Bill Gates.[9]

A top priority for Bloomberg is his antismoking initiative. There are around a billion smokers in the world today, 80 percent of whom live in low- or middle-income countries.[10] It's estimated that five hundred million of today's smokers will die from their habit.[11] To dramatically reduce the number of smokers in the world would be to make a major contribution to world health, freeing up resources for the ultrapoor and directly improving the lives of smokers and their families.

Bloomberg has also turned his attention to the urgent, if rather unsexy, cause of improving road safety. Vehicle accidents are one of the leading killers in the world, taking about 1.25 million lives worldwide every year (about forty thousand in the United States). Tens of millions more are injured or disabled.[12] That's not far behind tuberculosis, which is the largest infectious disease killer in the world, accounting for about 1.75 million deaths annually worldwide.[13] Bloomberg Philanthropies has so far invested $259 million for road safety in low- and middle-income countries.[14] By contrast, the World Bank–led Global Road Safety Facility, a partnership of foreign aid agencies that counts Bloomberg Philanthropies among its main funders, has spent only around $40 million since its inception in 2006.

Bloomberg's contributions are particularly valuable precisely because they fit the Good Ventures "neglectedness" criterion. Few governmental aid agencies have Bloomberg's resources to focus so deeply on a single issue: foreign policy priorities force them to work in many more countries on many more issues.

Road safety is also a "tractable" issue. There are known and cost-effective ways to reduce vehicle-related deaths, for example by passing laws and enforcing penalties for driving drunk, riding motorcycles without helmets, and not wearing seatbelts. In fact, over the past fifty years road deaths have gone down dramatically in many places, so there is plenty of data available to show that safety can be improved. Bloomberg now sets his sights on the total elimination of vehicle fatalities—a "zero goal," like ending child marriage or eradicating malaria or putting extreme poverty in the history books.

A third Bloomberg focus is noncommunicable diseases, such as diabetes. Because these are often thought of as rich-country illnesses—ailments that affect only those who already have a long life expectancy and that can be expensive to treat—they are woefully neglected by global health funders. Across low- and middle-income countries (which includes a lot of big countries with moderate incomes, admittedly skewing the numbers), 67 percent of deaths are attributable to noncommunicable diseases, but only 1 percent of global health funding focuses on them.[15] Bloomberg aims to change that and, given his personal resources, he likely can.

Bloomberg, as is typical of billionaire philanthropists who adopt at least some of the tenets of effective altruism, has a business background. He likes to find and grab arbitrage opportunities—neglected issues where he can make an outsized difference. Between his private foundation, his corporate foundation, and personal donations he's made, Bloomberg gave away $700 million last year to fight smoking, improve road safety, combat noncommunicable diseases, and more. So far, he's donated $5 billion of his wealth to charity over the years. Even after all that giving, his net worth remains $50 billion, and he still brings in over $3 billion a year from his privately held firm, Bloomberg LP, the provider of financial software and data.

Taking into account Bloomberg's age, seventy-six, and assuming he lives to the ripe old age of one hundred (beyond the actuarial tables, but, hey, he's a billionaire with access to the best medicine, and it's a safe bet he's not a smoker or a Big Gulp drinker), as well as the growing value of his eponymous firm, he still needs to ramp up his giving if he wants to give away a significant portion of his total wealth before he dies. Even if he sets a target of giving away just half his fortune during his lifetime, he'll need to donate around $2 billion *every year* for the next twenty-five years.

To put that in context, the Canadian government spends a third of that amount on global health aid annually.[16] And at that rate of giving, it would take Bloomberg just four years to reach the total amount John D. Rockefeller donated in his entire life—a philanthropic legacy that includes founding the Rockefeller Foundation, the University of Chicago, and Rockefeller University.[17]

ZERO GOALS

Despite the gap in their respective ages, Moskovitz-Tuna and Bloomberg represent the new wave of philanthropic giving, but they both owe a debt to the example set by the dominant billionaire philanthropists on the scene today: Bill and Melinda Gates, through the Bill & Melinda Gates Foundation.

Among other things, the Gateses have set their sights on a major health goal: to eradicate polio through the Global Polio Eradication Initiative. The idea that polio could be banished from the face of the earth forever seemed like an impossible task just a few decades ago.

Today, polio has largely been overcome thanks to an effective oral vaccine. It can be stored at room temperature, so it does not require expensive refrigeration equipment. It's also easy to administer: no injection is required, a child simply swallows a single dose of a few drops of liquid.

The vaccine was promoted through a massive communications effort and distributed through an equally ambitious administration campaign, both of which reached millions of children worldwide. It worked. Today there are only a couple dozen cases of polio recorded each year. These are almost entirely confined to the border area between Afghanistan and Pakistan, and in Karachi, Pakistan's largest city.

The border region is a particularly difficult place for health workers to operate because it is dangerous—more than forty polio vaccinators have been targeted and brutally murdered there since 2012.[18] These courageous health workers, mostly women, have faced even greater threats since 2010, when it was revealed that the CIA located Osama bin Laden in Abbottabad, Pakistan, in part by sending a doctor under the guise of providing vaccinations.

Still, we know that polio can be eradicated, even in countries where terrorist violence and resistance make immunization campaigns challenging. Nigeria, for example, has been free of polio for nearly two years as of this writing and it's likely that Pakistan and Afghanistan will succeed in wiping out polio in the next few years. The number of cases in Pakistan has fallen dramatically, from 328 cases in 2014 to 8 reported cases in 2017.[19] In Afghanistan, there were just 12 cases of wild poliovirus.[20]

So, though there are many barriers to overcome before we can claim total eradication, the achievement is within sight. When that happens, Bill and Melinda Gates and partner organizations such as Rotary International will have achieved a major milestone for humanity. Polio will be just the second human disease—after smallpox—to be dispatched from the world forever.

Perhaps the eradication of a disease with so few cases does not sound like an important or neglected goal. Indeed, the Gates Foundation's Global Polio Eradication Initiative has been questioned for spending such a huge amount on the cause—$1.1 billion in 2017, or around $50 million per known case of polio.[21] Bill Gates counters these comments by saying his critics are failing "a sort of math test." He figures that a big up-front investment in eradication will be far less than the amount spent on long-term administration and treatment. If there are no sick people to treat, all the costs of staff, facilities, medicines, outreach, and home care vanish. When the polio eradication campaign began in 1988, 350,000 kids were infected with polio every year.[22] Reducing those healthcare costs has saved the world $27 billion so far, not to mention the human lives saved.[23]

This particular initiative is also noteworthy because it says a lot about the kinds of projects that business-minded billionaires may prefer to invest in. Many, after successful business careers shaping entire industries, may want to be big players in the aid market. They'll want to have a demonstrable effect, and in that sense the idea of eradication could be particularly appealing.

Disease eradication is one example of what are known as "zero goals." From ending female genital mutilation to road deaths to polio, zero goals are definitive and measurable, and, in many cases, they have a clear end date. Investment in eliminating something harmful can generate long-term returns, in the form of reduced costs of ongoing aid, lives saved, and greater productivity of the survivors. As a result, from an economic standpoint, all the up-front investment required to achieve a zero goal can be worth it.

A zero goal can be an accomplishment of historic proportions, something that, I would imagine, could be deeply meaningful for billionaire philanthropists. Older ones in particular might find themselves thinking in these terms, including some of the top ten givers in the United States: Warren Buffett, George Soros, Michael Bloomberg, Larry Ellison, and even the controversial Koch brothers, David and Charles, all of whom are in their seventies, eighties, or nineties.

It is true that most members of the two-thousand-strong global billionaire club still haven't made public philanthropic pledges. Perhaps some prefer to keep their giving private, although my guess is those are people who are not donating much, as it would be hard to hide contributions of this size under the guise of anonymity. Others perhaps still prefer to pour large quantities of their money into yachts and aircraft, private islands, sports teams, and multiple homes and estates, and into running for political office. Still others might want to be major philanthropists but are focused on their business or family and don't know how to get started.

Warren Buffett, once the world's richest person, collaborated with his friend Bill Gates, also once the world's richest person, to establish the Giving Pledge in 2010. They made a public commitment to give away the majority of their wealth during their lifetimes or upon their deaths, and they invited other members of the superwealthy to join them. As of this writing, 186 people—billionaires or those who were billionaires before giving their money away—have been inspired to sign the pledge, and their commitments total over half a trillion dollars.[24]

The Giving Pledge is nonbinding, has no legal status, and there are no stipulations about where the money should go or how it should be deployed, but it is incredibly meaningful as a promise and a commitment, a statement of values, and a challenge to others.

The list of people who have pledged includes some of the most powerful, successful, and famous people on earth: Gates, Buffett, Ellison, Bloomberg, Zuckerberg, Icahn, Musk, Moskovitz, Branson, Gund, Rockefeller, von Furstenberg, Turner . . . the list goes on.

Billionaires sign the pledge for a variety of reasons. Some seem to deeply believe in the causes they fund and sincerely want to set an example for others to join them. Some may want to join one of the most exclusive clubs on earth. Some probably want to avoid the public awkwardness of *not* joining. At some point a journalist will almost certainly ask the question, "Have you taken the Giving Pledge?" Other attendees at the charity event will want to know, "Are you thinking of taking the pledge?" Grandkids, when they reach their teens, will likely pose the question more pointedly, "Why haven't you signed *already*?"

For those who have not yet achieved billionaire status there is another mechanism for potential giving, known as the Founders Pledge. It gives owners of stock in potentially valuable startups a way to make legally binding commitments to donate a few percent of their likely earnings to charity. Next-generation tech leaders like WeWork cofounder Miguel McKelvey and Shazam executive chairman Andrew Fisher have pledged, as have nearly a thousand others.[25]

A key element of the Giving Pledge is the strong suggestion (although it's not a requirement) that the money be given away during the donor's lifetime. Traditionally, wealthy people have specified the donation of the bulk of their estates in their wills. But that model has its drawbacks. First, it delays the application of funds to urgent issues that need addressing now. Second, some reasonably large percentage of any posthumous bequest will be eaten up by the overhead of the philanthropy that receives it. The Ford Foundation, for example, created with Henry Ford's wealth, spends as much as 20 percent of its giving on operational overhead. In the past decade, it donated around $4 billion and spent about $1 billion managing its own operations.[26] Ford has four hundred employees; by contrast, Bloomberg Philanthropies, which donates roughly the same amount each year, has around one hundred employees.

And, third, when wealthy donors personally participate in giving, they stand to learn a great deal about the causes they are involved with and about the challenges of administration and execution. Some are savvy businesspeople and public leaders who can effectively become skillful educators and powerful advocates for charitable giving and specific causes. They can help guide their friends and associates away from one-off donations and toward more strategic giving. What's more, as they begin to get that good feeling that comes from making a positive difference, and as they see that their dollars are achieving results, they may increase their commitment.

These pledges have almost no effect on the billionaires' capacity to do everything and anything they want. Let's face it, the level of wealth we're talking about is difficult to comprehend and is a symptom of a real problem in our society—income inequality. It would be difficult for any billionaire to spend all his or her money on consumption in a lifetime—or in ten lifetimes. Giving away an ample percentage of a fortune will have near zero effect on how a billionaire lives.

That is part of the genius of the Giving Pledge. A billionaire can retain his or her status in the billionaire club and attribute any reduction in net worth to an increase in charitable contributions. It's all public and reported. You may no longer be a billionaire, but you'll always be a Giving Pledge signatory. Nor will a commitment to the Giving Pledge have a negative impact on the long-term financial situations of heirs. Warren Buffett even claims the opposite: that children who inherit too much money often ruin their lives with overabundance. His own kids and grandkids—who have inherited only a small sliver of his wealth because of his philosophy—have nonetheless become major philanthropists in their own rights. His three kids' annual giving, combined, is at the level of the Ford Foundation and Bloomberg Philanthropies.

Facebook cofounder Mark Zuckerberg and his wife, Priscilla Chan, have not only signed the Giving Pledge, but, like Zuckerberg's former colleague Dustin Moskovitz, they have taken it a step further. Upon the birth of their first child, they committed to giving away nearly all their wealth—99 percent of their Facebook shares—through the Chan Zuckerberg Initiative (CZI). At today's share price, that would be approximately $60 billion. Just as I estimate that Moskovitz-Tuna will soon donate as much each year as the Ford Foundation, CZI will, by my estimation, ultimately reach the same scale as the Gates Foundation. That's because of the relatively small amounts CZI is spending today ($700 million to $800 million per year) and the time the younger Chan-Zuckerberg couple will have to grow their wealth.[27] The Gates Foundation will ultimately donate well over $150 billion, so that's saying something.[28]

Even with the negative backdrop of inequality, it's a positive step that so many of the best-known and most illustrious billionaires have made dramatic philanthropic commitments. They encourage others to come forward with commitments because of the good publicity, enhanced status, and important goals they can achieve with their philanthropy. But what about those who don't give? We have a powerful carrot in the Giving Pledge, but where is the stick? There is no champion, mechanism, or movement focused on naming those billionaires who hoard their wealth and don't make significant philanthropic commitments. I believe it's only a matter of time before this comes to pass. With growing income inequality leading to a rise in populism across the globe, it's only natural that people, billionaires and nonbillionaires alike, will confront the pressing issue of "giving inequality." Why should some billionaires give it all away for the betterment of humanity, while others only seek to further enrich themselves?

Jeff Bezos, founder of Amazon, could be among the first to face tangible consequences for a lack of philanthropic commitment. Despite occupying the "richest person" spot at various moments in 2017 and 2018, Bezos has made only modest commitments about his future philanthropy and, by comparison to others in his wealth class, he has been only a minor philanthropist to date.

Bezos recently sent out a tweet asking for ideas about how he could organize his philanthropic giving. He said he wanted suggestions that would help him "achieve results right now." He received forty-two thousand replies but has so far made no public commitment to any of them. Perhaps not coincidentally, the message went out just hours before Amazon announced it was buying the supermarket chain Whole Foods, which heightened concerns that Amazon was becoming too powerful in too many retail sectors.

Bezos has given away $100 million to charity, which of course is a lot. And in September of 2018 he pledged to donate $2 billion to address homelessness and early childhood education challenges in the United States.[29] But Warren Buffett, who is now outranked by Bezos in the billionaire parade (Bezos's net worth is approximately double that of Buffett), has donated $24 billion. Bezos has a libertarian worldview and so may be dubious about the value of aid and charity. Or perhaps he's simply too busy in his day job to think about these issues. (That should never be an excuse, since people are suffering now.) He has indicated that he sees his investments in space exploration as a kind of philanthropy, although I'd urge him to balance those with aid to help those whose lives are under threat back on Earth.

Bezos already receives plenty of criticism and backlash from people who believe that Amazon kills off small, local competitors and eliminates jobs. Especially as Amazon builds a greater local presence through Whole Foods Markets and Amazon retail stores and warehouses, Bezos may come under more fire for an apparent lack of commitment to social good. If he took the Giving Pledge or in some other way committed to giving away most of his wealth to the benefit of important causes, it would go a long way toward furthering his business interests. He would gain for Amazon what is sometimes called a "social license to operate"— permission from citizens for a company to do business in the society.

No matter what Bezos does, there is likely to be much more scrutiny of whether and how the superwealthy are living up to their commitments to social good. George Soros, for example, has donated billions during his lifetime, but the eighty-five-year-old was not on track to meet his commitments as calculated by actuarial predictions of his life span.[30] To bring his giving in line with his pledge, he announced donations totaling $18 billion to his foundation in 2017. Michael Bloomberg, at seventy-five, is technically not on track either and may make a similar lump-sum donation to his foundation in the coming years.

Today, there is no recognized authority for tracking billionaires' contributions and holding them accountable, nor is it a topic of much public debate. However, the tenor of the public discourse around philanthropy can change if we push to change it. It goes beyond holding the pledgers' feet to the fire about fulfilling a pledge or making one to begin with. As billionaire giving becomes more prevalent, and pledges more widespread, there should be detailed tracking of commitments. And, eventually, there ought to be scrutiny around the effectiveness and results of that giving.

The Laura and John Arnold Foundation is a great example of the future of philanthropy. Its focus is entirely on the United States, and from 2011 to 2018 it granted just over $1 billion.[31] It doesn't do the traditional things a foundation might do, like receive proposals from major NGOs and write checks to them. Instead, it takes a venture capital approach, seeking out opportunities to be more effective by making philanthropic grants that can shift government policies and spending.

Much of its work is in US criminal justice reform. For example, it created a public safety assessment tool that can replace the antiquated, expensive, and inaccurate approach to setting bail for criminal defendants. Under the current system, judges determine when a defendant is going to appear for a court date and, if he or she is released on bail, whether the person will be a danger to others. These assumptions are generally not based on data but rather on a judge's subjective determination based

THREE TECH BILLIONAIRE COUPLES WITH THREE DISTINCT APPROACHES

DONORS	PHILOSOPHY	APPROACH	OPERATING MODEL	ISSUE AREAS	WILLING TO COURT CONTROVERSY?	LEVEL OF TRANSPARENCY	SCALE (estimated annual/ projected total)
Bill and Melinda Gates (including Warren Buffett contributions)	Strategically wielding huge grants and influence, they aim to shape the entire aid industry to deliver much better results, saving and improving millions of lives	Data, evidence, and logic models drive decisions	Makes grants to organizations according to the foundation's strategy	Global health, global development, agriculture, financial inclusion, gender equality, education	Somewhat (promotes GMOs, education reform)	Moderate (most funding goes through foundation, which publicly lists all grants)	$5 billion in 2017 grants [32]/ approximately $150 billion (over $200 billion including Buffett contributions) [33]
Mark Zuckerberg and Priscilla Chan	By building tech tools, they aim to solve big problems themselves while using their influence to push government to make aligned and sensible policy changes	Technology, systems, and advocacy approach to solving big problems at scale	Not a grantmaking organization; creates and runs its own programs (which could make it the biggest NGO in the world)	Medical science, education, justice, and opportunity (criminal justice reform, economic growth, housing affordability, immigration reform)	Somewhat (promotes education reform, immigration reform)	Low (incorporated as an LLC, which reduces transparency requirements; nonetheless provides some basic information about its work)	$700–800 million [34]/ $100–$150 billion [35]
Jeff and MacKenzie Bezos	"Where are the opportunities to make things better?" is the closest thing to a stated philosophy so far	Unclear but so far picking just two local and popular issues	They will build and directly operate a network of preschools; and grant-fund existing homelessness organizations	Homelessness and preschool education	Less so (picks politically popular issues so far)	None (not even a website as of this writing)	$50 million [36]/ $2 billion

on facts they have been presented. The result is an unequal system in which people with money pay their bail and get out scot-free, and poorer people are stuck in jail awaiting trial, or have to take loans with sky-high interest rates from a bail bondsman. This can financially ruin an already poor family. Beyond the personal costs, keeping someone in jail is much more expensive for the state.

The Arnold Foundation did an analysis of 750,000 historical cases and was able to determine the nine factors that can best predict the likelihood that a criminal defendant will either not show up in court or will commit a crime in the meantime. (An example factor is whether a defendant has ever failed to appear in court, information not previously available to all judges.) The assessment tool helps judges to make more informed, humane decisions, and is now being used in thirty jurisdictions nationwide, including New Jersey, Arizona, and Kentucky. The bail industry feels sufficiently threatened by this tool sweeping the country that it is mounting an enormous effort to stop these kinds of bail reforms.

The Arnold Foundation is another example of low-profile billionaires strategically using their philanthropy to achieve outsized impacts, often by moving governments to focus more on what works. Arnold funds studies to find evidence of successful public policy and then pushes government to adopt the lessons. It's what I call "alpha philanthropy"—charity that seeks outsized impact—and it makes sense coming from a successful investor. ("Alpha" in the financial industry refers to returns on investment beyond the norm.) Of course, billionaires often try to influence public policy for personal enrichment too. Alpha philanthropy refers to truly charitable activity that's trying to do good for society.

THE GATES AGENDA

The Bill & Melinda Gates Foundation is by far the most sophisticated charitable operation in the world today and, I think it's safe to say, in the history of the aid industry. The Gates Foundation is, almost to a fault, all about strategy, key performance indicators, and data. It is disruptive, not simply donating to its own projects but forming alliances with other foundations and aid agencies and influencing the agenda. Bill and Melinda Gates are like heads of state, only more powerful than most. They

circumnavigate the globe, spreading a message aimed at aligning government aid programs, public policy, and charitable giving with their own
agenda for how to save and improve lives.

Their approach is so respected that Warren Buffett trusted the Gates
Foundation with managing the allocation and distribution of his wealth.
Buffett could easily have created a new foundation for that purpose, or
distributed all the funds among the several Buffett family foundations.
But he realized that no one in his family, even with their organizations,
would be able to effectively give away such massive sums. So he pledged
the bulk of his wealth—some 85 percent—to the Gates Foundation, and
the remaining 15 percent to Buffett-controlled foundations.

In effect, Buffett transferred the burden of giving away the money to
Bill and Melinda Gates, who are personally involved in their foundation's
direction. Even though Buffett determined that it would be too difficult
for him to handle making those contributions, that does not mean it's
easy for either of the Gateses to shoulder the responsibility of effectively
donating several billion dollars a year. (Buffett, who is eighty-eight years
old and has a net worth of $87 billion, has stipulated that his wealth must
all be given to charity within a decade of his death, meaning the Gates
Foundation will likely need to more than double its annual giving.)[37]

It's important to understand how different what the Gates Foundation does is from what a traditional foundation does. It isn't just writing
checks to credible organizations to work on worthy causes. It also understands that no one can write a check to end global poverty or empower
women all at once, so it isn't after silver-bullet solutions.

The Gateses want an aid industry that works. They have aims to eradicate diseases, not just manage them. But to achieve their goals, they need
everyone from UNICEF to the World Bank to do their jobs, to have the
funding they need and be able to recruit the best talent, to be data driven
and results oriented. The best way to do all that is to become indispens-
able to these agencies, to become the phone call they will always take.

To improve the aid industry as a whole, the Bill & Melinda Gates
Foundation has taken some unexpected actions that showcase its massive influence. In 2011, for example, the British government published
a review of all the aid agencies it funds and ranked the United Nations
Food and Agriculture Organization (FAO)—the UN agency responsible
for ending hunger—dead last. "Profound culture change is needed to

transform FAO into a modern, transparent and accountable institution," the report read.[38] At the time, I assumed this must have been discouraging to the Gates Foundation, given it had donated nearly $60 million to FAO since 2009.[39] But, rather than write the agency off, like a risk-averse government might, the foundation did something fascinating: it announced yet another grant to FAO. The foundation understands the aid industry better than most. It sees the need for agencies like FAO to exist, and saw in FAO's moment of weakness an opportunity to shape it into a more effective operation.

The foundation's influence can also be seen in the scale of its funding to the World Health Organization (WHO), the official standard-setting organization for healthcare around the world. The Gates Foundation's donations to WHO are greater than those of every country in the world except the United States.

When Bill Gates began his focus on global health, he was frustrated by the lack of data on which to base funding decisions. As a result, the Gates Foundation became the founding sponsor of the Institute for Health Metrics and Evaluation (IHME) at the University of Washington. The foundation's first grant to IHME was for $105 million in 2007.[40] A decade later, it upped the ante, announcing a $279 million grant for the institute's work over the next decade.[41] The data IHME produces is free and open to the aid industry, as is all the research the Gates Foundation funds. Its data is widely used at the World Bank, USAID, and National Institutes of Health, and it is but one example of how the Gates Foundation is pushing the entire aid industry to be more data driven.

The Gates Foundation took time to grow into its role as the leader of the aid industry. I first visited the foundation, based in Seattle, over a decade ago. The place was hard to find. The offices were tucked into a small, nondescript building near Lake Union. There was no sign out front, so I had to look for the street number. I gave my name to a security guard who let me in to the tiny parking lot. I had to know the phone number of the person I was meeting; the receptionist would not give me the extension. All this secrecy was no doubt born of experience: it must have had plenty of grant seekers dropping by unannounced with pitches for some cause or another.

Today, the Gates Foundation has grown into a public institution like the Ford and Rockefeller foundations, only much, much larger. It occupies a gorgeous complex that feels like a cross between the campus of a wealthy university and the technosprawl of a successful software company headquarters. There is a museum where visitors can learn about the foundation and its mission. I hear the Gates family is even engaged in an archival project akin to a presidential library to house their papers and memorabilia. The foundation's work is so structured that both Bill and Melinda Gates have found it necessary to create their own personal institutions (Gates Ventures and Pivotal Ventures, respectively) in order to pursue projects that don't fit its strategy. Bill Gates's personal office alone has a staff of about a hundred people.

That shift from anonymous startup to massive institution is emblematic of what's coming. One day soon, it's likely there will be dozens of foundations at least approaching this kind of scale, and almost all of them will have living donors behind them like Bill and Melinda Gates. The couple has stated they plan to spend down their foundation's endowment within twenty years of the death of the surviving spouse.[42] As a result, like a supernova, the Gates Foundation will almost certainly get much larger before winding down, only to be replaced by the next wave of billionaire philanthropists on the scene.

IT'S BIG, BUT IS IT GOOD?

As much as billionaires might like to think of their giving as an unalloyed good, their philanthropy will increasingly be a subject of controversy and a political issue itself.

In the United States, where more than half of all billionaires live, even our president among them, there is growing concern that our political system is being undermined by the divide between the billionaire class and everyone else. That has, in turn, put major US philanthropy in the spotlight, as three recent books make clear.[43]

In his book *The Givers*, David Callahan, a philanthropy critic, worries that massive private philanthropy is diminishing the role of government when it comes to public policy. Rich donors shaping society the way they like through tax-deductible political campaigning in the guise of charity and direct provision of social services runs counter to a democratic American society making its own choices. Similarly, Robert Reich, a Stanford University professor and author of *Just Giving*, sees the fast growth in private philanthropy as a subversion of government: the charitable-giving tax deduction reduced government revenue in the US by $50 billion in 2016. All that philanthropic giving could have been directed by government according to the democratic wishes of citizens. Finally, Anand Giridharadas's book *Winners Take All* examines how billionaire giving is part of a pernicious elitism that stops questions about inequality in their tracks. Writing big checks to good causes can take attention away from problems elites themselves are causing, he worries.

In Hungary we can see an extreme case of the politicization of billionaire philanthropy. There, the right-wing leader Prime Minister Viktor Orban has amassed power in part by positioning himself against that country's most famous billionaire, George Soros. A Hungarian immigrant to the US, Soros once supported Orban when he was part of the democratic opposition. But Orban has "evolved." As Devex has reported, Orban is promoting a law literally named "Stop Soros," which aims to undermine the NGOs, including those funded by George Soros's Open Society Foundations, that support refugees seeking asylum in Hungary.[44] Soros himself has become a major election and political issue in Hungary, and has been held up as a boogeyman by those who argue that outside forces are trying to undermine the country by bringing in large numbers of refugees.

Soros is having a hard time well beyond his native Hungary. In 2018 his Open Society Foundations plan to spend over $1 billion, more than Ford and Rockefeller combined, to further efforts to make the world a freer and more democratic place. Soros, eighty-seven years old with a net worth of some $26 billion, has already spent $14 billion on this issue, and he has pledged all of his wealth.[45]

Unfortunately, the battle against authoritarianism has taken a hit. While most global development metrics—life spans, incomes, education levels—have seen dramatically positive results over the past few decades, freedom and human rights are headed in the opposite direction. Freedom House, a research NGO, says 2017 was the twelfth year in row in which, by its measure, global freedom declined.[46] The bipartisan institution says only 45 percent of countries in the world can be fairly called "free." CIVICUS, which represents civil society organizations around the world, says as of 2017 only 3 percent of the world's people live in societies that have an open civil society.[47]

It may seem perverse that freedom and democracy must be supported by billionaire philanthropy, which itself flows from inequity. As a result, well-meaning philanthropists like Soros are finding that they have to be careful to avoid undermining the very causes they are promoting simply by attaching their names to them.

Similarly, when billionaires get involved in highly politicized issues like education, their involvement colors the debate. In Liberia, a major schools project was launched to develop something akin to charter schools in the country. These are privately run schools that would receive government funding. The program, called Partnership Schools for Liberia (PSL), became highly politicized, even though Liberia has the highest rate of out-of-school children in the world.[48] Two-thirds of Liberian kids don't get primary education.[49] The PSL program became a lightning rod for the broader question of private versus government schools in poor countries. International teachers unions and NGOs campaigned against it; major school reform organizations, some from the United States, argued in its favor. Politicization of the issue was due partly to the fact that some of the reformers backing the initiative were billionaire philanthropists. In fact, the most controversial of the private school operators involved in the PSL program was Bridge International Academies, which lists Bill Gates and Mark Zuckerberg among its investors, a fact often used by opponents to suggest the program lacks popular legitimacy.

Another issue where billionaire involvement has raised questions, but not controversy, is nutrition. Some billionaire philanthropists rightly think governments underinvest in nutrition. They see great potential to drum up more investment in this area by offering private money if governments and aid agencies increase their nutrition investments in turn. Two examples are the Power of Nutrition initiative, wherein private donors including the Children's Investment Fund Foundation and UBS Optimus Foundation are raising around $200 million in private contributions to encourage national governments and partners such as UNICEF and the World Bank to match four-to-one, ultimately leading to $1 billion in new, additional funding for nutrition.[50] Another example is the collective hundreds of millions of dollars contributed by the Gates Foundation, the Eleanor Crook Foundation, and the Aliko Dangote Foundation at the 2017 Nutrition Summit in an effort to push governmental donors to follow suit.[51] Some have questioned whether this use of private funding from billionaires to push governments to prioritize a certain issue, however laudatory that effort may be, ultimately undermines the representative nature of government.[52] They worry the voices of billionaire philanthropists, many of whom may be coming from overseas, are becoming stronger than those of ordinary citizens.

Those concerns may be valid philosophically, but it's hard to argue against providing nutrition to hungry children. Perhaps there are ways to mitigate the risk of undermining citizen voices while still addressing urgent needs?

Co-Impact is a promising new nonprofit organization set up by Olivia Leland, the former founding director of the Giving Pledge—the Gates and Buffett initiative to encourage billionaires to pledge half their wealth to charity. The purpose of Co-Impact is to help Giving Pledge members to pool their funds to tackle major global challenges together. It's "collaborative philanthropy."[53] This is especially helpful for billionaires who don't have big philanthropic organizations of their own and are newer to the world of global aid. By working together, billionaire philanthropists can make bigger, smarter bets to change the world for the better.

Banding together is also a potential solution to the problems of politicization billionaire philanthropists may face when they get directly involved. Nonetheless, pooling funds to create an arms-length distance between billionaire philanthropists and the issues they're funding can bring its own challenges. There is a risk of market distortion when large pools of funding pick one issue, one approach, or one set of implementing partners (NGOs and companies) over another. Move too far in that direction, and we could replicate the old monopsony model. It may also be harder to hold billionaires accountable for their giving if they increasingly move toward more anonymous giving through pooled funds.

As we face a coming wave of billionaire philanthropy, what's required are rules for the road, an example of which would be an admonition against anonymous giving. This is a historic opportunity to fundamentally change the world for the better, but we can only seize that opportunity if billionaire philanthropy is held to high standards of transparency and effectiveness. Those standards might need to be enshrined in law if billionaire philanthropists don't act quickly to demonstrate they are engaged in responsible giving.

Those seeking solutions to broader inequality are on the right track. Left unchecked, inequality can lead to "state capture"—a situation where a few wealthy people or interest groups effectively control the government. That can happen even in countries that hold elections and are technically democracies. As a result, there are tax, regulatory, and campaign finance reforms that may be required to mitigate the worst aspects of our current "gilded age."

But even if, for example, funds could be raised from a billionaire tax, governments would certainly not deploy the money entirely to end extreme poverty or achieve other critical zero goals. Already we face the problem of governments in rich countries dedicating too little funding to foreign aid—in the United States, it makes up just 1 percent of the federal budget.[54] Mark Zuckerberg and Priscilla Chan have pledged their massive future giving to education and human health. If more of their money were to be taxed by the US government, according to its current budget priorities most of it would be spent on defense, entitlement programs, and interest on the debt.

That's why the debate about billionaires paying more taxes versus donating more to charity is important, but too shallow on its own. We can't focus only on the amounts. Just as there is scrutiny of what governments spend tax revenues on, there needs to be scrutiny of what billionaires do with their philanthropic investments. What kind of impact are they actually having?

Zuckerberg and Chan's initiative is a case in point. Organized as a limited liability corporation, CZI is able to operate with little transparency, even though it is growing to become one of the largest philanthropic organizations in the world and could one day even eclipse the Gates Foundation.

The operating model Zuckerberg and Chan have in mind is also unusual and potentially problematic: they don't focus on giving grants to achieve their objectives—as nearly all other foundations would. Instead, they want to launch and operate programs themselves. This means that rather than maintain a small staff for grantmaking and advocacy, they will need to build a large in-house implementation team. Already CZI has a staff of 250, two and a half times the staff size at Bloomberg Philanthropies, even though the funding levels are nearly identical. That team includes 125 engineers, as CZI aims to build technology tools to advance scientific discovery in the medical field and improve learning outcomes in education.

As CZI scales to an organization that spends billions of dollars per year, its staff size could end up in the thousands. Funds that could have gone to social entrepreneurs and NGOs competing against each other to present the best ideas and results may instead end up building a massive institution that faces no competitive pressures and can't easily be scrutinized by the public. The approach might be practical, given CZI's central focus on technological innovation and the unique skill sets of its founders, but it could also be a mistake that distorts the aid market. Ultimately the public will need to be able to have an open and transparent debate about CZI's approach, even though CZI is organized as a private corporation.

The debate over whether billionaires should spend more on philanthropy or taxes isn't restricted to the rich countries where most of them live. A big part of the global development challenge is increasing the tax base in low-income countries, improving the capabilities of governments there, and pushing those governments to spend more of their limited resources on health, education, and infrastructure. Part of this agenda entails better tax enforcement, especially for the richest citizens of the poorest countries. But that's hard to achieve, and alone won't close the gap. And there are some foreign aid programs that have these goals, but private philanthropy has the most flexibility to attempt to influence and incentivize the governments of countries where most extreme poverty exists.

Mo Ibrahim's foundation does something no government aid program could: the African billionaire offers a $5 million prize to any African president or prime minister who leaves office when his or her term ends. It's an incentive to prioritize democracy and the rule of law, and just this year it was awarded to the outgoing president of Liberia, Ellen Johnson Sirleaf.

Like the Gates Foundation's funding of FAO and WHO and Ibrahim's prize, private philanthropy might just be able to make United Nations agencies, international organizations, and governments more effective in a way that just increasing taxes on billionaires can't.

The idea that trillions of dollars in new funding could soon become available to end extreme poverty, eliminate disease, and improve our planet and our lives strikes me as a good problem to have. That some of the most talented new economy leaders like Bill Gates, Michael Bloomberg, and Mark Zuckerberg would use their credibility, political clout, and expertise to move the needle on polio, smoking eradication, and education is a good thing. We need to both push more billionaires into that column and hold accountable those who don't act. We need to call out billionaires who give just to popular causes or pet projects and encourage those who instead fund proven, cost-effective interventions that maximize impact.

It won't be enough to sit back and watch more billionaires slowly sign up to the Giving Pledge and make their mark against the issues they care about. We'll need a highly engaged public encouraging results-oriented philanthropy and holding billionaires accountable when their giving isn't generating or even targeting the results the world needs. And we may well need laws and rules around transparency that allow us to do that. In the quest to end poverty, nearly eight hundred million ultrapoor adults and children are urgently counting on our ensuring their lives are on top of the global agenda.[55]

2. THE DEMAND FOR RESULTS
Good Evidence Is Hard to Find

IN 2005 MIT PROFESSOR Nicholas Negroponte, a well-known guru of the digital world, announced that he would deliver 150 million basic, rugged, crank-powered laptops to children in developing countries by 2007. His initiative, known as One Laptop Per Child (OLPC), was taken seriously in the media and got global attention. Who could argue with giving poor children a chance to learn by providing them with a free computer? And in this era of technological revolution, why couldn't an initiative this ambitious succeed?

The program, perhaps unsurprisingly in retrospect, fell far short of its goals. As of 2009, fewer than three hundred thousand laptops had been deployed.[1] When Uruguay and Peru placed large orders for the OLPC computers—900,000 to Peru, 570,000 to Uruguay—studies soon showed that the computers were having no impact on the children's ability to learn reading or math. In the rush to deploy the laptops, teachers had not been adequately trained. Curriculum had not been developed specifically for computer-based learning. There was not enough technical support. The machines fell into disrepair and eventually into disuse.[2] Later studies showed that, in general, the program was simply not getting good results.[3]

It's hard not to applaud OLPC for its ambition and good intentions. But, as we'll explore shortly, even university students traveling overseas to do something good can wind up causing harm. Blockbuster solutions that arrive from above, like OLPC, can be even worse. Ideas like this one can soak up funding from aid agencies and developing country governments, displace local markets, and disrupt locally rooted sustainable programs.

A results-oriented approach would have unfolded very differently, perhaps starting with a study to see whether the use of such laptops would actually result in specific defined outcomes, such as improved literacy rates, and would carefully consider any risks. If the results of the trial were positive, the initiative would then be rolled out iteratively, and only where there was community demand. Each deployment would be evaluated, tested, and the learnings applied to the next phase. In addition, the initiative would have focused on creating incentives in the market to produce the laptops (ideally in the region where they'd be used), rather than creating an organization to design and build a new machine.

One example of an aid intervention that took a more results-oriented approach is the use of road safety stickers in Kenya. In sub-Saharan Africa, road accidents are the leading cause of death for people fifteen to twenty-nine and the second leading cause for five- to fourteen-year-olds. The cost of all those accidents and deaths is estimated to be $10 billion per year.[4]

A major contributor to this urgent situation is dangerous driving, particularly by the operators of the minibuses locally known as *matatus*, which ferry millions of people to work and home every day. There's a culture of speeding, passing, and otherwise unsafe driving to get ahead. For passengers stuck in the back of a bus that's careening down the road with a reckless driver, it is easy to feel helpless.

Traditional approaches to improving road safety are expensive. They include installing lights and speed bumps, increasing police traffic enforcement, and establishing hotlines people can call to complain about drivers. The blockbuster approach might have been to design a safer vehicle. But William Jack and James Habyarimana, of the Georgetown University Initiative on Innovation, Development, and Evaluation, or *gui2de*, came up with the clever and cheap intervention of putting stickers inside every public service vehicle, like the *matatus* and buses, with motivational messages encouraging passengers to speak up when the operator is driving unsafely.

As is becoming typical in this new era of aid, the professors didn't propose an immediate global rollout. They began by doing a small pilot and running a randomized controlled trial, which showed remarkable results. Encouraging passengers with these "Zusha!" messages (which, in Kiswahili, means to "speak up" or "protest") appeared in the first randomized trial to have led directly to a 60 percent reduction in insurance claims involving injury or death in minibus accidents.[5] Overall insurance claims fell by a half to two-thirds compared to those of a control group. All this from simply placing some stickers in buses.

Two positive evaluations led to a tiered rollout of the program, and as evidence of its success grows it continues to spread. As a result, USAID backed it through its Development Innovation Ventures program. In 2015, Zusha! was launched nationwide in Kenya, and it is being tested in Uganda, Tanzania, and Rwanda.

THE COMPETITION FOR RESULTS

Zusha! is a far cry from the kind of ambition OLPC declared, but it may well have more of an actual impact and be a more cost-effective intervention. Cost-effectiveness is not an abstract concept. Funding for one activity could have gone to another with much lower potential to save and improve lives.

In fact, there have been so many successes in the past two decades that we should have a real sense of the opportunity cost of investing in the wrong kinds of aid. These successes establish a benchmark for effort that follows, regardless of its scale. When things go wrong, it forces us to ask: could the money and effort have been better spent elsewhere?

Many big successes relate to global health, and one of the most exciting cases is little known. Meningitis A was rampant across a wide swath of sub-Saharan Africa, from Senegal in the west all the way through to Ethiopia in the east. There are twenty-six countries in that region, and 450 million people live there.[6] Children and young adults are the most susceptible to the disease. People who contract meningitis A have a one-in-ten chance of dying within two days, even if they take antibiotics. Twenty-five percent of those who survive the disease are permanently affected by blindness, intellectual disabilities, hearing loss, seizures, or paralysis.[7]

In 1996, there was a particularly large outbreak of meningitis A. Two hundred fifty thousand people were infected, and twenty-five thousand died over just a two-year period.[8] Health ministers in the region appealed for international help. Ultimately, the Gates Foundation partnered with the World Health Organization and the global health NGO known as PATH. Together, they and other partners did something novel. They developed the first vaccine specifically for Africa. They designed it to be cheap—just forty cents per dose, or one-tenth the cost of a typical vaccine. Taking into consideration the conditions of the areas where it was needed, medical experts designed the vaccine to be rugged—able to last four days without refrigeration or an ice pack.

The vaccine was ready to go in 2010, and the partners began testing it in Africa's meningitis A belt. By 2016, more than 270 million people had received the vaccine. By the end of 2018 they expect to have vaccinated 430 million people and made meningitis A largely a disease of the past.[9]

Another remarkable success story is the fight against guinea worm. (The formal name is *dracunculiasis*, which comes from the idea that these worms are, from the Latin, "little dragons.") The disease has been around since ancient times and is even described in an Egyptian medical paper from 1550 BC.[10] Guinea worm is a disease straight out of a horror story. Drinking water can be contaminated with minuscule water fleas called copepods, which are themselves infected by worm larvae. Once the contaminated water reaches the stomach, the worm larva attaches itself and begins to grow. At first, there are no symptoms. It takes about a year for the worm to grow, and the female worms can grow up to a meter long. They are spaghetti-noodle thin—only a millimeter or two wide—but once fully grown they try to leave the body by burrowing through the subcutaneous tissues until they eventually form a blister on the skin from the inside. This process of the worm burrowing through the body is so painful that it's hard to walk or work. It can go on for weeks. The pain can be severe for months afterwards. One way many people remove the worm is by taking a small twig and slowly, painstakingly winding the worm around it as it exits, usually through the leg, sometimes between the toes, and, rarely, through the eyeball.

In 1986 three and a half million people were infected with guinea worm in twenty countries across Africa and Asia.[11] That same year the Carter Center, led by former president Jimmy Carter and his wife, Rosalynn, began the Guinea Worm Eradication Program. The Carters traveled around the world, pushing countries to focus on eradicating this disease. The interventions were basic, but effective. Putting a cloth filter over water buckets and other drinking water sources to prevent flea ingestion. Wearing a straw with a filter in it around the neck on a lanyard so one could safely drink water when away from home. Putting a chemical that kills the larvae in drinking water sources. Telling people to not dip their legs in water sources when the worm is forming a blister, which they do as a pain reliever. In 1995, Carter negotiated the longest humanitarian cease-fire in history in Sudan, known as the Guinea Worm Cease-Fire. This political maneuver allowed guinea worm eradication efforts, along with other global health work like vaccine distribution, to continue.[12]

After three decades of careful work, guinea worm is nearly eradicated. In 2017 there were around thirty human cases globally, in Ethiopia and Chad—down from 3.5 million when the Carter Center began its work. Even in war-torn South Sudan, there were no cases in 2017, although three were reported in 2018.[13] Since the parasite's life cycle is about a year (from flea to human and back to flea again), that means the disease is likely gone from South Sudan. When the eradication program began in South Sudan twelve years ago, there were 20,581 cases.[14] One simple tool health officials used in South Sudan was to offer a cash incentive of over $300 to anyone who came forward showing infection.[15]

It's highly likely guinea worm will permanently leave planet Earth in the next year or two, which could make it just the second human disease—smallpox was the first—to be eradicated. Jimmy Carter, who at this writing is ninety-three years old and in good health after battling cancer, may well live to see the day. But the eradication of polio could come first. Bill Gates has spent two decades battling polio as part of the Global Polio Eradication Initiative, which started in 1988, two years after the guinea worm initiative. It's possible polio may end also in the next year or two. After polio, Gates has malaria in his sights as the next major eradication target, and he's aiming to do it by 2040. He would be eighty-five years old.

Perhaps the most important global health success story of the past two decades is the rapid expansion of AIDS treatment for people living in poor countries, especially in Africa. Since 1999, sub-Saharan Africa has been the epicenter of the AIDS epidemic (it was that year the WHO declared AIDS was the number one cause of death in Africa).[16] Some seven in ten people living with HIV are African.[17] In the early part of this century, effective "cocktails" that combined multiple AIDS drugs were being developed—so called ARVs, or "antiretrovirals"—that could keep a person alive and healthy while living with HIV. But the cost of just one year's treatment was around $10,000.[18] In countries where annual incomes are in the hundreds, not thousands, of dollars, people were dying of AIDS in large numbers without access to these lifesaving drugs.

To date, 35 million people have died of AIDS, the vast majority of them in Africa. Without expansion of treatment, millions more African people would be dead today. Those deaths are not just individual tragedies—they have also decimated families, communities, schools, businesses, agricultural productivity, and entire economies. There are an estimated 11 million children in Africa today who have lost at least one parent to AIDS.[19] In Zimbabwe, three out of four orphans lost a parent to AIDS.[20] It's no exaggeration to say that Africa's entire future hung in the balance if AIDS treatments were not expanded.[21]

Millions of lives were saved by expanding access to treatment. The success was due to two main factors, interestingly led by two US presidents from different parties. The first was a massive effort spearheaded by the Clinton Foundation via its CHAI arm—the Clinton Health Access Initiative—to lower drug prices to around $100 per year per patient by coordinating massive bulk purchase agreements with governments, donors, and big pharmaceutical companies for African countries. The second was President George W. Bush's President's Emergency Plan for AIDS Relief (PEPFAR), which has grown to become the largest single commitment in human history by any country to combat a single disease.[22] More than $72 billion from American taxpayers has gone into saving the lives of millions of people around the world, and ensured that 2.2 million HIV positive mothers were able to give birth to healthy children.[23] Today the past successes in the fight against HIV are at risk, as a demographic boom of adolescents comes of age in sub-Saharan Africa and funding to fight the disease wanes.[24]

These global health success stories—meningitis A, guinea worm, polio, and HIV—are still works in progress, but they show what the aid industry, even with all its imperfections and failures, can do. They also highlight a chilling possibility—what if funding for any of these projects had gone into less effective, doomed projects?

▪ ▪ ▪ ▪ ▪

What makes someone donate to one charity versus another? Until now, it's been a charity's mission, story, and overall brand that matter most. After all, while we've all heard of the big brand-name charities, who among us could compare their cost-effectiveness on outcomes like child literacy or maternal health? My father would hear that Catholic Relief Services was working to help people after a particular disaster that was in the news, and he'd mail a fifty-dollar check. He knew its mission and backstory and felt his donation would go a long way there. In turn, Catholic Relief Services would send a glossy calendar with pictures of its work and the kids it was helping around the world, and he would rightly feel they were a serious organization trying to do good. I don't think he or many other donors ever considered demanding more information about the specific impact of their donations.

I got an eye-opening view of charity brand competition when I made a reporting trip to the Philippines not long after Typhoon Haiyan struck in November 2013. I traveled to a fishing village to see how recovery efforts were progressing. Most of the little houses, which had been built right at the water's edge, had been damaged or washed away by the storm surge. By the time I got there just a few weeks later, the village had largely been reconstructed thanks to the efforts of a number of NGOs, including Oxfam and World Vision. At least on the surface, the village was in better shape than it had been before the typhoon. It was postcard gorgeous, with its new, simple plank-board houses silhouetted against a dark ocean and the setting sun.

Picturesque houses were not what struck me most forcefully about the scene: it was the array of huge placards and colorful banners, displayed throughout the village, each one emblazoned with the name and logo of an aid organization that had participated in the reconstruction. They were essentially advertising billboards, trumpeting the goodness of the organization, competing for attention, vying for credit, and putting the organization forward for the next relief "job." I soon discovered that the advertisements were everywhere—in the major city in the area, Tacloban, as well as in the little fishing villages.

Competition is key to an effective market and is an important feature of the new aid industry. The issue is competition based on which factors? In the Philippines, it was competition for organizations to be seen as the most effective. USAID does the same thing: emblazoning the American flag on bags of food aid to show off our country's generosity.

This kind of branding falls into the category of "old aid." It's all about good intentions. It says, "Look, we're here, and we're trying." It has nothing to do with results.

When nearly all the aid money available to work in poor countries came from a few government agencies, brands only mattered for the biggest NGOs, such as Save the Children and World Vision, who raised funds from individuals and companies. For everyone else, relationships and reputations with the key decision makers in agencies like DFID and USAID were all that counted.

Today, in an industry with so many potential funders, including individual donors, brands have taken on a new importance. Small, nimble companies and NGOs are taking advantage of this shift, building global brands even when their operational scale is a fraction of that of some of the traditional players.

What's new is that brands will increasingly be built around good results rather than good intentions. Organizations are beginning to showcase their cost-effectiveness at a granular level by using independent, serious research. In the aid industry, the era of the glossy brochure and vinyl banner is ending fast. Even ordinary people making small donations are beginning to see themselves as "buyers," and want to know not just that organizations are putting their dollars to work in the effort to end extreme poverty, but that the organization is more cost-effective than its peers and is making measurable progress.

To understand just how seriously people are beginning to take the idea of focusing on results rather than intentions, we need only to look more closely at the heated debate that has become known as the Worm Wars.

All over the world, hundreds of millions of children are given deworming pills every year, whether or not they actually have the parasitic worms that can cause infection and seriously harm a child's health. The idea is that by preventing kids from getting worms, they'll be more nourished, will do better in school, will be generally healthier, and ultimately will earn more money over their lifetimes as a result.

At the center of the controversy is Michael Kremer, a Harvard economics professor and one of the originators of the move toward using randomized controlled trials (RCTs) as the gold standard for determining the effectiveness of development interventions. Like Tuna and Moskovitz and other new aid leaders, Kremer is an effective altruist.

Kremer and his colleague Ted Miguel did an RCT study in 2004 in Kenya that aimed to show the impact of giving deworming pills to kids in school. This study became famous because it showed that a pill that costs pennies could have an enormous impact in fighting global poverty. Everyone was intrigued, more studies followed, and distribution of deworming pills took off. Then over the years, as is quite normal, the original authors and others reviewed the raw data and the findings from the study and noticed some errors. In 2015, another review of the data was conducted and questions arose as to the accuracy of the original study. This led to in-depth journalism by medical reporters, and a firestorm on Twitter and in the blogosphere, with economists getting heated debating the details of how to analyze the results of the study and whether or not deworming ultimately is all that it was cracked up to be.

After years of emotional argument among normally reserved academics, the Worm Wars continue, but deworming remains a widely accepted global development idea. That's in part because even if critics are right and the program is a fraction as successful as the original studies suggested, it would still be among the most cost-effective aid interventions in the world. More than 280 million children participate in school-based deworming programs around the world at a cost of under fifty cents per child.[25]

This insider debate about the effectiveness of deworming initiatives showcases the transformation happening in global development. Ordinarily, the study may not have been revisited, even by experts in the area. Instead, the entire aid industry was watching and hungry for specific, data-backed evidence that this effort had been worthwhile. Those who might have simply sent a check were invested in the outcome.

Conducting careful studies—including RCTs like the one focused on deworming pills—has quickly become a standard approach in the aid industry. Such studies have been done for US social policy for decades, but only began to gain tremendous popularity in the global development community in the past decade as the industry became more focused on results.

IMPACT EVALUATIONS

YEAR	REPORTS	YEAR	REPORTS
2016	146	1998	25
2015	536	1997	18
2014	485	1996	25
2013	489	1995	13
2012	555	1994	13
2011	489	1993	9
2010	371	1992	3
2009	338	1991	3
2008	240	1990	3
2007	193	1989	2
2006	159	1988	3
2005	151	1987	1
2004	98	1986	2
2003	88	1985	1
2002	57	1984	0
2001	51	1983	0
2000	35	1982	1
1999	40	1981	1
		TOTAL	**4,644**

Source: "Impact Evaluations," International Initiative for Impact Evaluation, www.3ieimpact.org, accessed October 25, 2018.

People who came to believe strongly in the importance of these studies are known within the aid industry as *randomistas*. And for good reason. Their initial fervor propelled a massive increase in the use of RCTs.

In recent years, doubts have begun to emerge as to whether this methodology is being overapplied and its downsides underestimated. Drawbacks include cost and lost time, and the inability to translate lessons from one context to another. While the focus on results that RCTs exemplify remains undiminished, *randomistas* have lost some of their zeal.

Results-oriented aid workers have begun to favor approaches that are more integrated into projects themselves, such as real-time data dashboards that allow for course-corrections while a project is ongoing.

Unfortunately, some donors are still seduced into immediate feel-good donations without seriously considering the results. Orphanages are the classic, and sadly still pervasive, example of this. They are the literal poster-children of charity, the archetypal idea of what giving is all about. Like so much else, a closer look shows that orphanages are not the optimal solution to homelessness or poverty, and can even be part of the problem. They don't meet the test of "do no harm," yet thousands of people—including well-intentioned high school and university students in Western countries—donate and volunteer to support them.

According to the United Nations, some 80 percent of the 150 million children living in orphanages today actually have living family members, including at least one parent.

Why are kids abandoned? Often because of poverty. Their parents are alive but can't afford to care for their own children. In fact, a child can be an "orphan" according to the official UN definition and still have one parent around.[26] Other kids are abandoned because they have a disability. Parents may believe they can't afford to properly care for and raise kids with special needs and that they will be better off in an orphanage. However, it actually costs more to fund orphanages than it would to give parents the money they need to care for their own kids.[27]

But here's the rub: donors love orphanages. A church-affiliated survey in Australia conducted in 2016 showed that over half of all churchgoing Australians (51 percent) said they donated to orphanages. Another report from Griffith Law School in Australia found that 57.5 percent of Australian universities were advertising orphanage volunteer opportunities among their international program opportunities for their students.[28]

Orphanages are such attractive charities that unscrupulous operators have devised a variety of scams to relieve do-good donors of their cash. In Cambodia, for example, the civil war ended in 1975, leaving one in four Cambodians displaced.[29] People all over the world followed the plight of the Cambodian refugees.

The number of orphanages in Cambodia has steadily risen since the war ended. Between 2015 to 2017, the number of Cambodian orphanages grew by 60 percent.[30] Parents are convinced through intentional misinformation that their children will receive a better education and will have access to better opportunities at an orphanage than they could get at home. Many Cambodian orphanages are scams, and regulations for orphanages are lax—38 percent have never been inspected.[31] The conditions in some of these orphanages are often horrific. Kids are forced into labor, including sex work. They are poorly fed so they don't have the energy to resist their situation. Even worse, their very visible hunger is strategic for the unscrupulous orphanage owners: it plays on the sympathies of visiting donors.[32]

Of course, not all orphanages are like this. Some do good and important work, and many children have no other options. However, the Cambodian government acknowledges that fully 30 percent of the kids in orphanages should not be there and ought to be returned to families.[33] That's five thousand kids, making it a kind of mass kidnapping of unprecedented scale, and that's just in one country. The worst part is that the rise of these unscrupulous orphanages has largely been fueled by good intentions of charitable people who donate and volunteer.

Who should be accountable for crimes of this kind? Governments could investigate, shut down, or prosecute crooked orphanage operators. Parents could be held liable for neglect. The thousands of university students who travel to Cambodia and other countries to work in orphanages, who raise money for kids, and who post about their experiences on social media can't be held criminally accountable, but we need to help people understand that this kind of unquestioning, if well-intentioned, behavior is not necessarily solving a problem, and may even be exacerbating the situation.

Some countries, especially in Africa, are in the position of needing to push back against the charity of foreigners. Many are banning or cracking down on orphanages, citing concerns that well-meaning foreigners coming as part of voluntourism programs are actually fueling the orphanage industry: the *Economist* cites a study that says 52 percent of orphanages in Malawi are actively recruiting kids who would not otherwise be considered orphans. Rwanda is a leader on this front—there are now just a dozen orphanages, down from four hundred a decade ago.[34]

Much of the reduction in African orphanages is due to the efforts of Hope and Homes for Children, a British charity dedicated to "deinstitutionalization," or transitioning kids out of orphanages and into family homes, whether with their own parents, extended families, or foster families.

In other countries, the separation of children from their families has become so institutionalized as to be extremely challenging to reverse. For example, in Haiti there are three hundred thousand kids known as "restaveks," who are essentially child slaves. They are domestic servants for other families. That's one in five Haitian kids living like this. *Restavek* in Creole means "to stay with" (from the French "reste avec"), and these are kids whose parents send them to stay with families that have slightly more money, in order to give them a better life in exchange for their labor. But it's a horrible life—apart from their family, made to work, given little food and no education (even though the host family may have assured the parents that the child would get some education). Haiti is the poorest country in the Western Hemisphere, and this issue persists because of the poverty and fuels continuing poverty. And discrimination plays a role: the majority of restaveks are girls.

The International Labor Organization (ILO, a UN agency) says that the average fifteen-year-old restavek weighs forty-four pounds less than other Haitian kids his or her age and is one-and-a-half inches shorter. This cycle—malnutrition leading to stunting and wasting and mental deficiencies—contributes directly to the continued cycle of extreme poverty. In Haiti, fully half the country is ultrapoor.

Child separation and slavery is precisely the kind of issue the aid industry should be focused on reversing, but, as the orphanages example shows, without a results-oriented approach it's possible to do more harm than good. That's why we need to consider the potential negative side effects of our charitable activities. To use another example, thousands of bed nets treated with insecticide have been distributed in areas where malaria is a threat, and they have successfully repelled mosquitos that bear the disease. However, the nets are also put to other uses, such as fishing. The insecticide leaches into the waters and ends up polluting lakes and rivers. Is this reason to discontinue the distribution program? Of course not, but we must acknowledge that the positive effect is discounted in part by the negative side effects. Should organizations budget for the costs of mitigating those negative side effects, for example educating people about how to use—and not use—the nets? Absolutely.

There are a number of agencies that have taken on the difficult challenge of weighing these issues of efficacy and impact, using a variety of approaches. For example, Charity Navigator, founded in 2001, focuses on the fitness of the organizations themselves. They rate a large number of the most important nonprofits in the United States—nine thousand out of a total of some 1.6 million—based on two key criteria: financial health and accountability/transparency.

Charity Navigator's promise is to provide "objective ratings" so donors can find charities they "can trust and support" and avoid the mistake of giving money to organizations that might waste it.

Waste can take many forms, the most obvious of which is fraud, and Charity Navigator clearly flags organizations guilty of not using their resources wisely. As of this writing, of the charities assessed on the Charity Navigator website, 413 include a warning to donors.[35] These might pertain to media allegations about overspending, pending criminal charges, or revocation of nonprofit tax status by the IRS. Charity Navigator also calls out organizations with dubious financial records. If a charity spends too much on executive compensation or fundraising activities and too little on the actual work it purports to do, as a percentage of its overall budget, Charity Navigator will let people know. This is all valuable and useful information, and most nonprofits are pleased to receive a positive rating from Charity Navigator. As a part of increasingly important branding efforts, organizations will include the Charity Navigator approval logo on the donation pages of their websites as a sort of seal of approval.

This rating method is basically a negative screen—it flags organizations that do not meet certain basic criteria. The tougher challenge comes in evaluating an organization's positive impact. Some of those criteria can be problematic or unhelpful. For example, Charity Navigator allots positive points to an organization if it increases spending on its programs year after year. There's certainly a logic to this. A charity exists to raise funds from donors to spend on its programs and projects. If spending goes up, we might assume that more money is devoted to the projects and more good is accomplished. However, the downside is that the reward for funding growth does not necessarily correlate with positive impact or desired results.

Charity Navigator does recognize the limitations of focusing on money alone and has been working to develop a positive screen—a way of rewarding organizations for the actual impact they're having—in its methodology. For example, it will sometimes include impact measurements developed by third-party organizations to test whether this information is useful to potential donors.

This kind of "impact data" requires careful study and a good deal of knowledge to evaluate properly. It's most useful for those who are already well-versed in the world of global aid. For people just beginning their philanthropic journey, the data may not reveal much about the cost-effectiveness of the work, the long-run versus short-run benefits, or real or potential negative side effects.

Another group, GuideStar, takes a more robust approach to impact metrics: it incentivizes organizations to share a good deal of information about their work and how they themselves measure their impact. Those that do share information are awarded a badge that ranks their transparency—bronze, silver, gold, or platinum. Even so, it's challenging for a GuideStar user to judge the cost-effectiveness of one organization versus another, as they may each measure their own impacts differently. It's certainly not like looking at standard financial metrics when considering buying a stock or a bond. The rankings are more subjective, and not based on an agreed-upon system of external reviews. Donors are left to decide whether their donation will do more good going to a "platinum-rated" organization versus one with a "silver" designation.

GiveWell is a San Francisco-based charity rating service founded in 2007 by Holden Karnofsky and Elie Hassenfeld, two young men who were working as analysts for a hedge fund. Unsatisfied with the lack of data upon which to make donation decisions with their own money, they set out to develop a rigorous methodology in order to determine how to do the most good with their contributions.

Seeking to replicate the kinds of financial metrics they utilized in their previous careers, GiveWell's founders hit upon a standard metric for evaluating aid interventions against each other: the number of lives they saved. (Technically, lives saved is spoken of in terms of QALYs—pronounced *qualeez*—and DALYs—pronounced *dolleez*. These are measures of the number of years of life saved or lost, adjusted for quality or disability, respectively.) The organization makes careful cost-benefit analyses to determine which interventions save the most lives—such as providing medicines to children afflicted with worms—and it considers only organizations it determines are underfunded. Rating the effectiveness of every single charity in this way would be extraordinarily difficult, perhaps even impossible. As such, GiveWell does not attempt to rate thousands of entities, nor does it easily hand out endorsements. As of this writing, just nine charities have a GiveWell recommendation and seven more have honorable mentions.

A great benefit of GiveWell is that it is radically transparent. On its blog, you can follow along as the cerebral staff wrestles with difficult intellectual and ethical questions in measuring the probability that an intervention will work, or determining how much additional funding a charity can take before seeing diminishing returns. Ultimately there are a lot of assumptions that GiveWell's analysts must make to determine which charities they support. Putting a value on saving a young life versus an old one, for example, might be a determining factor in their calculus for picking one charity over another. That's a hard determination to make, although they do it transparently and in good faith.

The biggest difficulty posed by impact measurements of the kind GiveWell uses is the time horizon. Again, immediate and short-term impacts always seem most attractive and are easiest to see and measure. People are dying daily from easily preventable diseases, so it would seem that prioritizing programs that reduce those deaths would have the greatest impact. That's what GiveWell's charities tend to do. They fund programs that provide bed nets to reduce malaria, distribute pills for deworming, or deliver chlorine to sanitize drinking water.

However, big problems, like extreme poverty, are tied to chronic, systemic issues. If efforts are focused on short-term projects alone, we may not be making an impact on poverty in the long run or in the toughest places. GiveWell charities help alleviate immediate suffering, which is critical. But other models exist that aim to stop the cycle of poverty itself.

THE GRADUATION MODEL

The graduation model is the idea of making a big investment in a single person that fundamentally changes his or her life over the long term—rather than going for the cheapest donation that will benefit the most people possible today. It's the basis of the Ubuntu Education Fund, now Ubuntu Pathways, a relatively small nongovernmental aid organization in Port Elizabeth, South Africa. Its self-described purpose: to help raise Port Elizabeth's orphaned and vulnerable children by giving them "what all children deserve—everything."[36]

One of those kids is Siya, a South African girl whose early life did not augur well for her future. An HIV-positive child, she "lived in a shack with an unstable family" whose members could not sustain themselves, let alone offer Siya the opportunities she deserved. Then along came Ubuntu Pathways. In a post Jake Lief, the organization's founder and CEO, wrote on Devex, he told the story of how Ubuntu had paid for Siya's healthcare and schooling from the time she was eight years old all the way through university. It even bought her the pink dress she graduated in.

Lief wrote the post to point out what he saw as the dangers inherent in focusing on narrow impact metrics. Some of Ubuntu's wealthy donors—many of whom made millions on Wall Street—would question Lief about whether it made sense to invest so much in a single individual. Was it really cost-effective to invest so much money in Siya when the same amount would have paid for a lot of insecticide-treated bed nets or necessary medicines, which would have helped a greater number of people and possibly created a higher return on investment?

Lief, himself the son of an investment banker, understands that Wall Street bankers have a return-on-investment mind-set. He also knows they think nothing of spending $50,000 just on annual preschool tuition for one of their own kids. And there's a reason for that: it pays off. It *does* deliver a return, if we take the long view.

The total cost to Ubuntu's Wall Street funders for helping Siya was about $62,400. The intent was not to make Siya's life better just for her personal gain but rather to create a virtuous cycle. An investment in education for a single person enables him or her to thrive, become a productive citizen, help others, and ultimately save enormous amounts for society and even create new wealth. Ubuntu claims its own model shows that its investment in Siya has led to a $195,000 "net lifetime contribution to society."[37]

That's the concept behind the "graduation model" that has been gaining currency in the aid industry. Rather than invest in interventions that incrementally improve many people's lives but don't do much, if any-thing, to get them off aid, people like Lief want to make up-front invest-ments that will help people like Siya get off aid forever. This approach is comparatively expensive in the short-run but can bring great benefits over time. So philanthropists now have to ask themselves: should I take the risk on the long-term investment or fund something that we know works and can reach huge numbers of people immediately?

Whatever the answer, what matters is asking the question. In the new aid industry, the debate about results, not good intentions, is the debate worth having. We can argue about time frames and investment models, so long as the competition is focused on results.

■　■　■　■　■

As we've seen in our discussion of these charity-rating tools, it would be most useful—indeed the holy grail of impact measurement—if we could develop a set of standard, universal metrics that would allow us to make true apples-to-apples comparisons between different kinds of organiza-tions and different scales of initiatives.

If we could create a model or algorithm that takes into account both immediate needs and long-term challenges, that includes risk assess-ments and probabilities of success, and that considers life span, quality of life, and lives saved—and then comes up with a relatively simple and universal cost-effectiveness rating for every charity or intervention on earth—well, that would be incredibly exciting. Bill and Melinda Gates would use it to make grants. The World Bank would rely on it to approve loans. The effectiveness of the aid industry would soar. Seemingly in-tractable problems would no longer look impossible to solve. We'd race toward our goal of eradicating extreme poverty.

Though it certainly wouldn't be a silver bullet, checklists like the one developed for hospitals by Dr. Atul Gawande might also be effective for measuring project effectiveness and tracking accountability. Gawande's approach is to influence human behavior to ensure that a certain set of basic tasks or procedures is always done in surgery situations, so that a doctor never leaves instruments inside the patient or a nurse always washes his or her hands. It turns out these checklists are both simple and profoundly impactful.

For aid workers and organizations, a checklist could help avoid mistakes of oversimplification or succumbing to the draw of good intentions. A checklist for the aid industry might seek the following:

❑ *A clear definition of the success factors being measured (e.g., literacy rates or incomes or maternal deaths or reduction in conflict or human trafficking)*
❑ *A logic model, explaining in very concise form the theory of how this intervention is going to move the needle on those factors being measured*
❑ *A listing of risks to the very people you're trying to help: what could go wrong that would actually hurt them?*
❑ *A listing of risks to others: could there be unintended consequences for others in the community or the family?*
❑ *A projected cost-benefit ratio*
❑ *An itemized list of the data points that will be tracked and publicly released (along with information on how often each will be released)*
❑ *A statement of how lessons learned will be shared and acted upon (and how often)*
❑ *A checkbox on sustainability: whether the project or initiative aims to be sustainable over time by generating its own source of funding or through transfer to a national government or local institutions, and, if so, how*

In addition to checklists, there are many other tools we could use for improving the effectiveness and impact of the aid industry. We could push every development project of a certain size to adopt a voluntary, standard reporting procedure. We could insist that major philanthropists sign on to a set of basic principles of responsible giving, perhaps as part of the Giving Pledge. We could expect every aid organization to provide real-time information on its funding and activities, rather than delivering such information in the form of an annual report, which is the norm in the global development industry today.

These kinds of tools are improvements in the realm of the possible. On the other hand, I called a standard, universal metric the holy grail for a reason. We're not going to find it. But the more transparent and thoughtful we get about measuring results, the closer we'll get to impact metrics we can invest against. That, in turn, will lead to more aid.

DEVELOPMENT IMPACT BONDS

One intriguing mechanism designed to attract more private capital to fund global development goals is known as the "development impact bond" or "social impact bond." In this model, an investor agrees to take a risk on a development project in exchange for a potential payoff if it succeeds.

An example of this model is the Utkrisht Impact Bond. In India, the majority of mothers access care from privately funded facilities. The quality varies substantially—from gleaming hospitals operating at the highest global standard to local quacks writing prescriptions willy-nilly. But how to improve the overall quality of these private facilities? Funding organizations like USAID have a goal to make sure more women safely give birth and have children who survive. The old way of doing that would be for USAID to try to tackle the entire issue at once: they would study the problem, design a solution, and hire an NGO to deliver that solution. This felt like a way of controlling risk, but actually the donor owned all the risk: if a donor made a mistake in understanding the true problem, in designing the solution, or in hiring the organization to execute it, the whole project could fail. The only people holding the bag would be the funders—USAID, and the US taxpayers who support it—and the poor mothers not getting the care they and their babies need.

To give a sense of the urgency of the problem, in Rajasthan, a state in northwest India, almost 5 percent of babies born alive don't survive.[38] In comparison, in the US, the infant mortality rate is one-half of one percent, and even that is high for advanced countries.[39]

A development impact bond (DIB) is an instrument that basically tries to pay for results while spreading the risk around, which allows funders to fund more projects. More importantly, it creates and aligns incentives so everyone is working hard to get to the best solutions for those moms and babies.

In the case of the Utkrisht bond, the idea is for aid organizations to work with two highly regarded NGOs—Population Services International and Hindustan Lever Family Planning Promotion Trust—in order to find ways to improve the private providers of maternal and newborn care. If they can do it, and hit certain targets, they'll get paid not only what it costs to do the work but a success bonus, too.

Instead of telling aid organizations precisely what to do, these bonds let the NGOs do their own thing: try, experiment, make mistakes, and try again. They'll stay laser-focused on the end results rather than try to execute a plan designed thousands of miles away.

If these NGOs meet their goal of saving ten thousand lives, they'll get paid that success bonus by USAID and Merck for Mothers (a program of the pharma company Merck aimed at saving maternal and newborn lives). That makes sense for USAID and Merck, because they only pay if a specific goal is met, greatly reducing their risk. Because they are only paying for successful initiatives, they can take on more projects than they otherwise would if they were paying out all along the way regardless of results.

But it costs a lot of money to do this work, so who is going to front all the cash? Surely the NGOs can't afford to just pay all their staff for years hoping they are successful?

The financing comes from investors. In this case, UBS Optimus Foundation, a part of the largest wealth manager in the world. The Swiss bank pays the money up front in exchange for getting its money back and a rate of return—in the case of Utkrisht, several percentage points on its investment.

The beauty of this model is that there's lots of investor money out there, far more than there is philanthropic money. Think trillions rather than billions. Rather than risking philanthropic grant money up front, in this model it's investor money that's at risk. Only if the results are achieved do the donors pay.

As of this writing, there are fewer than ten DIBs operating in the world, but if these kinds of pay-for-results models work it could create a revolutionary market for development aid and push traditional aid funders to adopt more innovative, results-oriented approaches. Already the World Bank, an institution that has been giving loans to governments for decades, is pivoting to become more of an innovative finance institution. In 2015 it was part of the creation of the innovative funding mechanism known as the Global Financing Facility, designed to get middle-income countries to invest more in healthcare. In 2016 it created a financing mechanism to provide cheap loans to countries where there is a sudden influx of refugees, such as Jordan and Lebanon. In 2017 it issued "pandemic bonds," a kind of insurance scheme designed to pay out to countries when they are hit with an outbreak of disease, such as Ebola. By 2018, the World Bank was announcing a Famine Action Mechanism that front-loads funding to countries where famine is predicted using advanced analytics tools. Partners in the effort include Amazon, Google, and Microsoft.

There will still be a critical need for philanthropic money, and there's much more of that flowing now. A tidal wave of billionaire and ordinary giving is coming. DIBs and other innovative financing mechanisms could mobilize that funding and make it far more effective.

CELEBRITIES CLAIM COUNTRIES

That tidal wave of giving is at least correlated with the growing involvement of celebrities in the aid industry. Their role is a subject of some controversy. They can attract tremendous attention and quickly raise awareness for projects and causes. They can also make a mess. That's because celebrity culture is more closely aligned with old aid, in that it prizes easy answers, good intentions, and stories of individual heroes. Theirs is a simplistic world of good guys versus bad.

In the real world, global development challenges are extremely complex. "Complex adaptive systems" is the technical term for how things actually work. Push a button in one area (say, building a school for underprivileged youth) and you may make an unintended problem in another (say, exacerbating ethnic tensions because the school is seen as a benefit to one group).

Even the benefits that celebrities can deliver—raising awareness, mobilizing fans, and opening doors in the halls of political power—are not unalloyed positives. As Tufts professor Alex de Waal argues, celebrity lobbying can undermine local leaders and simplify complex issues, leading to misguided policies. *Mother Jones* has a cheeky "interactive map of the celebrity recolonization of Africa" that shows which countries celebrities have "claimed."[40]

While it's easy to be cynical about celebrity involvement, healthy skepticism rather than downright cynicism is warranted. Celebrities can be part of the focus on results, if they are serious about wanting to help and if organizations they work with don't simplify complex problems or undermine local leadership and activism. If they can avoid those pitfalls and still raise money and awareness for a cause, celebrity involvement can be a good thing.

In that context, it's interesting to consider why one of the best-known celebrity-driven projects—Madonna's school in Malawi—failed so badly. In 2006, Madonna created a nonprofit called Raising Malawi to support orphans and vulnerable children in one of the most impoverished countries in the world. On the organization's website she says, "When I discovered that there were over a million children orphaned by AIDS, living in one of the poorest countries in Africa, I felt an overwhelming sense of responsibility to get involved and do what I could to help bring awareness to the situation."[41]

In some ways, Madonna's efforts have succeeded. She has effectively brought global media attention to Malawi and raised significant sums of money using her name and connections. But one major project she sponsored—a school for four hundred girls—ran into trouble. Madonna seemed truly committed to the country (she adopted four Malawian children and still visits twice a year) but despite multiple trips there did not realize the classic folly of trying to build a school from halfway across the world. Rather than work with a locally rooted, credible organization that already provided education in the country, Madonna's initiative essentially started from scratch. The proposed budget for the school was astronomical for Malawi—$15 million. According to the *New York Times* and other sources, some $3.8 million was swiftly spent on building designs, architects' fees, even cars for employees who had yet to be hired.[42]

In 2011, the school project collapsed and was abandoned. Madonna, in a 2018 interview with *People*, blamed the failure on local mismanagement, and described what it was like to endure such a massive and incredibly public failure.

"I'm the biggest philanthropist in Malawi, but I was being treated like a criminal. It's crazy. But all my work in Malawi's been like that," says Madonna, who didn't give up. "People would say to me, 'Oh, you're so naïve—who do you think you are?' Then I would go, 'Maybe they're right. Who do I think I am?' After a couple days, I'd think, 'Everyone who's criticizing me: What are you doing to make the world a better place?' At the end of the day, you just have to get on with things, if you believe in what you're doing."[43]

Despite Madonna's doubts and reservations, her commitment to Malawi appears to be genuine. Her latest 990 IRS filing for the organization shows that it received over $9 million in grants in 2016, up from just over $600,000 the prior year.[44] The Raising Malawi website details a number of areas where it claims impressive successes, including educating 5,600 children through schools Raising Malawi constructed (apparently through partners) in 2013, two years after the original school project was abandoned.[45]

Madonna is just one of many big-name celebrities who have thrown themselves into development projects and philanthropic causes—including Bono's ONE Campaign, which fights for foreign aid; Richard Branson's Carbon War Room, which fights against climate change; and the Enough Project, which is most closely associated with George Clooney and fights against genocide and conflict. All these are examples of celebrities using their ability to get attention and open doors to lobby for important policy change.

So many of the global goals ultimately do connect to policy and politics. Keeping steady support for foreign aid is one example; pushing for reducing greenhouse gas emissions is another. But complex issues require thoughtful policy changes. For example, new trade rules can help some impoverished people but unintentionally hurt others. Something similar appears to have happened with a law, passed in 2010 by Democrats and Republicans, that was heavily promoted by the Enough campaign.

That law is colloquially known as the Conflict Minerals Law, but really it's just a brief addendum to the massive Dodd-Frank law regulating the financial industry.[46] That add-on (section 1502 of the bill) essentially says that companies using minerals in their products have to certify that those minerals aren't fueling the war in the Democratic Republic of the Congo (DRC). By 2010, the war had claimed an estimated five million lives over a decade and a half, and was still going on, thanks in part to the money militias could extract from the artisanal mining of tin, tungsten, tantalum, and gold. DRC has an estimated $24 trillion worth of these minerals under the ground. They are heavily used by companies including Apple, Google, and Intel for electronics, and in the manufacture of jewelry and automobiles. Enough and its many celebrity supporters, along with other activist groups, thought it found a way to help end the war: regulate the minerals that militias were using to fund it.

After years of hard campaigning by Enough, section 1502 passed. Though the law was written with the best of intentions, these are complex issues and even what appear to be practical solutions can have unintended consequences. The law seems to have been successful in some areas, including putting a spotlight on an important issue, getting Europe and China to agree to also regulate the minerals, and choking off some funding to violent militias. On the other hand, one in six jobs in the country are tied to the mining industry, and the bill may have had the unintended consequence of cutting income to some impoverished miners, leading to economic recession and hardship for many Congolese people.[47] The Conflict Minerals Law may have even provided a new source of income to unscrupulous actors willing to go around the law. Rwandan media has reported that the country has now surpassed Congo as the world's largest exporter of the mineral used in electronics (tantalum, or, more precisely, its precursor coltan), leading some analysts to believe illicit dealers are simply smuggling the product out of Congo.[48]

Not all celebrity activism takes place in front of cameras or Congress. Forest Whitaker, the Oscar-winning actor, took his role as UNESCO Goodwill Ambassador so seriously that he ended up forming a peace-building organization that works in some of the toughest places in the world. He has made many visits to South Sudan and Uganda, personally working with young people of different ethnic groups to bridge differences. His organization, the Whitaker Peace & Development Initiative, has so far trained over four hundred young people to be "peacemakers." When I interviewed him in 2016, Whitaker shared how he saw the "same look in the eyes" of child soldiers in Africa as he had seen when he worked with young gang members in the United States.[49]

I'm told Whitaker was once called upon to help broker a meeting with rebel leaders in South Sudan. As the executive director of his nonprofit crouched out of sight in the backseat of their car, Whitaker had to walk past piles of dead bodies and drugged child soldiers holding guns.

HARD TO MEASURE BUT IMPORTANT

There's another way good intentions can lead to unintended consequences: thinking that focusing on metrics automatically leads to results. As we transition into a results-oriented era, there is a danger that we'll prioritize what is easiest to measure, while underinvesting in less tangible impacts, such as the leverage and influence that can be generated by the power of advocacy.

Consider, for example, the case of Yegna, the now infamous girl band. The UK *Daily Mail* tabloid derided Yegna as the "Ethiopian Spice Girls" in an effort to delegitimize it by depicting the band as an example of wasted foreign aid. Britain's foreign aid agency, DFID, had given around $7 million in grants to the group of five young Ethiopian women, who had attracted a huge following of girls and boys with their music about troubling, complex issues related to gender stereotypes and cultural behaviors, such as child marriage.[50]

The music video for their first hit—"Abet"—opens with a young woman in a headdress doing laundry in a metal vessel full of soapy water. She stands in front of her home, a ramshackle mud and brick affair, with goats at her feet. This is in many ways your typical girl band—five members, all in their twenties, each with a distinct "personality" designed to attract young girls to see themselves in one or the other and to identify personally with their stories—but this is Ethiopia, a wonderful country I've been honored to visit but where, according to UNICEF, three out of every four girls have their labia and clitoris ceremonially mutilated when they reach puberty. One in five girls are married off before the age of fifteen, and a third of all girls don't attend school. In other words, this is a country where it's no small thing for young women to serve as role models or leaders.

On an Ethiopian talk show in 2015, the Yegna band members were filmed among their fans. Young girls came up dressed like their favorite members of the band—some uncannily matching their hairdos and clothes. One girl said she identified with the character Lemlem because "she's poor and she's nice." Another, tearing up while speaking of Mimi, the tough girl character in the band who has her arm around her during the interview, says, "Mimi is courageous—she doesn't care about anything. She is very confident. I love you Mimi, and thank you!"[51]

Yegna, which means "ours" in Amharic, is Ethiopia's first girl band. The group was conceptualized by Girl Effect, a nonprofit spun out of the Nike Foundation, which uses the best Hollywood and media industry techniques to change attitudes about girls and women around the world.

The band hosts a weekly radio show telling the story of five unique girls forming a band and the challenges they face. It provides a venue to bring up issues like domestic abuse or sexual harassment and discuss those issues in a way that resonates with young listeners—both girls and boys.

What the creators of Yegna didn't realize is that they would be a juicy target for a campaign that had nothing to do with Ethiopia. The conservative *Daily Mail* has been on the hunt for years for ways to make the case against increasing British foreign aid, arguing for a Britain-first approach in the face of domestic spending cuts. In the end, it convinced DFID minister Priti Patel to drop funding for the group—the celebratory headline read "Aid: *Now* They're Listening."[52]

Listening to what? The danger in focusing only on wholly tangible results is that it provides an opening for aid opponents with isolationist, us-versus-them agendas to criticize work that's essential but more difficult to measure. Was Yegna good value—as Girl Effect claims—or a waste of money? In its "investigation," the *Daily Mail* hammered home the point that Girl Effect could not prove what British aid was ultimately buying with Yegna. After the British government pulled all aid to the group, the *Daily Mail* headline huffed, in part, "Did Listening to a Girl Band REALLY Stop 40,000 Young Ethiopian Girls Getting Married Too Early?"[53]

Girl Effect worked to show results, including polling that demonstrated 76 percent of girls who listened to Yegna saying they felt inspired to continue their educations.[54] But these kinds of results may not be enough for skeptics. That's why pay-for-performance approaches hold so much promise: imagine if the British government was paying for a specific reduction in child marriage or female genital mutilation? Those results are much easier to measure with precision. Instead of prescribing approaches to achieving those goals, and having to heed the opinions of tabloid journalists, the government aid agencies can allow the market to work: the most cost-effective ideas, which may well include ideas like Yegna, will win out.

SHAKEOUT

The note written by the Harvard Business School professors at the height of the dot-com bubble suggests that today's period of experimentation in the aid industry will end, as seems logical, with a shakeout. A shakeout of this kind, they found, typically takes around a decade. Some established organizations working in this space for many years may go under or shrink dramatically. Projects once heralded as ambitious and exciting may land in disgrace as rigorous metrics are applied to the aid industry overall. As diseases are eradicated and lives saved, making the case for your NGO or aid project may get more and more competitive.

An early case was Merlin, a storied UK NGO that nonetheless faced financial challenges linked in part to this emerging shakeout. Merlin was huge by earlier standards: it had five thousand employees and an annual budget of around $100 million.[55] Growing competition was putting Merlin in a precarious position. It was too big to rely on small grants but too small to compete against much larger organizations for the biggest aid contracts. Even if it won those contracts, it couldn't afford to pay up front to do the work and wait to be repaid later by DFID or other donor agencies.

Plus, the market for individual donations, while growing fast, was also getting more competitive. New NGOs with smart social media strategies and modern messaging, such as Charity: Water, were popping up and raising tens and even hundreds of millions of dollars. Merlin simply couldn't compete. In 2013, Merlin was acquired by Save the Children to avoid insolvency.[56]

Traditional NGOs or development consulting companies could be in for a rude awakening. Some are innovating and changing, learning to shift their cultures and approaches to the new focus on results, and even admitting to mistakes. And these organizations typically have so much experience and technical expertise that they are in a position not just to survive but to thrive if they can get their business model right.

But others are trapped in a way of thinking that's fast becoming extinct. They have the wrong customer in mind: in the new era, it's the ultrapoor, not your largest funders, who are your key customers. Many established implementers of aid projects, among them billion-dollar nonprofits that are household names and for-profit government contractors that take in hundreds of millions in foreign aid revenue but are not so widely known, may find themselves caught in a storm as the results revolution gets stronger.

As results become easier to measure and data more transparent, the new aid industry will grow. Donors who might have sat on the sideline—including ordinary givers who donate in tens and hundreds of dollars, not millions and billions—will be encouraged to enter the market. What billionaire wouldn't want to end extreme poverty in an entire country if such a result could be more certain? Who among us wouldn't save a life if we knew with certainty our donation would work?

3. PEOPLE, NOT WIDGETS
What Do People Really Need?

IN A JOURNALISM CLASS I took in college, our professor showed a clip from a TV news broadcast of the Vietnam War era. It featured an American foreign correspondent, dressed for the part, in a khaki safari jacket, looking directly into the camera. Behind him we could see, as backdrop, a stream of Cambodian refugees listlessly trudging along. The correspondent leaned into the camera and intoned in a deep baritone, "One can only imagine what must be going through the minds of these fleeing refugees."

After showing the clip, the professor asked a simple question. If the correspondent wanted to know what was going through the minds of the refugees, why didn't he just ask them? It was as if they were aliens from another planet who could never be understood, let alone communicated with.

That describes one key problem with the traditional aid industry approach: decisions were made by people in large institutions at great remove from the people they sought to help. There were many reasons for that, one of which was that it was very difficult to communicate with people who did not have access to phones or televisions or mail, who spoke a vast array of languages, but not all of whom could read or write, and who were often scattered in remote areas.

But, of course, the internet, widespread connectivity, and cheap communications devices have changed all that. There are no more excuses. For the first time in history we can communicate directly with the people we're trying to help, and do it at massive scale. If we take full advantage of this new opportunity, it could make the aid industry more effective than ever before.

To do that, however, we have to use this connectivity to ask the question that on-camera journalist didn't: What are you thinking? What do you really need?

Only by asking those questions, listening carefully, watching how people actually behave and react in the real world, and then designing programs to address those realities, will we be able to get the kind of results we want. Poor people should have the strongest voice in what's happening in their own lives. To borrow a term from economics, they should have "agency" in the decisions made about the aid they receive. This is a problem even in the expanded and more competitive aid market, because the decision-making power—the agency—is still largely in the hands of rich people in San Francisco, Seattle, and Sydney. Even with the best of intentions, that divide can lead to huge mistakes.

There are many initiatives trying to address this issue, of how to give people in need more of a voice in the aid industry, but most aren't realistic. Sometimes surveys are conducted before or after a project to get input from the people who are affected. In my experience it's rare for a development project to be based around what poor people themselves are actually asking for. This is because decision makers bring a number of biases to the table, including an assumption that they know better, and a sometimes unconscious desire to not give up control.

I know that mind-set because it applies to me, too, and perhaps to many people who have been involved in some of our most cherished charitable activities. In high school I participated in a Thanksgiving food drive. It was an annual tradition, and we loaded up cardboard boxes with a frozen turkey and all the sides that go with it: boxes of stuffing and cans of gravy, cranberry sauce, and green beans. I was given a list of families in need, compiled by the church, and drove to their houses (some were classmates of mine) to drop off the boxes. People seemed appreciative, and everyone associated with this initiative felt great about it. I still see these drives all the time: for toys and food during Christmas, turkeys during Thanksgiving, canned goods during natural disasters.

What's underpinning this great tradition, however, is a dark underbelly. One assumption is that poor people can't be trusted with cash: they might spend it on booze and their family would go without a Thanksgiving meal. So, better to buy them food. Another is that the way for us to feel good during highly consumptive times of year like Christmas and Thanksgiving is by giving a little away to others. If it were really about the needs of the poor, why so much focus on just a few days a year? Plus there's the sense that we're not really providing something of value—we can just dig into our cupboards for an old can we haven't used, perhaps of something that's high in sodium or fat. And many people purchase new food for these food drives, and they're doing that at high retail prices instead of buying in bulk nationwide.

What if we had actually turned away from the camera (to return to our Vietnam War correspondent) and asked the people trudging along behind us? Together, we might have designed a very different initiative. I could imagine it would extend beyond a few holidays and that it would give the recipients choices about what food to buy and when. Chances are it would look a lot more like a cash transfer program—perhaps with appropriate restrictions and safeguards—than a food drive. And what about all those volunteer hours associated with food drives? All the time spent shopping for canned goods and dropping them off at the local library or firehouse? Well, maybe those hours would be better spent in other ways: helping a poor family fix up their home, or helping their kids do their homework, or helping them fill out the paperwork for government services. That would entail volunteers spending more time directly with poor families, strengthening our bonds of common citizenship and reducing the idea that there's "us" and "them."

To know what will really improve people's lives in the real world, you have to talk to them and deeply understand how and why they make the decisions they do.

My uncle likes to tell a story from his days as a medical student. As part of his university training in India, he had to provide medical service in rural and underdeveloped areas for some time. He recalls patients coming into his clinic. He diagnosed them, and then provided them with pills for their ailments. Looking out the window, he saw a strange sight: patients conferring with each other, palms open, looking down. He realized what was happening: they were trading pills with each other based on their color ("I'll give you a blue if you give me a yellow . . ."), not realizing each contained a different kind of medicine for a different ailment. It's a story that makes us wonder: are we designing health, education, employment, and other projects in global development in a way that actually takes into account how people behave and make choices?

A behavioral sciences approach to aid uses human psychology as a tool instead of an impediment. Traditional economics-based approaches focus on provision, access, and pricing. For example, should everyone be given an insecticide-treated bed net to combat mosquito bites that cause malaria infection? If the cost-benefit model shows it makes sense, OK. The next step would be making sure everyone who actually needs a bed net can get one, focusing on things like distribution systems to rural areas. Finally, we consider price: should the bed nets be free? Or should we institute some kind of sliding scale based on ability to pay?

These are all critical issues, but by adding a behavioral science perspective we're more likely to ensure this bed net program actually works. The bed nets work in a laboratory setting, but what about in real life? A behavioral approach might begin by interviewing people about how they feel about using a bed net, and asking them if they ever fail to use it and why. Aid groups may learn that bed nets can make it too hot to sleep, they can be hard to hang, or that it's a pain to get in and out of bed, especially with little kids.

Behavior-based approaches would take these kinds of issues into account, ensuring not just that bed nets are provided but that they are actually used. This is known as *adoption*, and is related to similar issues like *uptake* (how many people start using the net), *utilization* (how well they use it—tucking it in properly and hanging it correctly), and *regularity of use* (every night or just sporadically?). A review of several studies from the early 2000s showed that only half the households that owned insecticide-treated bed nets in Africa actually used them regularly for kids under five years old—the most susceptible to deadly malaria.[1]

These adoption issues are prevalent across global development interventions, from medicine to education to agriculture. Is it enough to offer farmers better seeds? Perhaps not, if they don't understand how to use them. Are free IUDs going to lower birthrates? Perhaps not, if women are embarrassed to ask for them.

The World Bank has a Mind, Behavior, and Development (eMBeD) team of about a dozen behavioral scientists, started in 2015. The same year it was founded, the team conducted a randomized trial to prove that experiential learning is more effective than just trying to tell people to do things.[2] They used the national lottery in South Africa as the example. They asked regular lottery players to roll dice. They asked them to roll one die until they got a six. Once they did, they gave them two dice and asked them to roll until they got two sixes. Then they explained that winning the lottery would be getting all sixes on nine dice at the same time. Then they measured whether these people kept playing the lottery after this experience. What they found is that people who took longer to get the two sixes learned the point more clearly and reduced their lottery playing.

An amazing example of the power of behavioral approaches comes from popular Brazilian soap operas.[3] One-quarter of the country tunes in to watch soap operas at 9:15 p.m. every evening.[4] By contrast, only one in ten Americans watch the Oscars. The soap operas—called tele-novelas—have huge cultural resonance. The main producer of these pro-grams—Globo—purposely designed the story lines so the characters had no kids, or just a few kids, very much unlike the actual situation of the average Brazilian family. Globo did this to limit the number of characters on screen and thus the number of actors it had to cast, and perhaps to fit writers' conceptions of an idealized family.[5] A study from 2012 shows that this change in telenovelas led to a dramatic and measurable decline in birth rates in Brazil. The researchers were able to measure this by looking at fertility rates a year after certain municipalities got access to the soap operas. The effect was strongest for women in the same age cat-egory as the main characters in the soap opera (thirty-five to forty-four): for those women, there was an 11 percent decrease in fertility. In behav-ioral science, this is known as the role model effect.[6]

In addition to the behavioral science approach of studying what drives human behavior, another approach with tremendous promise is employing human-centered design (HCD), or directly engaging with the people you aim to serve. The key distinction is that behavioral science involves people in identifying a problem; HCD actually involves the peo-ple you're trying to help in designing the solution. For example, asking someone why they don't use a bed net and then taking into account that the nets make it too hot to sleep in designing a solution—that's behav-ioral science. Actually setting up a prototyping session with the bed net user, in which they are helping to design a product or message that will help counteract that problem, makes it human-centered design. HCD requires more than just conducting surveys or listening, it involves directly working with people to design, test, and refine an approach.

An example of an HCD project is Lab.our Ward, an initiative to redesign the physical architecture of maternity wards in poor countries. The architects involved in the project seek to understand the entire experience of a woman giving birth in a maternity ward. How would women themselves design a ward that meets their needs?

At the Women Deliver conference in Copenhagen in 2015, I witnessed Lab.our Ward set up a maternity ward experience for conference attendees to showcase what they normally do with the expectant mothers they typically serve. We could walk through the setting to experience what it would be like to be a "customer" of a maternity ward, and were able to offer feedback at every step, from the check-in process to what the beds would be like, to how to call for help if something went wrong, to how a medical professional would actually deliver in such environments. The project is all about getting input from women and medical professionals who would actually use these wards in order to design a maternity ward of the future.

This HCD ethos of seeing people as "users" is exactly aligned with the new aid industry approach of seeing people not as beneficiaries or "the needy" but rather as customers with a voice in the process.

Behavioral science helps develop deep insights—really understanding the problem from the perspective of the customer. Where HCD takes this further is by working with those customers—often through a process known as rapid prototyping—to figure out what might work to help solve the problem.

All this can seem like an extra cost, an extra step. Why not just give the money directly to people? Well, for complex issues—like maternity wards—it's not enough to give people money to pay for medical services when those services just don't exist. You actually need to step into the market and help design a solution.

CONNECTING WITH THE CUSTOMER

One of the barriers to ensuring that poor people have agency in their own aid has been fundamental: we did not know enough about them, or have a way to reach them even if we did. It is estimated that about 15 percent of people on earth are not identified—they are not registered with any agency or listed on any voting roll, and do not have any identifying data, such as a Social Security number, a credit score, or even a bank account.[7] That's 1.1 billion people who are essentially anonymous. When it comes to connectivity, just over 50 percent of the world's population has access to the internet, which means that four billion people are *not* connected to the greatest source of information and communication ever developed.[8]

A growing realization that the problem of unidentified and disconnected people can be rapidly solved with new technologies has led to a range of initiatives. The most ambitious program to identify the unidentified is the Aadhaar program in India, a massive effort to biometrically identify all the country's 1.3 billion citizens.[9] The program is nearing completion—some 1.2 billion now have an ID based on their irises or fingerprints. Aadhaar puts government agencies in a position to more efficiently provide social services, and Indian banks can more easily open accounts while complying with know-your-customer rules.

Getting an accurate fingerprint scan, however, is not as simple or foolproof as it sounds, for a number of reasons. For example, farmers who toil long days in the fields using manual tools often wear down their fingerprints to a point where conventional scanners can't read them. A Cambridge University startup, Simprints, has developed an advanced fingerprint scanning technology that is more sensitive, which has also proved useful for healthcare initiatives. In an area of Bangladesh, the Simprints scanners have been used to identify thousands of mothers and their newborn babies to help build a complete record of their healthcare and ensure greater continuity of care over time. Simprints is part of a growing movement to professionalize delivery of health, education, agriculture, energy, and other services, treating the poor not as nameless and helpless but as identifiable consumers.

As far as increasing connectivity, some of the big tech companies are beginning to see the potential of innovating to serve customers in markets where connection is a problem. Of course, these monster technology companies don't think of the drive to connect all humans—including the lowest-income among us—as a purely humanitarian activity. To them, it's core to their business model. Microsoft wants every human being to use its software. Facebook isn't satisfied with two billion users—it wants all of us. Google can't stomach the idea that people would search for information anywhere else. In fact, the *Wall Street Journal* recently reported that technology companies are rolling out entirely new software that uses images instead of words, designed specifically for the poorest people who have no formal education.

While internet connectivity is essential, it can also have significant downsides. Among them are the potential for political destabilization, cultural loss, proliferation of scams, and consumerism. Recently, for example, Facebook users played a significant role in the tragedy of the Rohingya people of Myanmar. Anti-Rohingya sentiments spread like wildfire on Facebook, which is where a majority of people in Myanmar get their information and communicate. Most people in Myanmar use Facebook in part because of Facebook's program to provide free access to the internet through the Facebook Free Basics program. The normalization of hate speech has been at least partly responsible for an alarming rise in hate crimes against the Rohingya people. As a result, many have fled to Bangladesh, in what has become another refugee crisis. Facebook eventually shut down Free Basics in Myanmar, although many observers, including the former US ambassador to Myanmar Derek Mitchell, who spoke to Devex on the topic, have criticized the company for acting too slowly and reluctantly.

Another example of the risks of sudden and widespread interconnectivity can be seen in the Philippines. Facebook users may have played a role in political fragmentation there.[10] Similar to American complaints of living in "news bubbles," these divisions can have effects that are even worse in countries like the Philippines that are already divided along ethnic and language lines.

Beyond divisions within societies, traditional communities unused to interaction with the outside world may not be prepared for what will happen when their young people join a new global culture online. Similarly, people suddenly exposed to the internet may be unprepared for the kinds of sophisticated scams that are so rampant online. Finally, internet access can lead to a culture of consumerism, which may be deeply destabilizing for traditional communities.

Even as we grapple with the concerns related to internet connectivity, remarkable efforts continue to expand access to the half of the global population that is currently disconnected. For most unconnected people, those efforts are really about making the internet more affordable, because there is availability where they live, but it's just too costly for them to use it. On the other hand, around 10 to 15 percent of the unconnected people have no internet access at all, even if they had the money to pay for it.[11] For those people, there are high-tech solutions in development. Facebook's solar-powered Aquila drone, with a V-shaped wingspan larger than that of a Boeing 737, aimed to bring wireless internet to places that are currently cut off, including in rural sub-Saharan Africa.[12] But the project was shelved in 2018, even as similar efforts by aerospace companies are under way.[13] Google's similarly ambitious Project Loon, which brings internet to remote areas using large balloons equipped with wireless routers that float above off-the-grid parts of the world, has gained more traction and is being made commercially available for purchase by telecom companies.[14] Finally, Microsoft is pioneering TV White Spaces, which is a long-range wireless internet technology that utilizes unused portions of the television spectrum. Its first such project, in Kenya, now offers unlimited internet access for three dollars per month. Microsoft also has similar projects in Ghana, South Africa, Tanzania, Botswana, and Namibia.[15]

These and other initiatives make it likely that connectivity will continue to grow rapidly, and in the relatively near future this could be a universally connected world. That connectivity will be a key element in fundamentally transforming the way the aid industry operates.

LOW FINANCE

Perhaps the most disruptive trend in directly connecting with poor consumers and creating solutions that meet their real needs relates to personal finance.

In the United States everyone has a credit score, like it or not. Globally, only 30 percent of people have one.[16] Credit scores have a big impact, determining our fitness to buy a house, and how much interest we pay on credit cards. In many less advanced economies, there is no such thing as a credit score, and many people don't have formal jobs with pay stubs and the kinds of banking histories that would make it easy to generate a score. These people are often referred to as the "unbanked."

Innovative entrepreneurs are racing to utilize machine learning and artificial intelligence, combined with ubiquitous information on people's cell phones, including social media activity, to create a new kind of credit score for customers in these economies. Tala, a loan company founded by a twenty-four-year-old former UN employee, Shivani Siroya, developed a proprietary algorithm to determine who is creditworthy and who is not. It starts people off with a small loan—say fifty dollars delivered to their cell phones—and lets them build up a credit history over time. Just four years since its founding, Tala has already given small loans to 1.5 million customers in Kenya, Tanzania, Mexico, and the Philippines who couldn't otherwise have walked into a bank and asked for one. In fact, for Tala's potential customers—three billion unbanked people in the world—often the only alternative is to visit a loan shark.

That's one reason M-Pesa, the Kenyan mobile money platform, has been wildly successful. It gives people the option to transfer money among family and friends through their mobile phones, and increasingly is used for sophisticated financial services like insurance and savings. Today, it processes transactions for at least one individual in 96 percent[17] of the country's households—that includes the vast majority of households living in extreme poverty.[18]

M-Pesa is one of the biggest global development success stories. It started as a partnership between the massive telecom company Vodafone and DFID. Each contributed around $1.3 million to get M-Pesa, which is run by Vodafone's East African company Safaricom, off the ground. Because of its success, the Gates Foundation has funded several other telecom companies around the world to help them develop similar mobile money platforms.[19] In addition, Gates granted $11 million to Mastercard to support a lab in Kenya that designs innovative financial products for the poor. In 2014, the Gates Foundation announced it would provide up to $8 million to support the commercialization of any financial products developed there for the poor.[20]

What has happened in Kenya can happen in other parts of the world that are still relying on ancient methods of banking and financial accounting. Take for example, Colombia. My wife was born there, and we have family there as well as many relatives who moved to California like she did. Her grandmother, now eighty-five, raised eight children as a single mom and is retired in a mobile home community in Sonoma County. When we visited recently, I came across an odd piece of loose-leaf paper: it had several names on it and dollar amounts next to each name. I showed my wife and she explained this was the old-fashioned savings and insurance system called *rueda* ("wheel" in English) still in use today. Her grandmother and her friends put a set amount of money each week into the pot—say $20. Every month the full amount is paid out to a different person. If someone gets sick or has an emergency and needs money, they can withdraw early, jumping ahead in line.

Systems like that one—or the *hawala* system ubiquitous across the Middle East, North Africa, Horn of Africa, and the Indian subcontinent, which allows the transfer of money among brokers without connecting to an actual bank—remain widely in use around the world. But once formal financial systems reach the poorest of the poor, it becomes not only possible but better—cheaper, more secure, more reliable—to get insurance, savings, and credit products from reputable banks. At the very least, it will be more efficient to get money from friends and family using systems like M-Pesa. The days of loan sharks and money traders controlling the financial stability of the world's poor are numbered.

DISASTER CASH

The expansion of mobile money will be especially beneficial in times of disaster. In Tacloban, the Philippines, after the typhoon struck in 2013, major aid agencies handed out cash in exchange for cleaning debris and for other helpful activities. They knew that providing cash after a disaster is often much more effective and much cheaper than trying to cart in everything on their own. It helps local businesses to get started up more quickly and get people back to work. People can decide what they need to buy, instead of being handed whatever supplies are available. Supply chains can be remarkably resilient, so sometimes there are goods available to buy, even shortly after a crisis.

In fact, one aid worker told me that right after the typhoon, even before the relief agencies were really set up to start helping, one supply chain was up and running. On nearly every corner in downtown Tacloban there were vendors selling liquor. Some enterprising businesspeople knew that there would be a market with all the Filipino soldiers coming to town for the rescue and recovery, and amazingly they were able to get the supplies into the city.

Handing out cash isn't easy. For one thing, there are security concerns. For another, cash is tough to administer. You need to be sure you're not giving it out twice to the same person; if you give it away all at once, prices can rise and money can be wasted, but giving it away slowly over time is an administrative headache.

Increasingly, bringing cash to people in need is done electronically through mobile money platforms, designed with all kinds of safeguards and features that improve on paper money. Already Syrian refugees in Lebanon receive a kind of debit card that they can use in certain stores, allowing them the independence to pick out the brand of cooking oil they prefer or the type of rice that their family usually eats. There's dignity in being able to make those choices. It's also practical for the humanitarian agency involved—in this case the World Food Programme. They can know in real time what products people prefer, what quantities are required, and how much funding they may need to sustain this support. All of this points to a future in which humanitarian aid is delivered electronically far more efficiently than shipping bags of grain across the ocean.

Around $28 billion is spent each year for humanitarian relief, but another $15 billion is required.[21] This funding gap will need to be bridged with more donations—from governments, companies, and individuals—but that alone is unlikely to do it. The amounts required are set to grow each year as the number of climate refugees grows and political conflicts rage on. The only way to make ends meet in the humanitarian sector is to both increase donations *and* get more cost-efficient.

That's possible thanks to technological advances which are increasingly coming to even the most remote and underresourced places. Infrastructure designed to withstand floods and storms, energy sources that are renewable and portable, ubiquitous internet connectivity, digital IDs, and, as we have explored, mobile money, are all getting cheaper, more available, and easier to deploy.

These technologies alone won't fill the gap if the aid industry doesn't figure out how to use them. When it comes to delivering electronic cash, we need to ensure banking regulations contain emergency clauses to allow for aid to be delivered via electronic currency without the need to rewrite the rules in times of crisis. Issues of privacy and data security need to be sorted out well in advance of the tsunami or conflict so that NGOs know what data to collect from those in need and how to keep it secure. Metrics and tools for evaluating impact in real time need to be well-developed and staff need to be trained to use them. Emergency funds must be pre-positioned, ready to deploy.

None of this will happen without a mind-set shift. We need a redefinition of "humanitarian aid" to include the years of peacetime, of calm seas and sleeping tectonic plates. Every country, every business, every village chief, even every family should have their own crisis plans. And that process of thinking through what to do in a time of crisis—alongside the best practices from the world's leading NGOs and humanitarian agencies—can lead us down the path to a future where emergencies are less destructive and communities can bounce back faster.

A mind-set shift must apply to refugees, as well. The lingering image of the refugee is someone fleeing war or oppression. They arrive on the shore in tattered clothes and with immediate needs. That's certainly the case for many refugees, but it's not the full picture. Today the average refugee has been living in exile for around ten years.[22] In places like Lebanon where there are more than a million refugees, most live in apartments in the city.[23] They're often well-educated and computer literate, and have a smartphone in their pocket. In other words, they may need help, but they're not helpless.

Seeing refugees as agents of their own futures, not as victims, humanitarian organizations are beginning to operate differently. They may still give away food, but they buy it from local businesses and farmers. They focus on helping refugees find jobs. And they increasingly give cash, vouchers, or limited debit cards directly to people who can use the money as they see fit. At this point, less than 10 percent of the $28 billion spent each year on emergency relief, including for refugees, is provided in the form of some kind of currency to people who need it. But since that's been proven to be so much more effective, it's an area ripe for rapid disruption, and it's emblematic of a shift to a more consumer-centric approach to aid work.

MAKING THE GLOBAL, LOCAL

Climate change is a complex problem that many people are concerned about. Yet it can be hard to mobilize people to take real action. At the conceptual level, it's easy for some highly tuned-in people to get energized around doing something about the looming disaster for the planet. That small minority of people will change their behavior in difficult ways that require real lifestyle modifications: eschewing meat, for example, or composting leftover food. For most others, it takes a local problem like a flood or a wildfire to begin to see the threat as so significant that personal sacrifices might be called for. Even then, human behavior is such that most people will fall into the trap of moral hazard: knowing that their own lifestyle modifications will have such a vanishingly small impact on the planet that they can wait for others to change their own lifestyles first.

We interviewed the prime minister of the Maldives, a small Indian Ocean island nation, and he described how he held a cabinet meeting on the ocean floor, complete with scuba gear and a submerged conference table, in order to focus global attention on what rising seas could do to his lowland country. That's a compelling photo op but for most people probably not enough to make them change out their lightbulbs for LEDs or start bicycling to work.

What does work is connecting people to their local environments. Even fishermen who are overfishing their own waters can change their behavior if they're all brought together around the shared goal of preserving their community and way of life. When governments and well-meaning conservationists declare areas nature preserves, there's every chance the local people making their living by poaching turtles or clear-cutting forests won't heed the new rules. But if those same poachers and loggers come together around a solution that works for them and their families—a bottom-up campaign of sorts—there can be lasting change.

That insight—getting people engaged in protecting their own local environment—is the kind of human-centered design approach that is critical to the new way of doing global development work. Not incidentally, it involves actually talking with people and making them the center of their own transformation. An app or a global database or a slick advertising campaign designed in London or Frankfurt can be critically important, but these approaches must begin with a deep humility and understanding of the local context and what drives people.

A good illustration is the issue of overfishing in the Philippines.[24] It might sound like an environmental problem: too much fishing has depleted the stocks of fish around the country's shores. In reality, this island nation of one hundred million people is facing a looming humanitarian disaster. Over half of the animal protein that Filipino people eat comes from the sea, and millions of people work in the fishing industry to feed the huge appetite of such a big country. Almost all those workers are artisanal, working for family operations as opposed to big commercial ones, so they're particularly vulnerable. Fish populations have been on the downturn for sixty years now and could be nearing a total collapse that would put millions of people out of work and take fish out of the diets of many millions more.

Rare, a leading conservation organization, was looking at this coming disaster and trying to figure out how to approach it, knowing all the pitfalls of a top-down approach. It found a model that has worked elsewhere, called TURF (for "territorial use rights for fishing") and is applying it in the Philippines at the local level. This behavior-based approach seeks to understand what drives overfishing to begin with in order to adequately address it.

When fishing is a zero-sum game, fisherman must compete viciously. They have to fish more hours and in more places to get those remaining hard-to-find fish before another fisherman catches them.

TURF changes the equation to a collective effort. In exchange for not fishing in certain areas that are protected—so-called marine-protected areas, or MPAs—fishermen gain the right to fish in the surrounding areas. They're giving up something but getting something valuable in return. The protected areas allow fish to get big and fat, creating positive spillovers into the areas where fishing is allowed. As a result, local fishermen see value in banding together to enforce the rules so that they all benefit together. Most importantly, they play a key role in deciding which areas to protect and which to fish in, so they can devise a plan that's realistic to follow.

This example from the Philippines is a good one, because it encapsulates all that the new approach to development entails: putting people at the center of devising their own solutions, taking into account human behavior and what drives it (including market mechanisms), and thinking of the broader system—in this case, seeing the conservation of marine life not as a narrow stand-alone issue but rather as one that is integrally connected to employment and nutrition for an entire nation.

CULTURAL CHANGE

In India, a big reason for the high child-mortality rate is the fact that so many people—almost half the population of the most populous country on earth—still defecate in the open. We can transfer cash to the poorest people, but if we don't address the factors that lead to 117,285 child deaths from diarrheal disease in 2016, the problem will persist.[25] Addressing something like 524 million people practicing open defecation isn't a simple technical matter.[26]

I can say from personal experience in India—and social scientists have confirmed this in studies—that toilet ownership is not aspirational and sanitation is not prioritized culturally. It's even taboo.[27] Millions of Indians are born left-handed but trained out of it because the left hand is associated with cleaning oneself after going to the bathroom. My own father's chicken-scratch handwriting was because of this—his parents forced him to become right-handed.

Even in a relatively rich country like India, where the gross national product is over $2 trillion, simply transferring wealth is unlikely to end extreme poverty on its own.[28] We'll need to focus on what we now know works by talking with local people to better understand their interests and by getting them involved in designing their own solutions. In other words, developing not just an affordable toilet but one they will want to use. Within this process, it's imperative to understand systemic challenges, like gender discrimination, to consider whether women will utilize public toilets even if they are ubiquitous: Will they continue to wait until nightfall because it's not seen as dignified to use the bathroom? Will they feel safe going there? What else could be done to meet their cultural needs while ensuring they are able to use toilets?

Another complex challenge common in India and in many other countries where extreme poverty is high is child marriage. (Some groups make a compelling argument that this should be known as "forced marriage," since minors are not in a position to consent to marriage.) My own grandmother, for example, was married at just thirteen years old to a groom she had never met. By all accounts, theirs was a typical and happy marriage. It was also the norm at that time. They were married in the early 1920s. The Indian law raising the legal age to fifteen for girls and eighteen for boys was passed in 1929. After several modifications over the years, the law was changed in 1978 to make marriage illegal for girls under eighteen and for boys under twenty-one.

The Indian census shows real improvement—child marriage is steadily decreasing. Even still, UNICEF's data indicates that one in four Indian girls (27 percent) are married before they reach eighteen years of age, and 7 percent before fifteen years of age.[29]

Besides the human rights violations involved, why should we care? Because child marriage traps families in poverty. It's no coincidence that girls from poorer families are three times more likely to marry young than are their counterparts from families that are better off. There are certainly cultural drivers, but desperate financial conditions are a major factor: families marry off their daughters to reduce the number of mouths to feed and perhaps bring in extra income in the form of a bride price. (In India, the opposite custom prevails even though it's against the law: in many cases a bride's family must pay a dowry to the groom's family.)

Once married, girls typically receive no more education. A century ago, my grandmother received no schooling at all. Statistics demonstrate what should be obvious: girls who don't get an education earn far less as adults. They also have children at a younger age and ultimately have more of them. This too exacerbates poverty for the entire family, repeating the cycle.

Some creative initiatives may be helping, among them government crackdowns on the wedding industry in the Indian state of Telangana, demanding that florists, caterers, printers, and even priests check birth certificates or face legal consequences.[30] The most widespread undertaking designed to combat child marriage—ongoing for two decades now through separate initiatives in various Indian states—are financial incentives. This approach, in which parents receive a cash subsidy if their children don't get married until the legal age, has worked. In southern Bangladesh, Save the Children has piloted a similarly cost-effective approach—offering cooking oil every four months if girls remained unmarried.

Providing money to the poorest people in order to delay marriage is logical. Unmarried girls still living at home cost money to feed and support. Dowries are typically costlier for older girls. The incentives are simple and make sense—if parents don't force their daughters to marry they will be rewarded for it. But here's where clarity of goals is so important in global development and where complexity can creep in: the money is working to keep girls from forced marriages while minors, but studies have shown that many parents just delay the forced marriage until girls turn eighteen, and then use the financial windfall to partly fund the wedding.[31]

In other words, girls and young women in this scenario are not really changing their status in society. In this equation they remain a cost, something to be subsidized; a kind of property whose most important life choices will still be made by someone else. Delaying marriage is an important step and should be seen as a partial success of these programs, but ending the cycle of poverty will require something more. According to one study, cash transfers are no substitute for educating girls and connecting them to good jobs.[32] When that has happened—as has been the case in India's massive outsourcing industry, which employs millions of young women—their families begin to see them as "assets rather than liabilities."

LISTEN FIRST

With growing recognition of the importance of hearing directly from people about their own needs, it's not surprising that the world's largest social network has found it has a role to play. In Colombia, 1doc3, an organization that answers medical questions online, anonymously, and for free using doctors, accessed Facebook demographic tools to identify a major uptick in young women talking about "condom water." An internet rumor spread among teenage girls that if they boiled condoms in water and then drank the water they wouldn't get pregnant. The old approach to aid—say, distributing condoms in schools without really listening to young people—might have actually resulted in more teenage pregnancies had this rumor not been heard and rebutted. The organization, 1doc3, was able to use its platform to connect these girls with health professionals, who could then understand what was happening and counteract the myth with real information. It's an example of what's possible when the social-good community expands to include unlikely players with enormous scale, like Facebook.

Obviously privacy issues related to Facebook are an important topic today, which of course relates to ethical questions about monitoring activity on the platform, even for public health purposes. These serious privacy questions need to be addressed in part because there is tremendous opportunity to use Facebook for good in the developing world.[33] UNICEF is now using WhatsApp (a Facebook property) to communicate with young people under a UNICEF initiative called U-Report. Youth across fifty mainly low-income countries can share their views on schooling, healthcare, and other important social and development issues, helping to propel their voices into the political process when the U-Report poll results get published on radio and in the press. Five million young people use this *every day*.[34] That one data point offers a sense of the scale and functionality Facebook can provide that no aid agency can replicate on its own.

A social network with two billion members isn't the only tool for listening to young people and other marginalized groups. The Surgo Foundation—which counts the author and behavioral science expert Malcolm Gladwell among its funders and trustees—is another organization that prizes communicating directly with the people it aims to support. In Uttar Pradesh, India's largest state, with approximately the same population as Indonesia, Russia, and Brazil, Surgo took a low-tech survey approach that might just have a big impact.

Surgo's goal was to find out why many young women there are not using family-planning methods. Sema Sgaier, who heads the foundation, found the old model—creating awareness about the importance of family planning and then giving away family-planning methods, like IUDs, for free—wasn't having the desired effect. It turns out that cultural norms in the state made young women feel they couldn't go to the clinic alone, and when they went with their mothers-in-law, as was typical, they felt ashamed to ask for birth control because of taboos around sex.

By listening first and putting the young woman at the center of the equation, Surgo is able to study what kinds of interventions, such as sending nurses to make home visits, might change behavior and serve needs. In some ways it's a subtle shift, but it's one that can have profound results, including, as we'll see below, for the world's largest NGO.

EMBRACING FAILURE

Traditional aid industry players face real risks in this transforming industry. They are well known, which makes them targets for the upstarts. Many of their donors still expect to get calendars and tote bags and might not respond well to talk of failures and lessons learned, something the insurgents have made de rigueur. Some of the new players even have a tab labelled "mistakes" on their website.

BRAC, based in Bangladesh, is the largest NGO in the world as measured by staff size, with over 120,000 employees. Like the more famous Grameen Bank—only far larger—BRAC does a lot of work with microfinance, health, education, water, and sanitation. BRAC, founded by Sir Fazle Abed, began by making big mistakes. One of its first projects, after its founding in 1972, was opening adult literacy centers in small villages in Bangladesh. Unfortunately, it picked locations inconvenient for the villagers, and the curriculum—math and reading—didn't help their day-to-day lives. After eighteen months, of the five thousand villagers who had originally signed up, only 5 percent kept attending the classes.[35]

BRAC recognized its failure and listened to its customers. Rather than retreating, it learned from it. It changed the curriculum to be useful to people—teaching subjects such as animal husbandry, nutrition, and childcare. Parents were so pleased that they asked BRAC to open schools for their kids. Now BRAC operates forty thousand schools in Bangladesh and has graduated ten million students—making it the largest private, secular school system in the world.[36]

4. THE "PURE" SOCIAL ENTERPRISE
Products with Purpose

WHEN I WAS ABOUT TEN YEARS OLD, I visited a dairy factory in Anand, a town in the state of Gujarat in India. I didn't know until two decades later that I had seen up close the largest social enterprise in the world.

I went there with my uncle and aunt, A. H. and Geeta Somjee, both of whom held PhDs and were global development researchers and authors. They had an interest in India's dairy cooperative movement because of its significant effect on Indian society, particularly on the millions of Indian women it helped pull out of poverty. The Somjees were—to put it mildly—obsessed with this story. They were personal friends with the visionary leader of the dairy cooperative movement, Dr. Verghese Kurien, who founded the Kaira Union and became known as India's "beloved" milkman. The Somjees traveled all over India, staying in villages and interviewing the women who raised cattle and sold milk.

I remember the dairy factory with its huge stainless-steel tanks and freezers. I was probably enticed to join the tour by the idea of tasting some *kulfi* (Indian ice cream) and *badam* milk (an almond-flavored milk common in India), but the overpowering stench of dairy products fermenting is the main memory I came away with. I held my breath and waited impatiently to leave.

As I later learned, Amul Dairy had been built and supported by people living in poverty in the Kaira district of India. Founded in 1946, and formally known as the Kaira District Co-operative Milk Producers' Union

Limited, its mission was to bring together poor, local, independent farmers and provide them with a way to market their milk directly to buyers rather than through middlemen who were draining away the farmers' profits. The initiative started slowly with the participation of just a few farmers in the area. Then, in 1948, the union made a deal with the city of Bombay (now Mumbai), whose leaders wanted to improve the quality of milk available in the city, in what became known as the Bombay Milk Scheme. The Kaira Union set up a pasteurization facility to provide a regular flow of milk to the city. Enticed by the guaranteed market, Kaira farmers rushed to join the initiative, and by the end of that year, more than four hundred farmers were involved in what eventually became known as Anand Milk Union Limited, or Amul.

As the cooperative grew and gained success, it served as a model for other such organizations throughout the country. In 1969, India's National Dairy Development Board (NDDB) was established at Anand and launched a program to replicate the Amul approach nationwide. This led to the creation of a dairy development program that became the largest of its kind in the world, catalyzing India's "white revolution."

Today, Amul is going strong. In fact, it's the largest social enterprise in the world, by my estimation, with annual revenues of over $5 billion.[1]

The cooperative offers a wide range of products, including butter, milk, cheese, ghee (a clarified butter product widely used in India cuisine), cookies and other sweets, breads, paneer, ice cream, chocolate milk, and yogurt. It's a multifaceted organization, offering services and programs for its members on subjects including animal healthcare, dairy management and operation, and sanitation.

The Amul model has been so successful that India is now the largest milk-producing nation in the world, responsible for almost 10 percent of the world's milk production.[2] (India does not have the greatest number of cows, however, because a large percentage of its milk comes from buffaloes.)[3] Today, there are some 185,903 dairy cooperatives in villages across India,[4] and their milk products are exported to over twenty countries, including Afghanistan, South Korea, Nepal, and the United Arab Emirates.[5]

Amul takes great pride in the role it has played in building the milk industry in India and "alleviating hardships of millions of dairy farmers."[6] But, Amul says, "we remain humble in our approach . . . firmly believing that the true development of an organization or nation lies in development of people—our farmers."

Amul is what I call a "pure" social enterprise. By that I mean it was established with the sole purpose of meeting an important social need, and it creates shared value for all those involved—the producers, the organization, customers, and the broader society. It is about creating a company (nonprofit or profit-making) with a social mission embedded in the business model itself. The more it produces, the bigger it gets, the more good it does.

UBER FOR TRACTORS

Amul was one of the earliest social enterprises, and today there is a wave of mission-driven professionals founding their own. They are men and women who might once have had to pick between traditional aid-industry jobs or business careers but who chose instead to establish entities with the explicit goal of doing social good, usually informed by the practices of for-profit enterprise.

Jahiel Oliver, for example, is an American who started out in investment banking in the United States but soon got bored. He learned that Nigeria has one of the largest inventories of uncultivated land on earth, and that most of Nigeria's poor eke out a living through subsistence farming. They work with hand tools to till and sow their fields because they can't afford to buy tractors, even used ones, which severely limits their ability to increase their planting, improve their yields, productivity, and, incomes, or realize some profit. On the other hand, there are some farmers who do own tractors but don't use them full time. They may still be paying off a loan they used to buy one, which cuts into their profitability. Further, there are businesses that manage fleets of rental tractors, and they need better management tools to increase tractor usage and reduce idle time.

Oliver developed an app that is based on the Uber model, but, rather than scheduling car rides, it enables the sharing of tractors. Called Hello Tractor, it allows farmers who can't afford to own tractors to rent them at reasonable rates only when they need to. Oliver also worked with partners to develop a "smart tractor." This is a small, open, three-wheeled, one-person tractor, without all the bells and whistles of the massive machines that we see in American fields. These are designed specifically for work in the small, rugged plots typical in Nigeria, and they come with a variety of attachments that can be swapped out to do all the tasks of farming: land preparation, irrigation, harvesting, and transport. And, of course, they are "smart"—internet connected—capable of sending and receiving performance and usage data.

The boost in productivity that a tractor brings a poor farmer is almost unbelievable. According to Hello Tractor, a farmer who used to spend forty days preparing a field manually can get it done in just eight hours with a tractor.[7] Farmers can cut costs by as much as fifty percent. Those who own tractors can list them on the Hello Tractor app and create new income streams for their families. Owners of tractor fleets can use the app to better manage the rentals of their tractors for optimal usage. The app provides a variety of reporting and data analysis features, so that owners can check usage, schedule maintenance, and calculate income generation. It also has a feature that alerts the owner if the monitor is removed from the tractor. This helps prevent fraud by renters who want to make it appear that the tractor has been used for fewer hours than it really has been. Hello Tractor can also provide financing to help farmers purchase their own machines, which can then become part of the sharing system. Oliver believes that he can take the Hello Tractor model to other African countries and, eventually, the entire continent.

Hello Tractor is part of a surge of such social enterprises, founded by innovative and energetic social entrepreneurs, all of which aim to contribute solutions to the world's most pressing problems. SoilCares, for example, is a high-tech company founded in the Netherlands now working in some of the lowest-resource countries in the world. In coffee-growing regions of Africa, SoilCares works with global agricultural companies to provide local farmers with the SoilCares technology—a handheld device about the size of a shoebox—for free. The farmer simply points the device at a section of his or her field, the software captures an image of the soil, and the information is uploaded via cell phone to the SoilCares data center. There the image is processed to identify the chemical elements in the soil and to determine which fertilizers and treatments could be added to improve crop growth and yield. The farmer downloads the analysis to a phone and then follows the recommendations. The result is a more profitable farm at virtually no added cost, and the sponsoring companies are assured of a more reliable source of high-quality coffee beans.

Not every social enterprise is founded on the application of new technology, although most entrepreneurs leverage the capabilities of ubiquitous connectivity and cheap telecommunications. A great example is One Acre Fund, an NGO operating in East Africa. One Acre Fund's main innovation is not software engineering but financial engineering. It was founded by Andrew Youn, an MBA student at Northwestern University, to address a gap in agricultural productivity. Like the founders of Hello Tractor and SoilCares, Youn saw the potential to improve the yield of African farmers who were producing far less per acre than were farmers elsewhere. For an MBA student, this looked like an arbitrage opportunity, one that could generate the funds required to scale the idea, while helping farmers live a better life and send their kids to school.

One Acre Fund had the simple, low-tech idea of providing farmers access to high-quality seeds and more effective fertilizer to increase their yields and cover the higher cost of the materials. The problem was that the farmers did not have access to the very small amounts of credit they would need to buy seeds. Indeed, most of the farmers had never seen the inside of a bank. Youn decided to create a microfinance institution that would offer seeds and fertilizer to farmers rather than cash. One Acre Fund would give farmers the seeds as loans and expect to receive payment only after the harvests were complete and the farmers had been paid for their crops.

The idea seems pretty obvious, but it took Youn's entrepreneurial thinking to make the leap from cash to seeds. A decade after its founding, I'm told by insiders that One Acre Fund had annual revenues of around $135 million in 2018. Well over half of that amount is money coming back to the organization each year as farmers repay the loans of seeds and fertilizer One Acre provided.

Social enterprises like Youn's have taken off in the past several years, for all the reasons I have discussed before, driven by new flows of big capital, the growing recognition of the potential for market-based solutions to poverty, and a wave of young people who refuse to choose between a business-oriented career and a purpose-driven life. In the era of Silicon Valley's dominance and the rapid rise of the internet, there is an unshakable sense of confidence that even the hardest problems can be solved by a few smart, committed people working together.

THE BILLION-DOLLAR LENDING PLATFORM

That describes the story of Kiva, which began when a twenty-something couple—Jessica Jackley and Matthew Flannery—were traveling in Africa and saw that it was almost as challenging for entrepreneurs to get loans for their new business ideas as it was for farmers to get advances to buy seeds. They had limited access to venture capital and short track records with financial institutions, and their networks of family and friends rarely had the resources to donate seed money. The result was that the entrepreneurs were often unable to get their ideas off the ground.

Given the growing appeal of online communities, Jackley and Flannery believed that a peer-to-peer lending network could generate funding from people anywhere in the world for projects posted by entrepreneurs anywhere else. They developed a platform that makes it easy to go online, find a project, and provide a loan as small as twenty-five dollars. Lenders can fund an incredible variety of projects, from helping a medical student in Paraguay earn his degree, to enabling a woman in Pakistan to buy materials to build her tailoring business, to bankrolling a village group in Myanmar that wants to buy a goat.

The model worked. Almost two million people have made loans to projects in more than eighty countries, including the United States. The loan repayment rate is about 97 percent.[8] The lender does not earn any interest on the loan but can follow the progress of the project and get the great feeling of helping someone, usually at no cost to the lender. As of 2017, Kiva lenders have loaned more than \$1 billion to small entrepreneurs and business builders around the world.[9]

What entrepreneurs realized in the last decade and a half was that there was enormous opportunity in even the poorest parts of the world. They could see something that was tough to understand from the vantage point of those implementing aid projects: the problems of global development were investment problems that could be financed.

The problem was that money coming from large agencies intended for people in need would often never make it there. Wealthy elites would take control of government for their own purposes, avoid or subvert tax laws, and impose rules that benefited their own businesses. Corrupt leaders would dole out government benefits to some groups but not all, and certainly not based on a long-term investment philosophy or a desire to benefit the society as a whole. The aid industry has struggled with these issues for years—a problem known to political economists as "elite capture." Social entrepreneurs seek to bypass them. They create ventures that can serve as models that can be replicated—just as Amul Dairy and Hello Tractor have done—and can be self-perpetuating even as politics crackle and regimes change.

Water.org is another social enterprise founded for a social good. Its goal is to ensure that all people have access to clean water and toilets, and it was founded by a rather unlikely pair of social entrepreneurs: Gary White, a water engineer, and Matt Damon, the Hollywood actor. As the duo explained to me in an interview in 2017, when they teamed up a decade ago, they thought the solution to water access was to build more water infrastructure. They developed an organization, raised money, and set about digging wells, laying pipe, and setting up public faucets in villages and poor urban neighborhoods.

But, over time, they came to realize that water, even for the very poorest people, is "investable." Even poor people have no choice but to spend money to get their water. They buy jugs of water from local vendors with what little money they have, or they take time they could have used for work in order to walk long distances to public sources, such as dirty rivers. To use the water for cooking or washing, they had to heat it, and for that they would buy firewood from a wood seller, or devote more work time to gathering it. If they did not have sufficient water for sanitation, they might be forced to put themselves at risk: women would venture into isolated places to defecate, making themselves vulnerable to sexual predators.

In other words, these people had money to spend—in the form of cash or hours they could have been working—but there was never enough at once to just pay for plumbing. A family could afford to buy a single jerry can of water but could not come up with the cash needed to pay a contractor up front to run a water connection. White and Damon figured that if a community could capture a sufficient amount of the money its poor people were already spending, it would essentially be equivalent to the amount needed to support a functioning, widespread water infrastructure. It might be as basic as a water pipe running to each home and a single, simple latrine. In most communities, that kind of infrastructure could easily be put in place. There were people or companies who had the wherewithal to run the pipes and build the facilities.

So, the two entrepreneurs gradually transitioned Water.org from a water engineering organization to a financial engineering venture. Now they focus on raising capital that can be used to make small loans to people who then invest the money in water projects. This approach required an entrepreneurial mind-set and the belief that poor people have resources but need help deploying them more effectively.

A traditional aid project, by contrast, would dig wells and keep on digging them until the budget was used up and the project came to an end. We know from painful experience that these wells are rarely self-sustaining. They might become contaminated or fall into disrepair, and there will be no money or system to fix them. A Jesuit professor of mine at Georgetown University once told me a story about his experience in Appalachia in the United States. He and some others on a charitable mission there had dug a well, complete with a rope, winch, and bucket for fetching water. When he returned some time later to visit the community, he found the well in disrepair. He was told it was no longer being used. Why? The rope broke.

A consulting firm called Improve International, which focuses on the water and sanitation sector—known as WASH in the aid industry—keeps a listing of reported WASH failures like that one. In Africa, the group reports, roughly a third of all installed hand pumps simply don't work. In some countries, it's two-thirds. Another source reports that fifty thousand wells across rural Africa are not working because communities were not trained or financed for their upkeep.[10]

The importance of clean water cannot be overstated. I visited a school in western Kenya that had instituted handwashing before lunch—a project done in partnership with Unilever's soap brand Lifebuoy. All the kids lining up and washing their hands was a happy sight. UNICEF analysis shows that handwashing after using the toilet and before meals at school can reduce diarrheal disease by almost 40 percent.[11] Yet a 2012 UNICEF study also estimates that in Pakistan, 43 percent of toilets in public schools require extensive repair or replacement; in Afghanistan it's 45 percent, and in India 50 percent. The point is that the aid industry has funded clean-water projects and latrines all over the world, but these projects often fail because there isn't enough community buy-in to manage and maintain the infrastructure. The designed solutions don't fit local government plans; funds aren't budgeted for upkeep; training to go along with the infrastructure isn't provided. In other words, these are failures of not understanding the system, not listening to people, not considering human behavior.

That's why the Water.org example is so different and encouraging—like all social entrepreneurs I know, they put a lot of thought into the endgame. If it's a well that produces water, social entrepreneurs know to take into account parts and maintenance, as well as training and management, in their model. Many traditional charitable approaches did not: the act of building the well was sufficient to make the givers feel they had done their part. A true social entrepreneur's mind-set is different—a photo op at a well doesn't cut it.

That entrepreneurial approach can create complexity though, as Water.org found after being criticized for its partnership with beer company Stella Artois. In a 2018 Super Bowl ad, the partners promised five years of water would be provided to a person in need for every special-edition Stella Artois chalice purchased. But critics found that claim hard to believe, even though it was found to be credible by independent observers. It turned out Water.org's complex financial engineering approach to providing water wasn't easy to communicate. Nonetheless, social entrepreneurs focus on the end result, not simplicity. That end result might be the amount of clean water used each year by the community or, more ambitiously, a reduction in the number of kids who contract waterborne illnesses, or even the higher literacy rates and better incomes that result from better health.

THE SHIFTING LANDSCAPE

Given the success of social enterprises, there has been an explosion of interest and activity around them. Insiders even have a special term for them: *slingo*, as in "sexy little NGO." Universities offer social entrepreneurism classes, clubs, and even degree programs, such as the social enterprise master's degree at American University; Duke University's MBA program, which offers a concentration in social enterprise; and immersion programs and projects offered to students through the Center for Sustainable Global Enterprise at Cornell University. What's more, the rise of social entrepreneurism has had an effect on the large, traditional organizations that are dedicated to doing social good.

Nearly every major NGO—from CARE to Save the Children to World Vision—has its own social enterprise and approaches its charitable work from a more entrepreneurial perspective than ever before. To me, it's a bit like what's happening in the auto industry with electric vehicles. There had been attempts to make and market electric vehicles for decades. Although the concept was exciting and attractive to many, none of the offerings became commercially viable until Tesla bridged the gap in 2003. It too was seen by many as a pipe dream, but Tesla eventually attracted enough capital to scale the company, even as it experienced product failures and cash shortfalls. Tesla's ultimate success is not yet assured, but as of this writing it is the largest automobile company in the United States, bigger than General Motors, based on market value.[12]

What has Tesla's growth meant for the rest of the auto industry? Now many companies are making electric cars, and even those that once shunned them are revising their vision of a future without combustion engines. Volvo recently announced that by 2020 it will no longer offer any vehicles with a pure combustion engine.[13] Taking innovation a step further in Tesla's direction, many are even developing self-driven cars. According to an analysis by Reuters, top automakers are now expected to invest at least $90 billion in electric vehicles, many of which will drive themselves, ultimately enabling an era in which people don't need to own their own cars but instead can use a shared transportation service like Uber.[14]

A similar shift is taking place in global development. Sure, there were social entrepreneurs over the past several decades, but few were successful in a risk-averse, bureaucratic, government-led industry. But as they flourished—Kiva in microlending, Khan Academy in education, One Acre in agriculture, the ONE Campaign along with its sister consumer goods organization (RED) in advocacy, and many more—traditional aid agencies and NGOs began to see that they too could benefit from being more entrepreneurial. In 2001 the World Bank created a "development marketplace" to support entrepreneurial ideas in global development; in 2009 USAID's chief called for hiring "development entrepreneurs" to staff-up the agency; in 2015 UNICEF set up a Global Innovation Centre, based in Kampala, Uganda. As with Tesla and cars, the game had changed.[15]

Social enterprises are diverse but tend to be structured around doing work that has a positive impact on people and society while generating revenue. They often take grants but are never designed to be purely grant-funded. They all have a similar vision of growth: the profits generated from the enterprise are at least partly applied to growing the organization to do more good.

Muhammad Yunus, the father of microfinance, however, sets an even higher and more rigorous standard for social enterprise, or, as he calls it, "social business."[16] He believes that a social business is one that creates products or services specifically designed for the poorest segments of society, or that employs marginalized people, or that builds profitable businesses that are owned by poor people. And, importantly in his mind, the original investors in a successful social business must do no more than recoup their original capital investment.

A social business by Yunus's definition is essentially a not-for-profit and a not-for-loss business. As he puts it: "I am trying to go to the ultimate point where you don't make any profit for yourself at all."[17] That's because, he argues, when push comes to shove, the drive for profits will always win out over the intention to do social good.

Few enterprises will meet this standard or adopt this model, for one obvious reason: profit is part of what enables an organization to attract talent and investors. Few entrepreneurs are in a position to risk their time and money without any prospect of financial return. Only the wealthiest people will have enough resources to create enterprises in Yunus's model. Only the rich would be able to afford the asceticism inherent in the idea. In fact, it recalls a famous remark about Gandhi by the Indian politician and poet Sarojini Naidu. He quipped that it cost a fortune—collected from India's wealthiest industrialists—to fund Gandhi in his chosen lifestyle of poverty and asceticism.

There is another reason the Yunus no-profit/no-loss model of social business will likely not catch on: the risk of loss. Investors and entrepreneurs who might build a social business in the Yunus mold would probably think of the money as a donation, rather than as an investment. As a result, they will be cautious. They will certainly not want to risk so much capital that its total loss would fundamentally affect their well-being or harm their families. So the amount of funding available for this social business model will not be as great as for businesses that generate profit and also do substantial social good.

This debate about what precisely defines a social enterprise or a social business or a socially-responsible for-profit is important because it shows how the traditional aid industry is wrestling with the implications of the new aid industry. What do these so-called social entrepreneurs really want? What are their motives?

Oxfam America recently issued a report which highlights the concern about intentionality. "There is a real risk of mission drift as funds—pressured by the lack of deals that can deliver high returns and full impact in a limited time frame—sacrifice intentionality, which is essential to impact investment."[18] In that word, "intentionality," there are echoes of do-gooderism, of placing disproportionately high value on good intentions. There is an implication that investors and entrepreneurs who seek a specific financial return in a defined period of time will end up cutting corners on social impact.

There's only one way to get past concerns about intentions. With the rise of new models of aid, the need for rock-solid impact metrics is more acute than ever.

5. BIG BUSINESS FOR GOOD

Corporates Becoming Social Enterprises

YVON CHOUINARD, the founder of Patagonia, is not the archetypal corporate CEO. This is a man who, like Cari Tuna, had no ambition to be rich or even to be involved in business. But Chouinard *is* rich—in 2017 he made the *Forbes* billionaire list. And he is indeed a businessman, a highly successful one who has built a wildly popular outdoor clothing and equipment company with a remarkable record of growth and profitability.

But at age seventy-nine, Chouinard still objects to the classification. As he writes in his book *Let My People Go Surfing: The Education of a Reluctant Businessman*, "I've been a businessman for almost sixty years. It's as difficult for me to say those words as it is for someone to admit being an alcoholic or a lawyer. I've never respected the profession. It's business that has to take the majority of the blame for being the enemy of nature."

Chouinard is a special type of business leader today, but one day his model may become the norm. In fact, he's a pioneer of a certain kind of business enterprise that is becoming essential to today's aid industry. His company, Patagonia, is built around the idea of shared value.

The concept of "shared value," as opposed to "shareholder value," was articulated in 2011 by Harvard Business School professors Michael Porter and Mark R. Kramer.[1] (That's the same Professor Porter who cowrote the 2000 note about industry transformation.) The idea is that businesses must focus on creating value not just for their shareholders but also for their employees, the communities in which they operate, society at large, and, often, for a specific cause or focus area. The concept of shared value runs counter to the long-standing view of hard-core economic rationalists, that the fundamental purpose of a corporation is to benefit shareholders. It also goes beyond the idea that corporate value is measured primarily by ever-increasing growth in financial return.

Chouinard started out as an outdoorsman and is still a mad surfer, rock and ice climber, kayaker, and practitioner of a particular kind of freshwater fishing known as *tenkara*, which originated in Japan.

As a kid, Chouinard dreamed of being a fur trapper. That didn't work out, but through his early years he adventured around the world as much as he could. He got into rock climbing and loved scaling the rock faces in California's Yosemite National Park. He was less thrilled with the mountaineering equipment available at the time, especially the heavy, expensive pitons made by European suppliers. So, in 1957, he bought a forge, learned blacksmithing, and began producing his own lighter, chrome steel pitons and selling them to his fellow climbers. By 1966, he had a business partner and a company with an official name: Chouinard Equipment.

The company soon became known for its quality climbing gear and well regarded for its attitude toward the environment. When Chouinard came to understand that the steel pitons that climbers drove into the rock crevices to affix their ropes were causing damage, he discontinued them and made removable aluminum chocks instead. The switch put Chouinard's business in jeopardy, since the steel piton was its foundational product, but the company survived. In the early 1970s Chouinard branched out into clothing, which soon began to exceed the hard-climbing gear in sales.

In the early 1970s, as part of the company's rebrand to Patagonia, Chouinard declared a "leave no trace" ethos—that humans interacting with nature should not harm or even alter it.[2]

The story of Patagonia since then is that of a relentless campaign toward shared value—for its customers and for the environment. In the early 1990s Chouinard switched from traditional cotton, whose production has a devastating effect on the environment (think pesticides and massive water waste), to organic cotton, which is easier on the earth. The strong demand for Patagonia organic cotton—and the company's efforts to encourage other companies to make the switch—helped the organic cotton industry grow.

In 2002, in response to the low rate of contributions by donors to environmental causes, Patagonia created "1% for the Planet" with a group of other like-minded companies. As the group states, "Currently, only three percent of philanthropic giving in the U.S. goes to environmental causes; and only three percent of this giving comes from the business community." All companies that join the group pledge to donate 1 percent of their sales to organizations involved in environmental issues. Today, dozens of companies have taken the pledge. Over the years, Patagonia has contributed over $89 million, and a total of $175 million has been raised and distributed to a variety of groups and initiatives.[3]

Patagonia has gone further still in its commitment to shared value. In an effort to ensure its core business does some good, or at least does no harm, Patagonia pushes a counterintuitive message: don't buy more gear. It is urging customers to purchase only what they really need, and has developed a recycling program in which used Patagonia gear is refurbished.

Patagonia has also taken steps to embed its belief in shared value in its organizational structure and corporate status. In January 2012, Patagonia was designated as a B Corp, the first in California to earn that certification. This designation is like the Fair Trade badge and is offered by a nonprofit entity called B Lab, whose mission is to serve the "global movement of people using business as a force for good." To be certified, a company must meet various standards set by B Lab, related to "social and environmental performance, accountability, and transparency." According to B Lab, some 2,500 corporations based in fifty countries are B Corp certified, among them new economy leaders such as Warby Parker and Laureate Education.[4]

Soon after being certified, Patagonia discovered it was in violation of the standards it had helped to establish. The company uncovered labor abuses, including forced work and human trafficking, at some of its suppliers, such as the mills that create the cloth for Patagonia outdoor wear.[5] Patagonia went to work on the issue but continued to struggle with the challenges of policing the vast and often unscrupulous supplier network in some Asian countries. As a reporter in the *Atlantic* put it, Patagonia's incomplete efforts are proof not of "corporate hypocrisy, but of the near impossibility of treating workers well at every step in the production process, even when a company is genuine in its desire to do so."[6]

Patagonia is not typical, but it does represent the future of business—as a not purely for-profit company or a purely not-for-profit one, but rather a blend. The World Economic Forum calls this emerging kind of entity, which is neither a for-profit business, nor a nonprofit organization, nor a government, the "fourth sector."

A SOCIAL LICENSE TO OPERATE

The concept of shared value—even with its challenges—can define the future of capitalism if we as consumers, employees, and voters make it so. In years to come, companies will, of course, still do their best to maximize profits, but they will do so with a new ethos that goes beyond the laws and rules that regulate industrial and business practices today.

A business is prohibited by law, for example, from employing children or dumping toxic chemicals in the river. But government regulations are only one of a set of parameters that businesses need to pay attention to—they also need to earn their "social license" to operate, by benefiting employees, community, and society. If the company fails to do so it can be compelled to improve, or be punished, or even be put out of business.

Nike is one of many companies that had to rethink its purpose. The sneaker maker ran into serious trouble in the '90s when an activist-led campaign highlighted the low wages and inhumane working conditions in some of its Southeast Asian factories. The company had innovated a brilliantly successful business model: it produced stylish products overseas at such low cost that it could afford to spend unprecedented amounts on marketing in the US and in other wealthy markets. When wages started rising in South Korea and Taiwan as those countries developed, Nike needed to move its sneaker production to neighboring countries with lower wages like Indonesia, Vietnam, and China.

At the time, Nike was thinking about shareholder return, not shared value. It was legally in the clear, using subcontractors to produce its products so it wasn't seen as really responsible when minimum wage laws weren't followed. When the controversies and protests started, including at the 1992 Barcelona Olympics, Nike's approach was to deny and obfuscate. But the activists didn't give up, and Nike's brand image and sales started to decline.

Finally, in 1998, CEO Phil Knight made a 180-degree turn and gave a speech in which he acknowledged what was really going on: "The Nike product has become synonymous with slave wages, forced overtime, and arbitrary abuse. . . . I truly believe the American consumer doesn't want to buy products made under abusive conditions."[7] Nike went on to make a number of changes—increasing wages and improving working conditions—that led to the creation of an entire industry of consulting companies that monitor and report on factory conditions all over the world. The days of abuse are certainly not over—the apparel industry and especially the fast-fashion market continue to rely on low wages and contract factories as a key element of the business model—but the situation has improved, and Nike's brand has largely recovered. The company has predicted revenues will reach $50 billion by 2020 (although some analysts think 2023 is more realistic).[8]

Today, corporations must think about their commitment to the "social contract," the term coined by the eighteenth-century political theorist Jean-Jacques Rousseau essentially meaning a commitment to shared purpose. If a company fails to act in accordance with that agreement, response comes much more swiftly and publicly than ever before thanks to the power and reach of the internet and social media. Consumers in today's advanced economies are extremely aware of their power and have much more information at their disposal than they did when activists first held Nike accountable. The reputation of a brand is essential in a world of endless choice.

It would be great if every company could follow the shared-value model, but companies like Patagonia enjoy some advantages that make emulation difficult. First, Patagonia is a private company, wholly owned by Chouinard himself. He is not interested in growth for its own sake and does not have to answer to Wall Street analysts and shareholders, who would almost certainly push the company for ever-larger returns. Patagonia also operates in a niche market and sells high-margin products, so it has significant profit to invest in its social causes.

Although there are precious few Patagonias in the world, other entrepreneurs have built for-profit companies around social good, with some intriguing models. One of the most appealing models, especially to consumers, is the "buy one/give one" approach, originated and best exemplified by TOMS shoes. For every pair the customer buys, TOMS donates a pair to an impoverished child. The company has sold millions of pairs of shoes and given away millions more in places like sub-Saharan Africa, where going barefoot can put a child at risk of disease. TOMS took off and soon expanded into eyewear, apparel, accessories, and coffee. The model became extremely popular, and today buy one/give one companies are everywhere. SoapBox donates soap; Warby Parker donates eyeglasses; Bombas donates socks.

The buy one/give one model, however, has its limits. The companies have been criticized for disrupting markets by dropping free products into areas where local businesses were employing people to sell similar products. TOMS, in particular, was roundly criticized by global development professionals for disrupting local shoe markets and putting people out of work. TOMS responded by shifting its shoe production to a few sites in the Global South—a partial solution—and moving away from a pure buy-one/give-one model in its other products, such as coffee. When you buy TOMS coffee, the company provides clean water—not a cup of coffee—to people somewhere in the world.

The success of Patagonia, Nike, and TOMS demonstrates just how important social good is to today's consumers—especially younger ones.[9] Consumers care deeply if a brand is known for taking good care of its employees or is a conscientious steward of the environment. Research bears this out. Nielsen's 2015 survey on corporate citizenship showed that 66 percent of all consumers—and 73 percent of millennials—said they would pay more for products from a company known for sustainability.[10]

Big, publicly traded companies are well aware of this trend and seek to proclaim their commitments to social good. The Governance & Accountability Institute reports that, in 2017, 85 percent of companies in the S&P 500 published some kind of statement whose purpose was to showcase the company's environmental stewardship and social commitment. Just five years earlier, only 20 percent of those companies issued such a report.[11]

But the question remains: how serious are these commitments and how deep do they go? The Nike example demonstrates that big, public companies can and do transform themselves. The company that built its success on exploitation now genuinely thrives on a social and environmental mission. In its latest sustainability report, Nike notes that, like Patagonia, it is focused on reusing apparel and has so far recycled 30 million pairs of shoes. It has also cut its water use by 20 million liters thanks to application of new technology to its manufacturing processes, and it is on track to achieve its goal of 100 percent renewable energy use by 2025.[12]

Nike has also demonstrated that direct response to customer concerns has become part of its management practice. When, in 2017, university students around the country protested the sale of Nike products in school bookstores, Nike didn't deny and fight as it might have done in the '90s. Instead it negotiated with activist Georgetown students to allow the independent labor rights group Workers Rights Consortium to monitor its factories in Vietnam as a condition of selling its products in the campus bookstore.

This virtuous cycle—activists calling out bad behavior, consumers pushing up the norms of good corporate behavior, and good corporate citizens realizing that behaving well is actually better for business—is what will ultimately lead corporations toward a kind of shared-value business.

There are many examples of major corporations—pushed by advocacy groups, customers, and their own employees—that have incorporated social good into their missions. Starbucks' customers, for example, demand great coffee, but they also want to know the beans weren't picked by kids who really should have been in school. In order to source enough high-quality coffee at reasonable prices, Starbucks has extended its supply chain to some of the world's poorest countries, such as Guatemala, Rwanda, and Ethiopia. Not only is Starbucks buying from farmers in these countries, the company is working with farmers to modernize the way they farm, helping them achieve a higher yield per acre and ensuring their kids are in school where they ought to be.

Unilever is another example. The giant food and consumer goods brand acquired Ben & Jerry's a decade ago, and fans of the quirky and socially oriented ice cream company worried it would lose the sense of mission its bearded founders had fostered. (Ben & Jerry's took its commitment so seriously it had, and continues to employ, a director of social mission.) Surprisingly, the Ben & Jerry's approach rubbed off on Unilever, and the company that sells nearly $60 billion of ice cream, tea, soap, and other everyday items has increasingly become a socially oriented business. One example: Unilever has declared that it will sell only tea that doesn't harm the environment or negatively affect tea farmers. Since

Unilever represents 12 percent of the world's tea industry—it owns many tea brands, including Lipton, Red Rose, PG Tips, Pukka, Brooke Bond, and several others—its efforts brought greater prosperity to millions of farm workers toiling in the world's tea plantations.[13]

McDonald's, too, is working on corporate social responsibility in ways that can mitigate some of the harmful effects of fast food. In 2004 it introduced sliced apples as a healthier alternative choice to French fries in the famous Happy Meal.[14] The company is so large, the action had an immediate impact. On the very day it made that change, enough parents chose apples over French fries that McDonald's immediately became the world's largest buyer of apples. That is the scale of social impact that a large company can have on our society when it is pushed to act.

Other companies have taken a different approach to social good. When Mastercard went public in 2006, it established the Mastercard Foundation and provided it with an endowment of 10 percent of the new public company's shares. Since then, Mastercard stock has skyrocketed, and today the Mastercard Foundation is one of the world's largest philanthropies. Based on the company's stock price in early 2018, the foundation's endowment is likely worth around $18 billion, making it larger than the Ford Foundation. Its work is highly targeted, focused exclusively on helping African youth get the education and skills they need to prosper.[15]

Mastercard has also worked to align its core business with important global development goals, particularly helping people around the world get connected to the formal financial system. This is critical for the administration of pension systems—the South African pension system now delivers payments to millions of South Africans using Mastercard technology—and helps to reduce or eliminate corruption and ensure efficiency in financial transactions. The formal financial system also facilitates a wide range of cash transfer programs, such as those that reward impoverished parents for ensuring their kids attend school. It enables better administration of taxation so that governments have the funds to invest in health and education. And it enables humanitarian transfers so that people in an emergency can get a quick infusion of cash to their mobile phone.

Google's original mission statement—"don't be evil"—suggests a larger, socially responsible purpose, but the company has found it's harder to do good than to avoid doing evil. Larry Page, a Google cofounder, was exuberant when he launched Google.org in 2005, just after going public: "We hope someday this institution may eclipse Google itself in terms of overall world impact by ambitiously applying innovation and significant resources to the largest of the world's problems."[16]

Page announced that 1 percent of profits and equity in Google would be dedicated to philanthropy, which is about $125 million per year from profits, a level the company appears to be reaching. The 1 percent of equity would be around $5 billion, and it's less clear if or how that pledge is being fulfilled.[17] A *New York Times* piece in 2011 suggested that Google .org's ambitions had been scaled way back and were focused more on engineering problems that Google's people were best suited to solving.[18] Since then, the company appears to have found its footing by engaging in something closer to traditional corporate philanthropy. The Google case shows just how hard it can be, even for immensely wealthy and talented companies, to make a significant impact in global development.

Even with these struggles, there is no doubt that companies are now a major part of the new global aid industry. There are relatively few companies truly transforming into social enterprises, so there is a long way to go. Though consumers care more about whether brands they use are ethical, the lack of standardized oversight and metrics to measure how much good a company actually does still makes it relatively easy to reap the benefits of appearing to do good without actually following up on promises.

What's more, there are still plenty of major corporations focused primarily on or only on shareholder value—just as there are plenty of billionaires who are late to the philanthropic bandwagon—and some of these are being dragged kicking and screaming into the world of social good. Koch Industries, for example, is the second largest privately held company in the United States, with annual revenue of $115 billion.[19] Koch makes its fortune from petrochemicals, mining, metals, and logging. The two billionaire brothers who lead the company, David and Charles Koch, are known for making massive donations to conservative political groups and candidates in the United States—but not so much for their efforts to create shared value through their products and businesses.

Even Koch has at least come to recognize that people care about social good and perhaps they worry that their social license is in jeopardy. Beginning in 2014, Koch launched an extensive TV advertising campaign that clearly sought to reposition the brand as an entity engaged with social and environmental issues, including energy efficiency and "food for all." As the company's chief communications officer, Steve Lombardo, explained in *Ad Age*, "We have seen in the last three to four years an increase in competition for talent. We're often competing against more well-known companies because they're almost always publicly traded. It benefits us if people have a better understanding of who Koch is."[20] The bar is being raised for everyone, like it or not.

In an era when talent matters more than ever, and millennials—who tell pollsters they prioritize purpose in their careers more than their elders do—make up more than half the US workforce, companies that don't transition into fourth-sector businesses will find it harder and harder to compete. Not only do millennials not want to buy from brands that don't have a social mission, they don't want to work for companies that don't have a social mission.

It's not just the big, established corporations that can be swiftly and negatively affected when they violate the social contract—even hot new companies can quickly fall afoul of consumers' expectations, as Uber did in 2017, when reports of an aggressive internal culture characterized by rampant sexism rocked the world's dominant ride-sharing company.[21] One could argue that the company's culture should be of no significance to the customer who simply needs a ride. Yet many customers were disgusted with Uber, lost faith in the brand, and switched to competing ride-sharing services. Lyft, Uber's chief competitor in the United States, reported a 25 percent growth surge during the height of the public relations crisis—around double the rate of Uber's growth during the same period.[22] The situation was so bad that Uber's board had little choice but to fire its founder and CEO, Travis Kalanick, who was roundly accused of fostering a toxic environment at the company.

There was a time when sexism and sexual harassment were tolerated, even expected, at many companies. While the fight is far from over, the effect of feminist activists over many decades, combined with the impact of the #MeToo movement of 2017 and 2018, is changing what is regarded as acceptable behavior. In the aid world, some of my female colleagues at Devex started the #AidToo campaign, which has brought some important stories from women aid workers forward and advanced thoughtful ideas for addressing these issues within the industry. Norms continue to morph quickly across a whole range of social issues that corporations engage with, including many that relate directly to the poorest countries in the world, including child labor, fair wages, working conditions, and environmental degradation.

Startup social enterprises like TOMS get a lot of attention in the aid industry. But the transformation of major corporations into social enterprises will be the true game changer. There are examples where it's happening, which is certainly encouraging. But for the 800 million ultrapoor in urgent need, will big companies change fast enough? How can we accelerate this trend?

INVESTING FOR GOOD

In addition to the effect of protest, activism, information, and the demands of a younger generation, there is another huge lever that can be employed to tilt big companies toward shared-value operations—and that is through the practice of "positive investing."

Today, investors who want to put their money into the stock of "good" publicly-traded companies mostly do so by buying so-called socially responsible investments (SRIs). These are investment funds composed of stocks chosen mainly through a process of negative, or exclusionary, screening. These screens filter out those companies that don't meet the fund's definition of being "socially responsible." Typically, these would include entities involved in the production, sale, or management of tobacco, alcohol, weapons, nuclear power, big oil, casinos, and the like. The fund takes those stocks out of contention and will then invest in any other company that does not engage in the "negative activities" and has potential for attractive returns or dividends. These SRI funds are extremely popular, holding some $9 trillion in investments because they tend to perform well compared to the market overall, the methodology is easy to articulate and understand, and the funds are not difficult to set up and manage.

Positive investment funds operate quite a bit differently. Rather than merely weeding out "bad" companies, managers of these funds actively seek out and invest in publicly-traded companies that are doing good and creating shared value—they use, in other words, a "positive screen." The criteria are not consistent from fund to fund and are a little harder to define than negative screening. Some positive screening funds will, for example, be heavily weighted toward companies that score better on environmental, social, and governance ratings. An analysis by the *Wall Street Journal* found that different investment funds purporting to prioritize the same issues—like the environment—score companies differently.[23] That can lead to strange circumstances, like a socially responsible fund that held a large amount of BP stock[24] at the time of the Deepwater Horizon oil spill, or another such fund that holds a large stake in British American Tobacco.[25] Because these funds are less black and white than negative-screened funds, the total amount of money invested in them is thought to be much smaller.[26]

Positive screening is also used to make investments in privately held companies in a practice usually known as "impact investing." This is an even smaller investment strategy with a total of about $15 billion invested in 2016, but it has big potential for growth. In 2017 the Catholic Church, under the direction of Pope Francis himself, announced its intention to devote $1 billion to impact investments.[27] The Ford Foundation is allocating $1 billion of its endowment for impact investing.[28] The Gates Foundation is diversifying a small part of its $40 billion endowment into impact investments, and some university endowments, including those of Middlebury and Tufts, as well as corporations such as Pfizer, are following suit.[29] But the amounts remain small compared to the challenges, including extreme poverty, that these investments purport to address.

What will it take to make positive screening and impact investing both effective and ubiquitous? Data. Companies need to measure their environmental, social, and governance impact and report it. They can agree to use standard metrics, such as those developed by the Global Reporting Initiative, an international standards organization, whose metrics are used by businesses and governments to assess and report on their activities relative to such issues as climate change, human rights, governance, and social well-being. Today 93 percent of the biggest 250 corporations in the world report on their sustainability, and 43 percent report on how their corporate responsibility activities advance the Sustainable Development Goals.[30] When people have this kind of information and consistency of data, along with transparency, it will be much easier for them to evaluate companies and their records on social good and make smart decisions about which stocks to buy.

We know that there is a huge amount of capital available for investment and that people want to put it into entities that further the social good. A Morgan Stanley survey conducted in 2015, for example, found that 84 percent of millennials thought their investments could help lift people out of poverty. Investment in SRIs is exploding, with 33 percent more invested in SRI funds in just two years, between 2014 to 2016.[31] There are dozens of exchange-traded funds (ETFs) that make it easy to invest according to social values. The incentives are beginning to align around all major corporations becoming shared-value businesses.

POOR PEOPLE AS CUSTOMERS

There is one more way that corporations can contribute to social good, and especially to the cause of reducing extreme poverty: by creating products and services that are designed and priced specifically for the world's poorest consumers.

The idea that the ultrapoor can be customers rather than aid recipients is fairly new. It can be traced to C. K. Prahalad—the late University of Michigan economist—and his 2004 book, *The Fortune at the Bottom of the Pyramid*. His concept caught on, and today it is common in the aid industry to refer to initiatives that address the people at the "bottom of the pyramid," or BoP. The idea is that the majority of the world's citizens can be found at the broad bottom of humanity's pyramid, not at the narrow pinnacle. They, too, need to buy all kinds of things. Because there are so many people at the bottom, their small purchases add up. As Walmart has proved, there is money to be made in providing low-income customers with the low-cost goods and services they need.

That said, there are not yet many examples of major corporations successfully selling to the bottom of the pyramid. Even so, companies are not abandoning this market because they understand that the eight hundred million people living in extreme poverty, and the couple of billion people who are above that income level, but still poor, represent an important future market. Pew Research Center has found that roughly 71 percent of all people live on ten dollars per day or less.[32]

The cases where there have been big successes selling to the BoP are when the company already has sales infrastructure in place, the product is already understood and desired, and margins are high. Prahalad's idea for selling to the BoP involved selling high volumes at low costs. The problem is achieving the high volumes. If that means creating a sales and distribution infrastructure to penetrate remote villages, where many poor people live, that can cut into margins. And high volumes are very hard to achieve if the product is not already well understood and demanded.

An example of success in this area is Wheel, a product offered by Hindustan Lever, a subsidiary of Unilever. Wheel is a clothing detergent designed for people who wash their clothes by hand, rather than with a machine. Wheel comes in small packages, produces fewer suds than machine soaps (which is helpful when you don't have much water), and is cheap. Hindustan Lever already had a sales and distribution network in place to reach small stores, where it sold a range of more expensive products primarily to customers with slightly higher incomes. The benefits of the new product were easy to understand and poor people had easy access to the small stores, so the introduction was relatively easy and straightforward for Hindustan Lever. Wheel was a big hit. Today, Wheel is one of the biggest products in Bangladesh. "For millions of women across Bangladesh," reads the company's website, "Wheel transforms the tedious chore of laundry into a delightful experience lifting her spirits for the rest of the day."

In the Philippines, the country is dotted with mom-and-pop retail stores called sari-sari's. They're tiny but seem to sell everything. Ninety-five percent of the one million retail stores in the Philippines are sari-sari stores. How can a big company like Unilever reach so many small stores, especially in an island and rural nation like the Philippines? It created a program that provides discounts to the larger such stores if they agree to become distributors to the smaller sari-sari stores. The program works so well that distribution to rural areas has doubled.

Another example of Unilever's marketing expertise in rural areas is its use of a common practice in poor areas: the cell phone hang-up call. Around the world, people place a call to a friend or family member then disconnect before the person answers to avoid getting charged. They have achieved the purpose of the connection: to signal that the caller is OK, or has arrived somewhere, is ready to be picked up, or is available to meet, or some other pre-arranged message. Hindustan Lever picked up on the idea in India. Call the company's number, hang up, and you would instantly get a free call back, with several minutes of audio entertainment from popular Bollywood stars, interspersed with ads for Unilever products. By 2015, thirty-five million people had subscribed to this service, and now the company is rolling it out to other countries.[33]

Not every company has been so successful tapping into the aggregated wealth at the bottom of the pyramid. A classic failure is Procter & Gamble's water purification powder Pur. I've witnessed P&G executives take a glass of dirty, brown water, stir in the powder with a spoon, and gulp down the now-clean water. It's quite an impressive product. But they couldn't make it work from a sales perspective. Educating the customers was too hard, and it was too expensive to create the sales and distribution network. They ended up making it a philanthropic project.

There are many examples of successful BoP projects in telecommunications, as evidenced by the fast-growing number of poor people who have cell phones. Today, more people have access to a cell phone than to a toilet.[34] In Colombia, where I frequently travel, you can rent a cell phone for 200 pesos a minute (around eight cents) from local operators who set up their stalls in a plaza or on the sidewalk and sit in their plastic chairs all day doing a brisk business.

M-Pesa, the telecom-enabled mobile-to-mobile cash transfer system in Kenya, is BoP innovation that unlocked an entirely new way for the people of Kenya to improve their lives. M-Pesa operates through a network of agents, rather than banks, typically in small shops or pharmacies. The user can deposit money into their phone-based account, send payments by text message to other M-Pesa users and retailers, and redeem payments they receive for cash. Today, there are some 150,000 M-Pesa agents, and nearly everyone in Kenya is now connected to the formal financial system. A study from Innovations in Poverty Action suggests that access to mobile money financial services like M-Pesa might be a major factor in driving down poverty, especially among women.[35]

Access to financial services for poor people unlocks all kinds of development opportunities, allowing families to get help when they have a financial emergency, farmers to get insurance, women to save their money and even earn interest on it, entrepreneurs to borrow for their business, homeowners to lease solar panels and water filters, and so much more.

But while M-Pesa has been a big success in Kenya, it hasn't been replicated elsewhere at the same scale or pace. There are major obstacles to the rapid growth of financial inclusion technologies. The main problem is organizing the market to achieve financial inclusion objectives. What's happening in many countries is that a few big players—banks and tele-communications companies—dominate the market. They don't want to cooperate, they want to compete. So governments will need to step in to ensure the interoperability required to enable people to send money to anyone, even if they use a different cell phone carrier. Government action will also be required to create a regulatory environment that en-courages innovation—the development of services that go beyond basic money transfer, and enable customers to hold interest-bearing accounts, get insurance, and pay for a wide range of goods and services, from solar panels to health insurance.

Although in theory there's a fortune to be tapped into at the bottom of the pyramid, many companies still find it difficult to see the world's poorest people as an attractive market for their products, largely because of enduring assumptions about the poor—that they have nothing, can afford nothing, will buy nothing, and only want handouts. Anyone who has actually spent time with people with limited resources around the world knows that those assumptions are all wrong. People of all income levels are basically the same and want the same things for themselves and their families. That's why one of the most important aspects of the trans-formation happening in the aid industry is one of attitude: learning to see poor people as customers and partners able to make their own decisions and take action, not as helpless "beneficiaries."

6. AID GOES RETAIL
Crowdfunding and Direct Aid

IN 1969 THE NOBEL PRIZE-WINNING economist Milton Friedman wrote out an insane-sounding thought experiment about using a helicopter to drop a thousand dollars in cash over a community. It was just an idea to get people thinking, and in that sense it worked: there is an ongoing debate about whether a hypothetical program to drop cash from the sky could stave off deflation by encouraging people to spend money. Ben Bernanke, the former chairman of the Federal Reserve, even mentioned the idea of a "helicopter drop" in 2002, and he has since become widely known as "helicopter Ben."[1]

This idea of modern-day manna from heaven has been just that—an idea. That is, until a group of four MIT and Harvard graduate students in economics were researching philanthropy in 2009 and became frustrated that so many charitable initiatives offered little or no proof of impact. They thought using new technology like mobile money could provide answers about how much good aid can do. When they first explained their big idea—to give away large sums of cash, no strings attached, to people living in extreme poverty—people laughed. Michael Faye, one of those students, has told audiences that traditional aid donors "thought I was smoking crack."[2]

The foursome ended up founding Give Directly, an organization that, true to its name, identifies people living in poverty and sends them money. First, the organization finds people in need from a distance by using satellite imagery to select rural households that have only a thatched roof on their home. (Give Directly determined that a tin roof is a good indicator of slightly better economic circumstances.) Then it sends them relatively large amounts of money (via mobile phones, not helicopters). Coincidentally, it gives around $1,000 per household, which represents a few years of annual income for most of the recipients.

It's no surprise that the aid industry would be skeptical about Give Directly. Global development professionals have long assumed poor people given money with no strings attached would spend it on alcohol or sex workers. In fact, the $200 billion global aid industry exists in part on the premise that just giving away money doesn't work and may even be counterproductive. This is the assumption that drove the establishment of all these aid agencies and NGOs providing training and education, improving health systems and supply chains, tackling gender discrimination, and fighting for human rights.

But like using an app to hail a ride in someone else's car or communicating with the world via 140-character messages, Give Directly was a hard-to-believe idea that ultimately proved transformative. Give Directly has funneled around $100 million to poor people from donors such as Google and Good Ventures. Anyone can go to its website and give. There are no strings attached for the families who receive the money, and the overhead cost is extremely low. The model is relatively easy to scale and can keep growing so long as there are poor people in need of the cash.

What do the people getting the money say? Well, one of the most powerful innovations that Give Directly has brought to the aid industry is sharing the voice of its customers—the people being served. It's easy to visit a website it has dubbed GDLive and see a steady stream of feedback from thousands of aid recipients, something heretofore nearly unheard of.

This direct feedback is raw and unfiltered. It's very likely that the recipient of a grant through Give Directly may say unexpected things about the process, something very different from what you'd see in the glossy report from an NGO's communications department. Some might say they used the money to fix up their house. Some mention paying a dowry for their daughter to get married. One actual recipient of a Give Directly grant, a twenty-four-year-old man from Uganda named Penekas, wrote,

"My life is different in that I dress well and look like a man unlike before I got the transfer."[3]

One of the great advantages of a retail model like Give Directly is that you can get the straight story. Not only might you learn that your money is going to help a young man dress for success, you might also find out that a cash transfer is no panacea—a one-time cash donation does not end a family's poverty for life or protect them from disease forever.

In fact, Give Directly is quick to point out that giving electronic cash to people can really help them out, but it's not a substitute for the kinds of public services that governments provide, like schools and hospitals. Lant Pritchett, the Harvard economist, describes a similar idea: the important distinction between human development and national development.[4] You may be able to directly help an individual to a degree, but you can't avoid the fact that they live in an economy and a society. Even if they have a bit more money in their pocket, they ultimately still need roads, safety and security, healthcare, education, and a functioning government.

Nonetheless, there's something enormously powerful about Give Directly that's indicative of the new era of aid. It's not just that it's connected to the popular movement around advocating for a universal basic income. Nor that it riffs on the tried and true conditional cash transfer programs such as those in Brazil or Mexico that give money to millions of families if their kids are in school and vaccinated.

No, what's uniquely transformative about Give Directly is that it is making aid retail. Anyone can give and Give Directly can get the cash to anyone they determine needs it. The whole process is transparent, and you can hear directly from the aid recipients. It's like an open market, and Give Directly sets a benchmark that other, more complex and intensive programs providing, say, health or education have to show they can beat.

Connecting to aid recipients through a retail channel is compelling. It's eye-opening to hear from poor people directly; to step into their world, just for a moment. Much more money is likely to flow through retail systems like Give Directly that fundamentally change the relationship between donors and recipients. Conventional sponsor-a-child programs operated by big charities have been around for decades, but this is different: more authentic, more transparent, and more direct, all at the same time.

RETAIL AID

Give Directly would not have been possible without ubiquitous and cheap technology. Satellite imagery, mobile money, and connectivity are all essential to the emergence of retail aid. And cheap and ubiquitous technologies like these are opening the door for many more retail models.

If Give Directly is to sponsor-a-child programs what Uber is to taxis, then another disruptive idea is New Story, which has a decidedly different take from that of Habitat for Humanity. This San Francisco startup, hatched at the prestigious Silicon Valley incubator Y Combinator, has figured out how to build quality houses for poor people for around $6,500 each by contracting with local builders, not volunteers. Its CEO and cofounder had a life-changing visit to Haitian slums that opened his eyes to the dramatic needs of the people there. Traditional charities weren't getting it done. The American Red Cross, for example, collected $500 million in donations for earthquake relief in Haiti but managed to build only six houses—the rest of the money went to important services for people in need, but that's not what retail donors expected. Now New Story collects small donations from online givers and ensures that 100 percent of the money will go toward building houses for people who need them. In four years it's built over a thousand houses in four countries and every donor can see a video that shows the completed house they funded and the family whose life they have changed. It's even begun building houses using massive 3-D printers, an innovation that it thinks will fundamentally transform the way housing is provided after an earthquake or other disaster.[5]

New Story may be like many startups and never come to challenge the big traditional charities. But the powerful idea behind startups like these can ultimately move the entire aid industry in the direction of retail aid.

▪ ▪ ▪ ▪ ▪

Unlike New Story, Global Giving doesn't have one idea it wants you to fund: it's got thousands. Global Giving is the world's largest crowdfunding platform for donations, and it allows you to donate directly to a specific project run by a local nonprofit. You can search through thousands of worthwhile projects from dozens of countries, and make small donations to local nonprofits doing the work. The site has been successful, funneling $330 million in donations from three-quarters of a million ordinary donors to small nonprofits around the world.[6] As impressive as that is, it's also surprising that such a compelling offering hasn't raised even more money since its founding in 2002. By contrast, brand-name NGOs like CARE and Save the Children receive donations from hundreds of thousands of individuals each year totaling hundreds of millions of dollars. Many big NGOs like these have launched their own crowdfunding platforms. Why aren't more people donating directly to local nonprofits via Global Giving?

My sense is that Global Giving was ahead of the curve—launched well before public consciousness was ready for it and as the market for buying results was just beginning to form. Just as small upstart consumer brands are successfully competing with the likes of Heinz in ketchup, Gillette in razors, and Dove in soap, I see a period ahead of significant competition for charitable donations from ordinary givers. Platforms like Give Directly and Global Giving that can give individual donors the sense of connection they want, a frictionless customer experience, and a clear value-proposition based on results and not good intentions may eventually come to compete against some of the most storied brands in the aid industry today.

That competition is likely to be healthy, growing the number of people who are donating and increasing the amount they give. Reliable data[7] on crowdfunding is hard to come by, but one estimate is that a total of $34 billion was raised by the end of 2017 on all crowdfunding platforms globally since their birth, and, of that, $5.5 billion was donated to causes and individuals.[8] The site GoFundMe, which facilitates donations to individuals for everything from cancer treatments to school tuition, says that more than $5 billion has flowed through its platform alone, which makes me think the real figures around crowdfunded global donations may well be much higher than the $5.5 billion estimate. These opportunities to give small sums, often in $25 or $50 increments, and sometimes in place of a typical birthday or holiday gift, are catching on culturally and are likely to grow significantly in the coming years. In fact, one projection suggests the entire crowdfunding industry (of which global donations would be just one part) will grow to a massive $300 billion by 2025.[9]

It would be understandable if ordinary people making small donations wondered if their giving really matters in an era of billionaire philanthropists. But retail aid organizations are getting better and better at making the case that your money will have a specific, measurable, and important impact in the life of someone you can feel directly connected to. There's even a possibility of taking this kind of one-off giving around special occasions to the next level, turning ordinary donors into strategic philanthropists.

For example, already Americans of virtually any income level can create their own foundations in the form of donor-advised funds, receiving an immediate tax deduction while investing their donation in stocks and bonds to increase the value of their foundation over time. Then, whenever they're ready to make a donation, they can do so from this fund. Global Impact, a US nonprofit that helps companies set up employee-contribution plans, has developed a donor-advised fund called Grow Fund that requires a minimum balance of just $100 and allows for grants of as little as $25.[10] The idea that average Americans would engage in strategic giving is a potential game changer that could dramatically grow the amount of charitable donations and spur healthy competition among aid organizations.

As crowdfunding platforms get easier to use, become more culturally mainstream and more open and transparent, and provide more robust impact data, they could grow to be in the same league as the biggest foundations and foreign aid agencies. There could even be powerful crowdfunding models that emerge around narrow issues, like sports education or exclusive breastfeeding, that appeal to specific donor groups. Charity: Water, which focuses on clean drinking water, has proved this. After leaving a career as a nightclub promoter, Scott Harrison found his calling and created the startup nonprofit in 2006, working out of his apartment. So far, he and his team have raised an incredible $320 million, providing clean drinking water to 8.4 million people.[11]

The retail mind-set is powerful, and in the business world companies have learned that those who don't focus on new demands from customers often end up humbled by new entrants in the market. Disruptive startups find new ways to delight customers and end up transforming entire industries from hotels (Airbnb now has more rooms than Hilton)[12] to transportation (Uber is now worth more than General Motors)[13] to entertainment (the video game industry now has more than double the revenue of Hollywood).[14]

Just like those tech economy examples, the retail aid model has a great advantage against the traditional NGOs with their many layers of bureaucracy and large long-term projects: it can quickly scale.

GETTING TO SCALE

This issue of scale is dear to the hearts of billionaires and entrepreneurs, many of whom made their wealth in Silicon Valley. The goal in Silicon Valley is to build solutions that can ultimately reach every human, every business, every country. With the increasing cross pollination between Silicon Valley and philanthropy, this obsession with scale has entered the DNA of the global development community.

Real status in the aid industry now belongs to those who seek to create solutions that can scale to tackle problems like those outlined in the Sustainable Development Goals. Bill Gates is working to end polio; Mike Bloomberg, smoking; Mark Zuckerberg, disease; George Soros, oppression; Chris Hohn, the British hedge fund investor behind the Children's Investment Fund Foundation, child deaths. Smaller-scale tutoring programs are fine, but making them accessible to millions of kids in thousands of communities (say, through something like Khan Academy)—that's the Silicon Valley way.

Scale is important in global development and business for similar reasons: to bring down costs and build up capital. Walmart can't lower its prices much as a single department store. With thousands of stores, it has the buying power to change entire industries and supply chains, lowering prices for millions of consumers.

Traditional aid organizations can find it difficult to scale their activities. Yes, the cost per bed net would be lower if you bought millions of them, but the total amount of money required to buy that many is much greater and perhaps not within the project budget. The old aid mind-set is based on what the famed humanitarian doctor Paul Farmer, cofounder of Partners In Health, calls the "socialization of scarcity"— the idea that we are all competing for scarce resources and all have to make do with less.[15] Because this worldview was so embedded in organizations constantly appealing for more donations, aid organizations rarely thought big in the way that is so common in Silicon Valley. On the West Coast there's even a term for this mind-set—"abundant thinking." The predominant feeling among NGOs and aid workers was that money is always tight, so don't shoot for big things.

In a world where a single family—Mark Zuckerberg and Priscilla Chan—will likely contribute over $100 billion to charitable work, ordinary people have loaned $1 billion through the microfinance platform Kiva, and Americans donated $500 million via their cell phones to earthquake relief in Haiti in just a few days, or where some $9 trillion is invested in socially responsible investments, scarcity isn't the issue any longer.

There's enormous potential for tackling the biggest problems, extreme poverty included, in retail models. These models don't just have to rely on donations. The new money will also come from ordinary people in the form of loans, remittances, investments, or purchasing power. Foreign aid and billionaire contributions will still be critical—in part because they can fund important public goods but also because they can seed the kinds of organizations and models that will unlock this retail money.

It's not all about donations either. A key milestone for a poor country is when it can raise enough tax revenue from its citizens to fund its own health and education systems. A similar milestone for rich countries is when its consumers agree to pay a premium for fair trade coffee to ensure the farmers who grew the beans can send their kids to school. For the poorest individuals—without formal jobs or educations or savings to fall back on—a key milestone is when they can get an affordable loan directly to their cell phone in minutes. All this too reflects a retail shift where ordinary citizens and taxpayers are themselves part of the solution to global poverty.

THE POWER OF GETTING POOR PEOPLE TO PAY

It's incredible to think that thousands of ordinary people making small loans through Kiva could have already lent a total of more than $1 billion. It's a remarkable success. But in an era of retail aid, even Kiva may face serious disruption.

First of all, for sound logistical reasons, Kiva actually distributes money to individuals through local microfinance institutions and solicits online loans after the fact, to essentially "backfill" the loan that has already been made. That means that the transaction is not quite as direct as the donor might think when he or she picks out an entrepreneur on the Kiva website. In that sense, it's like sponsor-a-child programs or donate-a-chicken-or-cow initiatives. It appears that you are giving to a specific person or family, but since the money is fungible you don't really know precisely to whom your donation actually goes. This makes perfect sense today, since we should all want the loan to get to the person who needs it as quickly as possible and not create a kind of popularity contest for who has the most compelling online profile. But as retail aid expectations grow, competitors may arise who can better connect donors with the actual individual who needs the money.

A more serious challenge for Kiva is that microcredit itself is changing. These small business loans have long been plagued by their overapplication: not everyone will be an entrepreneur or be in a position to pay back a business loan. To make matters worse, administering small loans in challenging environments can entail high costs. In the US we chafe at credit cards that charge over 20 percent, but microloans routinely come with interest rates of 30 percent or even 40 percent. Kiva has helped to drive down those costs, refusing to work with lenders who don't charge reasonable rates, and reducing the cost of capital to the lenders it does work with by not requiring any interest be repaid to Kiva. But Kiva represents only a tiny fraction of the approximately $100 billion microcredit market, and abusively high rates have even led to farmer suicides in India that caused the government there to very publicly crack down on the industry.[16]

If new technologies emerge that make administering small loans much cheaper by bringing down the risks and transaction costs, the industry may balloon as demand rises and more private capital floods in. That could make Kiva and other nonprofit funders a less important source of funds for microfinance institutions.

Careful studies of microcredit have shown that, in general, the best that can be said for it is it does no harm. That's not an entirely fair assessment, as microcredit can be an important element of successful programs in targeted areas, such as One Acre Fund's seed and fertilizer loans to farmers. Microcredit could become vastly more powerful if only it were cheap: imagine if poor people everywhere could get small loans through their cell phones instantly at interest rates of less than 10 percent? They could use them not just for starting businesses but also for medical emergencies or for investments like school uniforms.

As I've mentioned, Tala is a startup trying to crack the code of credit scores for the poor, thereby facilitating and opening up lending to a vastly larger market, and lowering the cost of lending. Tala has developed a methodology that allows it to assess credit risks using ten thousand data points that even the lowest-income people have on their mobile phones, including their purchase and payment histories, their social connectedness on social media platforms, and their locations.[17] They've even found that people who organize more than 40 percent of their phone contacts by first and last name make for more creditworthy borrowers.

If companies like Tala can dramatically drive down costs by reducing credit risks, microcredit could be in for a revolution. Tala has already made loans to over a million and a half people, raised over $100 million in capital, and hired away Uber's chief data officer, who developed dynamic pricing for the ride-sharing giant. That gives you a sense of their ambition and potential scale.

As companies like Tala drive down microloan interest rates, peer-to-peer platforms like Kiva will be affected. That's because microcredit will become something more easily investable by financial institutions and won't require as much philanthropy. You might even be able to put some of your 401(k) into a microcredit fund and get a predictable and low-risk return on it. That's the big opportunity with microfinance—make it just like regular finance and thus reach many more people.

Kiva clearly sees the ground shifting and may well end up changing its model. Cofounder Matt Flannery left the organization in 2015 to start a Tala competitor called Branch, and in 2018 Kiva itself announced a new initiative to build a blockchain-based credit-score platform in Sierra Leone.[18] As credit scores for the poor upend traditional microfinance, Kiva could find a way to go around traditional microfinance institutions and lend directly to individuals. Or, it could become a powerful platform for both peer-to-peer grants and loans, using its tremendous scale to take on a platform like Give Directly.

Already, Give Directly makes a compelling case along these lines to ordinary givers. Unlike Kiva, it doesn't purport to allow you to connect to a specific individual—there's no true or imagined peer-to-peer functionality. But it does provide a real-time feed of survey feedback from the people who receive money from Give Directly, who, on average, live on sixty-five cents per day in Kenya and eighty-three cents per day in Uganda.[19] It's easy to see how even a small donation could be life-changing in those circumstances.

Crowdfunding does not always involve online loans and donations from another country: it can also mean people in need—even those living on less than a dollar a day—paying from their own pockets.

Toilets are a good example. My guess is that if you're reading this you have daily access to a toilet. Most of us have not had the experience of defecating in the open, as many poor people do, except perhaps on a camping trip.

I mention that only to help drive home the astounding reality that, nearly two and a half centuries after the invention of the toilet, one in three people on this planet live precisely the opposite experience to ours. It's maddening to think that such a basic problem—so tied up in human health, safety, and dignity—would remain to be solved. It's not as though toilets are some newfangled technology: they are cheap and straightforward. So why doesn't everyone have access to one?

The answer isn't as obvious as it seems. There's poverty: some people are too poor to afford a toilet, but that's a dead-end analysis. Maybe it's not that some people are too poor to afford a toilet but rather that toilets haven't been designed to be affordable. This shift in thinking is critical to the new world of aid we're in today. The old worldview sees poverty as an immovable object; the new one, in which poor people are consumers, sees poverty as another business issue to be overcome.

In this conception, there's an enormous market out there to be served: some 2.5 billion people who use pit latrines that have to be regularly emptied, often into waterways that people drink from, or who must defecate in the open. These are certainly people with the most modest of means, but even a penny a day from each of them would be a few billion dollars in purchasing power each year. More importantly, many billions more can be saved from health systems that treat related diseases like diarrhea, new money can be created when people save time and have improved health due to toilets, and lives can be saved from disease. There can even be valuable byproducts from human waste, including fertilizer, water for irrigation, and fuel. So while it won't be easy, there is a market to be built.

Some of the big players in the aid industry are trying to develop new solutions to this fundamental and age-old issue. The Gates Foundation, for example, has made the availability of toilets one of its signature challenges, developing a prize competition to award innovative ideas for affordable toilet technology. One of the key issues is building toilets that don't require being connected to a sanitation infrastructure, which is simply nonexistent in many places. One of the prize recipients, the bathroom fixtures company Kohler, has developed a closed-loop toilet system that treats and purifies the wastewater and then reuses it for flushing. Another recipient, a coalition led by Duke University, addressed a second key factor: being able to operate without electricity. This team figured out a way to automatically separate solids from liquids in human waste, burn the solids as a biomass fuel, and use the resulting energy to power the entire toilet system.

These challenging parameters are difficult enough for the engineers trying to win the prize. But the Gates Foundation added an additional factor, one that is essential to the new market-based thinking rightly taking over the aid world. The prize judges decided to require that toilet designs be affordable—so affordable that they would not cost more than five cents per person per day to operate.

Getting consumers to pay, even in tiny amounts, can dramatically change the economics of a problem like sanitation. It's a kind of crowd-funding by the poor for themselves. For those who see asking poor people to pay even pennies to use a toilet as a kind of cruelty, let's do the math. If toilets could be reduced in cost to a nickel per person per day, the cost to provide them to 2.5 billion people for free would be $46 billion per year. And that's just one visit to the toilet per day. To pay that bill would require more than half the total annual aid spending of all European Union countries combined.[20]

But if, instead, relatively small investments in new technology could lead to the development of a consumer-driven market that would generate financial returns, perhaps investors and governments would be willing to put up the money to ensure all people have access to a toilet. Like credit scores, new toilet technologies could unlock the ability for poor people to change their own lives for the better.

HOW WHOLESALE AID IS CHANGING

In Malawi I met a mother whose life had been transformed from a particularly bad situation. She told me that she had been the recipient of a direct gift: the local Red Cross had given her three goats. After caring for them and breeding them, now she had two dozen. Thanks to her hard work, her income had increased and she had been able to build a one-room house out of brick instead of mud.

She was an exception. Many of the other women I met in her village showed me the small, hard gourds they were eating. The rains had stopped and their more nutritious corn crop had failed. The goats had been good for a single woman who needed a leg up, but the community needed a broader and more fundamental solution to its farming problems.

In a situation like that, dropping in donations without talking to local people first can have limited results or backfire. It's a complaint some people make about Give Directly. Some of the results from evaluations of its impact are that those who get the money are like the woman with the goats, and those who don't, look at their well-off neighbor and feel more miserable than ever. Similarly, I've heard from executives at oil companies who have tried to help out the communities where they're exploring or drilling. The money sometimes gets distributed unevenly or unthoughtfully. When some people have more cash to spend, the price of goods at the local market can spike up. The people who didn't get a handout are hungrier than before.

What I call "wholesale" models of aid would work quite differently in this kind of context. As we've seen, the current focus tends to be on projects, not on individual aid recipients. These projects can be quite large—often in the millions or even tens of millions of dollars—and entail billion-dollar NGOs subcontracting and subgranting through a whole series of partners and local and national organizations. The goals of wholesale projects are often more connected to public goods like improving school feeding programs, and they're hard to compare to something as straightforward as handing out cash. They're often designed around a fixed plan that doesn't easily shift and change based on feedback from the people in need. In an example like that village in Malawi, a wholesale approach might entail an irrigation project to benefit the whole village as opposed to singling out just the neediest people.

Even with these key differences, the emergence of retail models where the voice of aid recipients is strong and can force immediate changes will change the way wholesale projects are executed too.

Like traditional retailers in the era of Amazon, even the most respected brand names in the world of charity will need to change. Increasingly they will be forced to do a better job showing authentic feedback from aid recipients and ensuring their project actually takes that feedback into account. They'll need to connect donors to the communities in need and they'll have to be careful to not position even the poorest people as helpless victims.

In this Malawian village example, it could mean something like a large irrigation project is executed quite differently, incorporating local input into the design, taking into account ongoing feedback and continually monitoring results to make changes as-needed, and maybe even implementing a sliding-scale fee so that the project can be self-sustaining over time. Even a large-scale project could entail direct connections with community members such that the success or failure of the project is judged by them and owned by them.

The retail aid model has the potential to unlock scattered trillions of dollars to support global development. The involvement of millions and millions of ordinary givers might just become a force as big as the billionaires in the new aid industry. For that potential to be realized, donating has to become more like retail purchasing: ordinary donors need to have choices, they need to understand value, and they need to know what they're actually buying with their money. That is exactly what Give Directly wants to do, including offering the option to make donations specifically to refugees.[21]

As more and more donors act like consumers, picking and choosing their philanthropies based on factors such as transparency, results-focus, and cost-effectiveness, the "suppliers" in the market will have no choice but to respond by improving their performance. No longer will donors be satisfied with the little acknowledgments and swag items that came with feel-good giving—they'll increasingly go with the organization that guarantees outcomes per dollar donated. As that happens, the market will shift so that the wholesale model—big projects aimed at providing public goods like infrastructure—is balanced with a retail one, in which there is a much more direct connection between the person giving and the person consuming the aid.

To me, this customer-focused mind-set is similar to that of huge retail companies. McDonald's serves billions of customers, but, for them, the individual customer is the key stakeholder. Customers matter to the retailer. What they say about a brand, a product, or an experience is incredibly important. If one customer tweets a complaint about a lousy hamburger, the retailer is obliged to sit up and take notice.

This has not been true of traditional charity and philanthropy operations. Technically, aid professionals in the field are supposed to be working on behalf of the people they serve—who are commonly referred to as "beneficiaries." Maybe this is true on paper, but the reality is that for on-the-ground aid workers, the entity that supplies the money is the customer. If, for example, the nonprofit receives funding from USAID or the Rockefeller Foundation for an education project in rural Kenya, those funders are going to have a lot of influence over how the program is designed and implemented—perhaps more influence than the people affected. As a retail approach to aid grows, that's going to change.

7. OPEN SOURCE AID

The Case for Openness

PLAYPUMPS WAS A MUCH-PUBLICIZED aid industry failure. Backed by AOL founder Steve Case and his wife, Jean, as well as former First Lady Laura Bush and others, PlayPumps were a clever low-tech innovation.[1] Much like One Laptop Per Child, the project was hailed as a kind of technological panacea—a whiz-bang invention that would solve the problem of providing clean drinking water in places that didn't have easy access to it.

The PlayPump was a merry-go-round connected to a water pump that would bring up water from a well. It did not need electrical power and it gave the kids a way to play. It also had room for advertising messages, and the revenue would supposedly help cover its costs. Like other blockbuster ideas, all sounded great.

PlayPumps was announced at a 2006 event, headlined by Bill Clinton and Laura Bush, and was well-funded with US foreign aid and private philanthropy totaling $16 million. The ambitious goal was to install four thousand pumps by 2010.[2] But, like OLPC, the reality fell far short of the intention. Only a few hundred PlayPumps were installed. Businesses did not sign up for advertising. Kids did not play on them. Most damning, an analysis by the *Guardian* showed that the PlayPumps could never have achieved their goal even if they had been used. Kids would have to play on the merry-go-round for an impossible twenty-seven hours per day to reach the target of providing 2,500 people per pump with water daily. It also turned out that PlayPumps cost four times more than a standard water pump.[3]

Where PlayPumps differs from OLPC is that once it was clear it wasn't working, it's funders—especially the Case Foundation—pivoted. They learned from their mistake. The South African company behind Play-Pumps—called Roundabout—transferred the technology to another water NGO so it could decide if and when it made sense to use it. The Case Foundation engaged in other projects to support clean water that had more evidence behind them—including ensuring running water in schools.[4]

So, although PlayPumps must be seen as a significant failure given how much money was lost, the initiative was shut down fairly quickly, mistakes were acknowledged, and the funders applied what they had learned to better, more effective initiatives. That kind of creative destruction is going to be much more common in the new aid industry, although less money will be lost as initiatives share results more quickly and respond to what their customers—the people in need they are designed to serve—are saying.[5]

When I consider the new aid industry—erupting with billionaire donors and big company do-gooders, social entrepreneurs with a retail mindset, new approaches like human-centered design, behavioral science, and systems thinking, all with a results focus—I see the outlines of a new ethos I call open source aid. It's not a single methodology, like randomized controlled trials or a robust philosophy like effective altruism but rather an operating culture. It's a combination of having the humility to assume no charitable idea is going to work out exactly as intended and the honesty to share experiences and results, good and bad.

The old aid industry has been held back by a fear of openness. The risk of highlighting wasted taxpayer dollars or of drawing attention to failures that individual donors might not appreciate makes charities and aid agencies clam up. One of the key reasons we started Devex was because we saw no open forum for the most effective ideas, people, and organizations—especially those from the countries where aid work takes place—to rise to the top.

OLD AID	OPEN SOURCE AID
Annual Reports	Real-Time Public Dashboards
Post-Project Evaluations	Ongoing Data Feed
Mission Statement	Logic Model

OLD AID	OPEN SOURCE AID
Problem & Solution Designed First	Agile, Iterative Process
Vertical View of Specific Issues	Holistic View of Whole Person
Decision-Making Close to Funding Source	Decision-Making Close to Funding Recipient
Ideological	Pragmatic
Idealistic	Realistic
Wholesale Project Orientation	Retail Business Model Orientation
One-Off	Systemic
Grants, Loans	Leverage, Incentives
Success = Budget Size	Success = Results

Open source aid, like open source computer code, seeks to change all that by enabling everyone involved in the industry to learn from and build on the experiences of others. It's not proprietary or centrally controlled. It values everyone's contribution—from the foundation president to the expert consultant to the poor person sharing feedback about an initiative in his or her own community. It's effectively altruistic in that it assumes all lives have equal value and that saving as many lives as possible should be our shared goal. It allows for a range of approaches, with the best ideas bubbling up to the top of a transparent and open community.

GitHub is the largest online platform for web developers, where they post and comment on each other's code. The site also hosts the largest open source community in the world. Over twenty million developers are part of the platform, and they work together to improve the quality of open source code that no one owns. Engineers on the platform take pride in the amount of code they publish and on how many people have given their code a kind of digital thumbs up. Whether you've heard of GitHub or not, chances are many of the digital products you love have benefited from that platform, as have ours at Devex.

Wikipedia, a similar platform, is another example of what is known as the principle of open collaboration, where people work together informally and without hierarchy but toward a singular goal. On Wikipedia, volunteer editors prune and add content to make the platform as robust and accurate as possible.

Similarly, global development is beginning to head in the direction of open collaboration. When aid projects are designed by the same people in the same conference rooms in London and Washington, DC, it's only natural that they'll turn out to be near facsimiles of what's been done in the past. Often, in pursuit of low-risk, high-impact results, they'll pursue straightforward, noncontroversial interventions like training healthcare workers or purchasing medicine. Because overseeing smaller projects can entail as much cost and time as larger ones, these projects will commonly be quite large—often millions of dollars committed over several years.

This approach leaves out risky but innovative opportunities like APOPO, one of my favorite examples of an intervention that only an experimental, collaborative approach could surface. APOPO is an organization that trains African giant pouched rats—who have an unbelievably precise sense of smell—to detect tuberculosis (TB) in laboratory samples. In Ethiopia, Tanzania, and Mozambique, people with symptoms of TB cough up sputum and the rats sniff it to see if it contains the disease. The samples flagged as positive by the rats then get full laboratory testing. It turns out a rat can check a hundred samples in just twenty minutes, something that would take a lab technician five days using a microscope.[6] In low-resource settings with high rates of TB, the number one infectious-disease killer in the world today, use of these rats might just be a game changer for detection of the disease and saving lives.

APOPO was funded by USAID but not through a standard government contract or grant. Instead, it received money through a program called Development Innovation Ventures (DIV, though known more commonly as "Div") specifically designed to test out risky but potentially hugely cost-effective ideas. The organization is funding APOPO to help build evidence of the rats' capabilities, and, ultimately, to scale the program up for more widespread use. So far, DIV has granted $90 million to innovations like APOPO in over forty countries.[7]

DIV uses a tiered system for awarding grants: $25,000 to $150,000 for an initial proof of concept period, which, if successful, can be followed by a $150,000 to $1.5 million grant for testing and preparing the innovation for the market. Finally, if the innovation really works and has market potential, it'll award a grant of $1.5 million to $15 million in order to take it to scale. This allows it to take measured risks and to focus most of its funding on innovations that work.

GRANTS AND COMPETITION

Another manifestation of open source aid is the growth of competition grants like XPRIZE. These kinds of grants seek to inspire a large community of people—including those outside of a field of practice who may have a fresh perspective—to bring their ingenuity to bear against a significant problem. The financial prize offered isn't meant to necessarily enrich the winners but rather to help take their idea to fruition.

As the aid industry has been shifting to a greater focus on evidence and results, these kinds of competition grants have been growing dramatically. Grand Challenges Canada, an initiative primarily funded by the Canadian government, seeks out what it calls "bold ideas with big impact" and has funded 854 since its inception in 2010. Scientists, healthcare practitioners, students, and anyone with an idea can make a case for funding as part of a competitive process. An example is a project to test pregnant women for urinary tract infections (UTIs) in low-income countries.

Around a third to half of pregnant women will get a UTI during pregnancy. They're often not serious, but if the infection is not treated it can have significant complications for the mother and fetus, from premature labor to low birth weight or even spontaneous miscarriage.[8] In low-income countries like Sierra Leone, poor women don't have the money for expensive lab tests to determine if they have a UTI. The alternative is use of test strips you pee on, like a pregnancy test, but those cost one dollar each, which is still too much for many soon-to-be moms. A Christian relief organization, World Hope International, won a Grand Challenges Canada grant to test out a new innovation it developed—a test strip specifically for UTIs that costs just twenty cents.

Ideas like that one are most likely to be hatched by smaller organizations and those closer to where the problems are. Competition grants are cropping up to help foster the development of these ideas and take them from small-scale concepts to commercial application.

What's incredible about competition grants is their efficiency. Given the causes involved, many people are willing to contribute their ideas and efforts without receiving a paycheck. Participating in a competition to solve an important problem is its own reward. Plus, using a tiered model allows funders to experiment with innovative ideas while reserving significant money for ideas that are proved and ready to scale.

The Global Innovations Fund (GIF), which made its first grants and investments in 2016, is one of the latest examples of the growth in this space. Among its projects is a modest effort to place twenty Syrian refugees currently in Jordan into employment with major corporations in Morocco and the United Arab Emirates.[9] At first glance, it seems like a drop in the ocean of twenty-one million refugees in need. But remember, these are not typical grants designed just to do immediate good but rather opportunities to collect evidence.

Like an early stage venture capitalist, organizations like GIF use small grants to study what works—in this case the process for identifying employers, matching and training the workers, securing visas—in order to build a robust business model that can scale. If it works—and it could well fail—GIF will ultimately provide loans or even invest directly and become a shareholder of a new company that connects global corporations with refugees who have the skills they need.

We are in a period of experimentation, as organizations work to define their impact in order to meet the new expectations of the industry. While I have certainly witnessed quite a few young organizations and projects given credibility they don't deserve by virtue of throwing around buzzwords that fit the moment, some of these experimental ideas are working.

THE ROLE OF EFFECTIVE ALTRUISM

A significant contributor to furthering open source aid will be the effective altruism movement. Think of effective altruists as the evangelicals of the new era in charity and global development. They tend to be true believers—not necessarily in divinity but in the power of pure reason. Born from the same philosopher who pioneered veganism, Princeton's Peter Singer, effective altruism is a utilitarian philosophy that sounds a lot like high finance. Effective altruists have a language quite unlike others in the global aid industry: "costs-benefit analysis," "expected value frameworks," and "diminishing returns" roll off their tongues. They are the Silicon Valley venture capitalists of the aid world, coolly analytical, with the key difference being that effective altruists are talking about saving huge numbers of lives, not making extraordinary profits.

Plenty of charity leaders I speak with are frustrated by the effective altruists: they are too sure of themselves and their spreadsheet-based models; too focused on what's easily measurable; too dismissive of those who don't sign on to their credo. But effective altruists have also injected an essential element of competition and ambition into this industry. It's the effective altruists who zero in on the very poorest people and what's killing them (because they see the greatest potential "return" in terms of lives saved there). It's their annoying questions that push well-intentioned charity executives to defend their work with a logical argument for why their approach deserves to be funded over others—a thought process that could help them to actually be more effective.

Some of Singer's views have generated intense criticism. A utilitarian philosopher, he has advocated infanticide as an option for parents when their doctors are certain an infant has such a severe disability that he or she lacks "rationality, autonomy, and self-consciousness"—a position decried especially by members of the disability community. Although this issue is separate from effective altruism, it's a sign of how zealous Singer and his supporters can be: they are willing to promote even deeply unpopular ideas if they align with the philosophy they promote.

The one way in which Singer's thinking is linked to effective altruism is that adherents to this movement need to make value judgements about human lives in order to run the numbers of what interventions are most effective. As such, they need to determine the value of, for example, saving the life of a child versus the life of an elderly person. Without making those judgments, it's impossible to do the calculations on the cost-effectiveness of various philanthropic interventions.

Making judgments like that may not sit well with some. As one critic put it in relation to his views on disability, "[Singer's] arguments are built intricately and beautifully, like a perfect mathematics equation, but at their core beats a single assertion, one that is still too difficult to concede: that this group of human beings aren't really people."[10]

Avoiding or ignoring the calculus doesn't actually help anyone either. What's important when making those kinds of judgments is total transparency so everyone can see the underlying assumptions driving effective altruist philanthropy—something GiveWell does brilliantly.

In my view, the emergence of the effective altruism movement is a good thing. Their focus on evidence and results is a step in the right direction for an aid industry long focused on good intentions. For example, effective altruism homes in on the fact that, on average, millions of preventable deaths can be averted for $4,000 each and that, since the world is awash in money and that is a small price to pay for such an important moral purpose, we should do more to save those lives.[11]

Where this movement can fail is in its disconnection from the lives it is trying to save. As the *New Yorker* writer Larissa MacFarquhar has pointed out, the effective altruism movement is "the drone program of altruism."[12] It's highly effective in the short run but perhaps doesn't address underlying issues and might even exacerbate them.

Others in global development, including groups like Oxfam and leaders like Paul Farmer, take a view that's more grounded in history and politics. They see in today's poverty the results of a colonial and imperial history that was designed to exploit countries and people. That exploitation continues in the lives of poorly paid workers in unsafe sweatshops stitching our clothing, in factories that pollute over there so we can have clean air over here, and in poor people using their bare hands to mine the metals that make our high-end smartphones work.

It's not that the effective altruists necessarily disagree with this kind of political analysis. But it's not something easy to diagnose and address, so it's not the focus of the movement. Instead, effective altruists treat governance and politics like any other problem that can be solved by thinking your way out of it.[13] But can you engineer a revolution? Can a distant, cold calculus drive local politics? Maybe not everything in human relations is a game that can be played from a distance without anything more than financial sacrifice.

I experienced this personally when I witnessed the Orange Revolution in Ukraine up-close in 2004 while conducting an exit poll. It was a euphoric atmosphere, with strangers embracing in the streets and raucous singing and dancing until the wee hours, but overthrowing the government didn't ultimately change the underlying situation. A decade and a half later, the country is still run by a few billionaire oligarchs extracting wealth. It's still subject to a great power game by Russia.

Effective altruism can do a lot of good, but it's unlikely to be the singular approach adopted by the biggest development agencies in the world. Those organizations, like the Gates Foundation and the World Bank, have learned they need to not just fund vaccines and bed nets but also to provide long-term support to civil society, good governance, and peace.

One way effective altruism can make short-term progress but imperil long-term success is by "skimming."[14] This is a term that refers to creating programs that benefit only the most mobilized of the poor. An example is charter schools that pull in some poor kids, but perhaps just the ones who have parents who are clued in to these opportunities. The result can be that the remaining government-provided services (hospitals, schools, feeding programs) don't improve, and those mobilized poor people now accessing private services don't have the incentive to push for broader government reform.

This argument is more compelling in the abstract at this point. The scale of need is so great that it's hard to suggest we do nothing and instead wait for poor people to rise up and demand better healthcare and education. Evidence-based intervention is better, so long as it takes into account the broader political system in which these challenges exist. That kind of thinking might lead, for example, to spending a bit more to ensure not just that healthcare outcomes improve, but also that local institutions can continue providing them over time. Effectiveness is an important principle; but even if it's hard to measure, we should include in it the idea of self-determination.

As one observer, political scholar Jennifer Rubenstein, has noted, the "effective altruism movement's primary strategy for attracting new members [is] showing how easy it is to save lives cheaply."[15] She describes how Singer argues to his students that donating to a cost-effective charity "can do as much good as a person who runs through flames to kick open the door of a burning building, saving one hundred lives." The analogy, Rubenstein argues, "encourages donors to think of themselves as heroes or saviors" and "overlooks poor people's central role in alleviating their own poverty and rich people's role in contributing to and benefiting from it."[16]

A similar philosophical debate bubbled up on stage when Paul Farmer and Jim Kim needled each other at a Harvard screening for the 2017 documentary *Bending the Arc*, about the storied nonprofit Partners In Health. The two medical doctors and close friends were among the cofounders of PIH three decades earlier but, as the moderator pointed out, had taken different paths since then. Farmer continually reminded the audience that while Jim, now president of the World Bank, was cutting big deals with presidents, finance ministers, and CEOs, Farmer was still visiting rural clinics in places like Sierra Leone, serving patients and getting his hands dirty.

Their friendly rivalry points to a serious issue: a technocratic model for ending poverty can be effective only if the assumptions it's based on and the data that feed it are right. After working for years in a rural clinic in Haiti, Farmer may have a very different idea about the key drivers of poverty there than a foundation program officer in San Francisco or even than the World Bank president would. He seems to have a healthy skepticism of big plans hatched in rich countries that may never really come to fruition where it counts. If we're to create new models and approaches aimed at ending global poverty in just over a decade, how can we be sure they're based on reality?

CHINESE AID: BIG BUT OPAQUE

There are some obstacles to the kind of collaboration, transparency, and pragmatism that are the hallmarks of open source aid. It may be difficult, for example, to move a few important participants in the aid industry, notably China, toward the open source model. China came in last (tied with the United Arab Emirates) in the Publish What You Fund index. China is among the largest foreign aid donors in the world, with some estimates putting it in the same league as the UK and Germany, which are right behind the US in terms of how much they give. Yet almost no information is available on China's foreign aid activities. A painstaking, but likely not exhaustive, study by AidData shows China gave more foreign aid than the US since 2000 to Cambodia, Cameroon, Ghana, Ivory Coast, Sri Lanka, and others.[17]

China is a major player, yet there's little detail on what its programs are funding and what the results may be. China's government is famously less than transparent: even the birth dates of its top leaders are a state secret. The assumption among expert observers is that China gives foreign aid with strings attached: for a combination of political (voting with China in the UN for example), commercial (helping Chinese companies), and economic reasons (like trade).

China, it seems, sees its foreign aid as a direct extension of its foreign policy. That must change if it wants to be part of the solution to ending extreme poverty globally as it has been doing so effectively among its own citizens. I recall attending the annual meeting of the African Development Bank in Shanghai in 2007. It was a lavish affair. At one point I was in line at the buffet table behind the diminutive finance minister of an African nation who had piled his plate so high with food he could barely see over it. That night the conference attendees were treated to a massive fireworks display.

Chinese companies win the majority of contracts funded by the African Development Bank to build roads, ports, and other infrastructure on the continent. It's not uncommon to see Chinese workers at construction sites in African countries, something I've witnessed in Kenya and Ethiopia. Clearly there's a lot of activity, and perhaps China has even done real good for African people. A 2015 survey showed a majority of citizens of thirty-six African countries think China is a positive force in their country.[18] Nonetheless, the secrecy inherent in its current approach will undermine the necessary movement to open source aid unless it changes soon.

In 2017 a senior Chinese diplomat, Li Hong, gave an interview to a Devex colleague of mine in which Hong claimed that the country's secrecy around its aid activities could be reduced in the coming years. He suggested much of the current Chinese approach has to do with the fact that it's new to the world of global aid, and that it's eager to learn from others. Even so, the April 2018 announcement of a new, unified aid planning agency in China, the China International Development Cooperation Agency (CIDCA), with the influential head Wang Xiaotao, has not so far been accompanied by a new approach to transparency.[19] While China is likely to continue using foreign aid for foreign policy purposes (just as the US, the UK, Germany, and others do, although nowhere near to the same extent), there's a real opportunity to push the country to make its aid more effective, particularly in the poorest countries.

In particular, advocacy groups spent decades pushing multilateral development banks like the World Bank to adopt environmental and social safeguards, urging them to ensure they don't finance projects like coal plants or infrastructure that displaces large numbers of people. We need to do the same with China. Those with leverage in the aid industry, from private donors to major corporations to reporting organizations including Devex, will need to push CIDCA to at least be more transparent if it wants to be a part of the fight to achieve the Sustainable Development Goals, and not just its own goals.

Chinese aid is often seen by the global development community as a problem. It operates in isolation, does its own thing. China is not funding big international NGOs but rather Chinese firms that build infrastructure like roads, bridges, and ports in poor countries. Much of the aid it gives is in the form of loans that must be repaid—an incredible $1 trillion in loans are planned under China's Belt and Road Initiative. There is deep skepticism about its motives and the way it operates. Most aid professionals I speak with assume China encourages corruption to make the deals it wants on access to raw materials and trade. Many also worry that China will saddle poor countries with unsustainable debt as it encourages them to take huge infrastructure loans.

But China's involvement in the global aid industry is also a massive opportunity. If Chinese aid is truly at the level of the UK and Germany and can be mainstreamed into the kinds of interventions we know work, it can have an incredible impact on saving lives and advancing human progress. Chinese aid directed toward the right goals, relying on the best evidence, and focused on results would be like cloning Bill and Melinda Gates three or four times over.

One important opportunity is the Asian Infrastructure Investment Bank (AIIB). When China created it, the first reaction in the West was that it would be somehow competitive with the Asian Development Bank (ADB) and World Bank. Cooler heads prevailed in most countries. While the Obama administration asked its allies not to join the bank, they did anyway, with the UK, Germany, and Australia among others paying-in capital and joining the board of directors. China still controls the AIIB, but now these Western countries have a seat at the table. The AIIB is designed to build much-needed infrastructure in Asia—including, for example, sanitation systems in Cambodia and power plants in Pakistan—that can quite literally save lives. As a result, Western partners correctly see it as an opportunity to cooperate with China around a shared goal, even though the US and Japan are still not members. The Western countries involved hope to push the bank to adopt the same kinds of environmental and social safeguards that activists pushed the ADB and World Bank to take on over the years. And they rightly realize that the infrastructure demands of Asia are so great that there truly is no shortage of projects that need to be done, no competition over good and important work. The real competition is one of ideas and values.

OBSTACLES TO OPEN SOURCE AID

The dream of a new aid industry that operates like an open market and drives a virtuous cycle of more funding chasing better solutions is far from assured. There are major roadblocks in the way. The largest is that despite all of the transformational work being done, most aid funding today still comes in the form of government contracting.

In the case of the US, reforming the way the federal government purchases goods and services is a challenge far beyond USAID and the other US government foreign aid agencies. There's reason to be skeptical that significant foreign aid funding will shift away from large-scale contracts and grants and toward more innovative pay-for-performance instruments.

There are also many examples of progress, including those I've detailed so far, from USAID's Development Innovation Ventures mechanism to the Millennium Challenge Corporation to development impact bonds. Nonetheless, these are just a few percent of the approximately $30 billion annual US foreign aid budget.

Achieving global development progress may get harder in coming years. For one thing, automation and digital disruption, including technologies like 3-D printing, could close off the traditional route to economic growth for the poorest countries. Instead of low-skilled, light-manufacturing, such as that done in garment factories, moving from places like China and Bangladesh to sub-Saharan Africa or Haiti or Myanmar, those jobs may be replaced by robotics. For another, accelerating climate change could lead to more migration and more water shortages and food crises.

Foreign aid agencies and foundations urgently need to open up, collaborate, and innovate if they are to be effective under these difficult new circumstances. In particular, they need to find a way to tap into the millions of people around the world working in all industries and professions who want to help. If we can crowdsource innovative ideas and solutions and crowdfund the necessary investment for implementation, we can redraw the org chart of the aid industry to include virtually everyone in the world who wants to be a part of it.

An important element of moving toward an era of open source aid will be innovators inside government agencies like USAID and DFID. We need more focus on the sometimes-unsexy topics of procurement reform—for example, moving away from buying big technology projects that become obsolete overnight and toward the kind of software-as-a-service rental models so favored in the private sector. In a moment of urgency, innovators will need to figure out how to take more risks and co-create solutions with private companies and online communities, and they will need to move more quickly. Who would have thought the future of the world, including critical challenges like ending global poverty, would be in the hands of procurement officers?

8. SYSTEMS THINKING
Embracing Complexity

IDENTIFYING GLOBAL DEVELOPMENT PROBLEMS can be deceptively simple from a distance. There are good guys like Malala to promote and bad guys like Joseph Kony to vanquish, effective new water filters to be installed and antiquated institutions like child marriage to be outlawed.

Up close, it's clear empowering poor people and countries isn't just about inserting money, technology, and innovative solutions into the equation. These are complex systems problems that connect to history, politics, and culture.

Consider Myanmar. Until recently it was a closed-off time capsule of a nation, like Cuba and North Korea. Cell phones didn't arrive en masse until 2014,[1] and at that time a SIM card needed to operate one cost upwards of $2,000.[2] But the military dictatorship, feeling the pressure of global progress and growing agitation among the Burmese people, recently began to open up. By 2015, SIM cards had dropped in price to around $250.[3] The following year, the same year that Nobel Peace Prize winner Aung San Suu Kyi won the presidency of Myanmar after decades of protest and house arrest, a SIM card could be had for one dollar.

I visited in 2015 at a time of near euphoria in the development community about prospects for Myanmar. The country was a year away from elections that could bring then-revolutionary Suu Kyi to power. There was much tension and uncertainty as to whether the military junta could be trusted to peacefully cede power in a democratic process, but there was also a sense that one of the world's last closed-off countries—a pariah state of over fifty million people strategically situated between China and India—could soon be thrust onto the world stage and its people could jump on a fast-rising wave that would propel them out of poverty and into modernity.

Aid agencies had plans to spend over $1 billion per year in Myanmar on development projects of all kinds, raising agricultural yields, building roads and ports, and modernizing the education and health systems.

In a country where international NGOs were almost entirely banned during five decades of authoritarian rule, there was practically no development community or cadre of trained professionals. Local organizations existed but were often small and difficult to vet. At the same time, business and investment was flooding into the country at a breathtaking pace. Shining tall buildings, ancient gold temples, and dozens of construction cranes dotted Yangon's skyline.

Practitioners of global development live for moments like this one. Here was a rare chance to witness the opening of the time capsule and guide the progress of a traditional society; and, let's be honest, to live for a time as a privileged expat in an inexpensive, beautiful, and safe (for expats) country.

What fascinated me about Myanmar was the idea that it could act as almost a natural experiment for various development approaches. Big loans to the government to build infrastructure could make sense, but would the money be stolen and the projects mismanaged? A series of controlled trials could take place around the country to determine the best interventions for Myanmar's unique context, but would the slow pace of that research satisfy the urgent demands of the government, donors, and the Burmese people? Planeloads of expats working for NGOs and aid contractors could arrive to implement health, education, and agriculture projects of all kinds, conceived in Washington and London and executed in Myanmar through a hierarchy of local contractors and staff, but would those projects address the actual problems on the ground and do so cost-effectively?

From Washington, DC, it seemed so obvious to send huge amounts of foreign aid to the country to take advantage of this unique opportunity to quickly improve people's lives. But once in Myanmar it was clear that the situation was much more complicated.

In a rural part of the country several hours drive from Yangon, I sat down for tea with a farmer who made that complexity apparent. He told me he was working his family farm some years earlier when an army officer showed up and told him he wanted to buy his land. The farmer refused, but the officer returned with police and forced him off the property. Angry but thinking that the law was on his side, the farmer set out on a twenty-four-hour bus journey to Naypyidaw, the country's capital situated far in the north, in order to submit a written complaint to the relevant government agency. But still nothing happened. It turns out this sort of land grab was quite common in a country where the military had so much power. Another farmer told me about a retired military officer taking over the land of several families in order to create a place for his own family to reside.

The problem wasn't that Myanmar lacked laws saying you couldn't be forced off your own land; it's that those laws weren't enforceable for common people like farmers. A project to build a road or to introduce better seeds and fertilizers to farmers or to improve the educational outcomes of kids in that rural area—all of these sound like sensible development interventions, but what are they worth when people's basic rights aren't secured?

I met those farmers through a remarkable grassroots organization on the forefront of a new systems-approach to aid. Called Namati, its members are known as the "barefoot lawyers" and, true to the name, the farmer I met was trained as a paralegal. Namati had trained many local people in what it called administrative law, the simple act of knowing which forms to fill out, how to fill them out, and where to submit them. This afforded ordinary people with essential basic knowledge that, for example, taking someone's land, even if you're a military officer, is against the law.

Namati's approach in Myanmar was not flashy and didn't require a big budget or a large expat contingent. They weren't running a series of controlled trials. They were doing something simple, based on what local people told them they needed and on how human behavior works, that was geared to the larger system at play. They had made their initiative something that could be run and owned by local people serving their own communities.

Something as in-the-weeds as administrative law is hard to make buzzworthy or encapsulate in a thirty-second television ad. It can even be easy to attack as ineffective compared to more easily measurable interventions like insecticide-treated bed nets. Administrative law certainly doesn't sound as transformative as a revolution against a military junta.

The global euphoria that surrounded the election of Aung San Suu Kyi and the end of military rule reminds me of something I have often heard said about the Philippines. After World War II, conventional wisdom held that the Philippines would rise from the ashes of conflict to become a fast-growing economy and an Asian success story.[4] By contrast, Japan, struck by two atomic bombs, with a capital city that had been burned to the ground, was thought to be the next "sick man of Asia" and a looming basket case.[5]

Of course, the opposite transpired: today the average annual income of a Japanese person is around \$39,000 compared to \$7,600 for the average Filipino.[6] One in ten Filipinos live in extreme poverty.[7] What could that reversal of expected fortunes tell us about Myanmar?

In one critical aspect, Myanmar is more like the Philippines than Japan: it is a sprawling country of several ethnicities, some of them in ongoing conflict with the dominant Burmese. One of these ethnic groups, the Rohingya, have experienced years of persecution—a situation which has escalated since the country's transition to democracy. Hundreds of thousands of Rohingya have fled the country as the shocked international community looked on, waiting for their heroine Suu Kyi to respond. She has not. Nearly one million Rohingya, more than equivalent to the population of Washington, DC, now live in the world's largest refugee settlement in Cox's Bazar, Bangladesh.[8]

It seems in Myanmar, as in the Philippines, democratic elections alone won't put the country on the path to development. Ethnic divisions are too strong and democratic principles and institutions too weak to automatically prioritize growth and development for all citizens. I recall meeting top Western diplomats in Yangon who told me they feared Suu Kyi's election could actually distract from the reform processes underway: her star power and cult of personality could become the locus of attention, instead of efforts to rebuild the country's institutions from the ground up.

HEALTH SYSTEMS

One of the most important and complex institutions in any country is its health system. Even the concept of a "health system" is relatively new and showcases the rise of systems thinking.

Until recently, specific diseases like polio or TB got the most attention in global health, or, sometimes, the kind of basic healthcare that can be delivered in rural clinics did. But, especially since the Ebola crisis in West Africa a few years ago, there's been a growing recognition that what matters most is the underlying health system and how strong or weak it may be.

When you hear "health system," it's right to think doctors and nurses, hospitals and pharmacies. But many other things should come to mind too, including how healthcare professionals get paid, what kinds of standards clinics follow, how health information gets shared with the public, and even how mothers care for their babies. It's all connected and has to work together.

One of the Sustainable Development Goals encompasses the idea of universal health coverage (UHC), and the newly elected head of the World Health Organization, Ethiopia's Tedros Adhanom, has embraced the UHC agenda as his primary focus. This is a fairly radical agenda centered on strengthening health systems, but it's now widely accepted as the most important overarching global health goal.

Two early revolutionaries with a similar worldview were Paul Farmer and Jim Kim, two of the founders of Partners In Health, now one of the biggest and most impactful global health NGOs. Then students at Harvard Medical School, their philosophy was way ahead of its time: "We go, we make house calls, we build health systems, we stay."[9] The two men approached their work as doctors, not administrators. They would see a patient who needed care and they wanted to offer the best treatment regardless of whether the patient had enough money to pay for it. Farmer and Kim would literally steal medicines and equipment from the well-supplied Harvard facilities in order to stock the clinic they had established in Haiti. They had little choice. At that time, donors had no interest in funding expensive healthcare initiatives in poor places like Haiti.

Today health systems are all the rage, but back when PIH was founded in 1987 the idea of universal health coverage was a long way from common acceptance. When you put the patient first, as PIH did, it's easy to see the need for a complete health system. In the course of a patient's life, he or she is going to have many needs beyond a single treatment and what a community health worker or rural clinic can provide. Imagine instead an entire health system that can handle everything people need, rather than a program or even a stand-alone clinic. That is how Partners In Health has progressed over the years. In Rwanda, for example, Partners In Health now operates a major teaching facility, two hospitals, a cancer center of excellence, a university with visiting Harvard Medical School faculty, forty-two health centers, and a team of 6,400 community healthcare workers.[10]

From the beginning, Farmer and Kim did not focus on money. They believed that the money could be found for what they wanted to do because lives depended on it. They willed it into existence, successfully convincing donors to fund seemingly illogical things like providing tuberculosis treatments that cost thousands of dollars for penniless patients in Peru. They did it through the force of their moral courage—their *satyagraha*, or "soul-force," as Mahatma Gandhi might have said.

In the new aid industry, money is much less of an obstacle than it was for Farmer and Kim back then. As a result, it has become more possible to create health systems that draw on the advantages of scale to drive down costs, increase the volume of care, and generate tax revenues to further underwrite healthcare initiatives. Medications can be purchased in large volumes under special agreements with pharmaceutical companies that dramatically lower their costs. Clinics can be linked to hospitals so that patients can be referred up the chain to more and more specialized services. Healthcare services can be provided by private companies and nonprofit service providers and paid out based on outcomes. Insurance plans can be developed that include a combination of government revenue from taxes, fees paid by patients—but set based on their ability to pay—and funds provided by aid agencies and foundations.

As a health system grows and becomes more capable, it can draw in more private sector investors and tap into market mechanisms that allow it to provide more and better services over time. It can be more responsive to what patients want and see them as customers, not as charity cases, no matter how poor they may be.

For decades, as Farmer and Kim, relying on donations and sheer will, provided world-class healthcare to the poorest patients, nearly all the profit to be reaped in healthcare was made in North America, Europe, and Japan. Eye-popping hospital bills and high-price branded pharmaceuticals are still a major political issue in the United States, the kind of issue that wins and loses elections. In recent decades, the same companies making fortunes in developed markets looked at the poorer countries of the world and didn't see significant business opportunities. There are enormous populations in places like China, India, Brazil, and Nigeria, but the healthcare markets in many developing countries haven't been geared to truly significant business opportunities for the world's biggest healthcare companies. So, companies often engaged in those markets from the perspective of philanthropy, limiting how much they could do.

That has at last begun to change. Where major healthcare companies once looked at poor countries as an opportunity to do some good without profit—bringing their medicines and innovations there as a kind of corporate citizenship—they are beginning to see that business models might exist that could warrant substantial investment as well. One example is a billion-dollar fund recently created by private equity firm the Abraaj Group to purchase hospital networks in places like Kenya, Ethiopia, Pakistan, and India. (As of this writing, the fund is reportedly slated to be transferred to the private equity firm TPG as part of its multibillion-dollar impact investment fund, Rise. The transfer was part of the fallout of a massive financial malfeasance scandal that spelled the end of Abraaj but is unrelated to the investment approach of the healthcare fund.)[11]

Another example is Philips, the Dutch health technology giant, which is aggressively pushing to expand its customer base in Africa from 5 percent of all African patients to approximately 25 percent by 2025[12] by building its own primary healthcare clinics, dubbed Community Life Centers.[13]

The immediate business opportunity in these countries is the large and growing middle class. Health insurance is woefully insufficient and government hospitals are often overcrowded, ineffective, or even dangerously unhygienic, and patients often need to pay out of pocket. In Kenya, 67 percent of health expenditures are paid by the patient, and in India it's 60 percent.[14] While elite patients may fly out of the country or visit high-end private hospitals in major cities, middle-class patients need, and can just about afford, effective but not gold-plated healthcare services.

Most people in the global development and global health community have spent their time focusing on the people who have no access to a formal health system—the more than one billion people who don't even have access to primary healthcare, and more than half of all people who don't have full coverage of what the WHO considers essential health services.[15] It's at that community level where 70 percent of preventable deaths happen, so it makes good sense to focus there.

These aid professionals work on things like helping expectant mothers deliver their babies in local clinics, and ensuring those clinics have basic items like rubber gloves and antiseptics. Many global health professionals I've met seem to regard the shiny private hospitals and clinics cropping up in capital cities of African countries as a symptom of the problem of income inequality: Why, they wonder, should we applaud hospitals for the elites and middle class when most people barely have access to a functioning health clinic?

This is part of the old view of aid. That way of thinking regards poor countries as so different from rich ones like the United States that comparisons are irrelevant. It doesn't make sense, in that worldview, to compare our circumstances in New York City with someone else's in Kampala. A philanthropist's own child might attend a $50,000-a-year private school in New York City, but why raise that in a conversation about funding a school for poor kids in rural Uganda? It's such a different world that it's irrelevant, right? At the same time, why not scoff at wealthy or middle-class Africans living among their poor compatriots where the disparities are so glaring and visible?

If we can get past these psychological barriers that keep "us" separate from "them," we can learn a lot. In the case of healthcare, the lesson is that it's all one system and every human being deserves access to it. If you design it right, you can leverage the market created by rich and middle-class people in order to expand services to the poor.

It can sound counterintuitive, and the current dichotomy of public hospitals versus private ones—patients who can afford care versus those who can't—makes it hard to see healthcare as one system. But if you want to serve the poorest people in remote villages with basic but high-quality "primary" healthcare, you also need to have good hospitals in the cities providing things like diabetes treatment and cancer care.

It's the high end of the market that can attract investment and build the facilities and trained workforce needed for an effective healthcare system. Since patients are already paying out of pocket in these places, it's often the private market that is most effective at driving down costs to win over those consumers.

Those same private operators are experienced at serving consumers no matter who is footing the bill and can be paid by governments and aid agencies to deliver better healthcare services to the poorest people, from primary healthcare at the community level to high-end hospital services. Instead of seeing primary clinics as one-stop shops for all healthcare needs, healthcare workers there can refer patients to hospitals in the cities when more comprehensive care is required. Since hospitals are where the money is made and they need patients, hospitals can become a means of financing better quality primary healthcare.

Now we can see the outlines of a market coming together: a system for serving the poorest healthcare customers near where they live and referring those who need the care to the costlier services. Money is, of course, required, and most of these patients don't have it, but that's where a combination of government funds, private insurance, and wealthier patients come in. Pretty soon there's enough of a market for major investors to see a reason to buy and build hospitals, to equip them with the latest technology, to send in doctors where they're needed and train more locally. None of that happens if well-intentioned aid agencies focus only on providing the most basic services to the poorest people without regard to the broader dynamic. What's needed is a market.

I don't mean this to be a paean to unfettered capitalism, and I'm well aware that many countries are a long, long way from having a truly functioning healthcare system. Markets like healthcare and education must be highly regulated and subsidized. But to view poor patients as entirely the domain of public or philanthropic services, top down and donor-driven, is to relegate them to their current circumstances. As I have heard Githinji Gitahi, the Kenyan business leader who is now chief executive of the leading NGO Amref Health Africa, put it: "We're not doing UHC because we're rich, we're doing UHC because we're poor."

Plus, the healthcare market isn't exactly standing still. By one estimate there will be twenty billion to thirty billion healthcare devices connected to the internet by 2020.[16] These include wearable devices and gadgets that plug into a smartphone. Already such devices can read blood pressure, perform cardiac tests, measure blood glucose levels, and perform eye examinations. They're getting cheaper and more ubiquitous and will soon be purchased directly by middle-class consumers in poor countries at tremendous scale. Combine these devices with machine learning and data analytics, and the potential for a massive disruption in the way healthcare is provided and paid for is not just possible but likely.

I met with Liberian health minister Dr. Walter Gwenigale just before Ebola struck in 2014. He told me that half of the healthcare provided in his country was controlled by international nonprofits and that he had no way of knowing what they were doing.[17] He wasn't upset; he was thankful that they were helping people in desperate need in a country torn apart by a decade of civil war. But he knew the situation wasn't on a path to improvement. His ministry, and the NGOs doing this important work, were treading water. They were doing triage and not much more.

A well-designed system, by contrast, has embedded within it a vision of growth and an idea for what is possible if everything comes together. That can't happen in places like Liberia without massive foreign philanthropic support, no doubt. But when those donations are tied to a market mechanism, especially at a time of unprecedented technological change, a virtuous cycle can begin.

EDUCATION AS A SYSTEM

A couple of years ago, I visited a part of southwestern Ethiopia far off the beaten track—Boreda Woreda. I was serving as an independent board member for a startup nonprofit called Nuru International, with operations in that area. Nuru is the kind of new organization born in this era of transformation: it's led by former members of the US Special Forces and funded by Silicon Valley billionaires. A dirt track led us to an area where farmers worked dry land to grow corn. I met a couple who had joined Nuru's farmer cooperative, which provided loans, expertise, and access to larger markets to several hundred local small-scale farmers. They invited me into their thatched-roof home, thick with smoke from their cooking fire, and served me the local version of coffee, brewed from the green leaves of the coffee plant, which of course are far cheaper than the beans we're used to buying, including from Ethiopia.

While they showed off their four children and told me their story, I was served two snacks: a kind of hard bread made from corn and the homemade equivalent of Corn Nuts. Corn, corn, corn—I was starting to get the picture! Through a translator, the father explained that last year his corn crop wasn't good and he couldn't afford to send his children to school. In many parts of the world, even public schools have fees or require uniforms to be purchased. This year, with some advice from Nuru plus some seeds and fertilizer he got from them on loan, he was growing not just corn but also beans. Having multiple crops with different harvest times helped to stabilize the family's income, and the kids were back in school. It's important to remember that while a lot of people can feel good about contributing to that result, in the end the key people in the equation are the farming couple who broke their backs planting the seeds and working the land, not the philanthropists who lent a helping hand from across the world.

That same principle—that development challenges need to be owned at the local level—applies beyond the individual family. In the case of something as complex as education, the solutions have to come from communities themselves. That's the idea driving one of the most influential social enterprises in the world—Teach for All, the global initiative born out of Teach for America. As Wendy Kopp, the Teach for America founder and education reform leader, has told me, transforming the educational system is a long game. There's no app for that. And whatever the answers may be, they have to come from local communities themselves.

That's why Teach for All focuses on building up local leaders with real experience in education. It tries to do what Teach for America did in the US across the globe, including in some of the lowest-resource settings in the world: it encourages the very best and brightest recent college graduates to put off other career opportunities in order to spend two years teaching. Some remain teachers. But many go on to be leaders in their own right, serving in government, business, and civil society. After learning so much about the challenges of education, they come to those roles with a newfound commitment to improving education in the communities where they live.

The sixty-five thousand teachers and alumni of the Teach for All program in forty-eight countries represent enormous leverage to change a complex system like education, especially in communities with limited resources.[18] Teach for All has a name for that leverage—"collective leadership"—and it sees a future in which thousands of local leaders become champions in their own communities for prioritizing education and improving the system over time.

For those with the Silicon Valley mind-set, this can be entirely unappealing. A multidecade slog toward training and empowering local leaders, so they in turn can make changes in their own communities, is slow and tough to measure. It has none of the immediately disruptive characteristics of the technology startup ethos. But it may just be that the most intractable human problems, including extreme poverty, operate more like broken systems than like broken markets. Perhaps Uber can go after taxis aggressively and win in that lightly regulated marketplace, but can Bridge International Academies—a network of independent for-profit schools operating in Liberia, Nigeria, Uganda, Kenya, and India—really hope to win in the highly regulated education marketplace by taking the same aggressive approach? Not if education operates more like a complex, emotionally fraught, politicized system that can reject solutions that might make sense from a narrow consumer standpoint.

I should note that Teach for All has its critics beyond those who think its solutions are too long-term. Much of the controversy stems from different worldviews—an approach protecting and improving public education versus a reform mind-set that doesn't hold sacred the existing public education structures.[19] Teach for All has a reform mind-set and sees training a legion of highly educated young people to be teachers well-versed in the challenges of poor rural and urban schools as a way of building local leadership that will ultimately fix the educational system. Critics want to improve schools, but they balk at the idea of fundamental reform, especially reform ideas coming from the billionaire philanthropists and corporations who back Teach for All.

The systems-thinking mind-set exemplified by Teach for All is key to the future of the global aid industry. It's a maturation from wide-eyed idealism to an embrace of real-world complexities. In my mind, all development practitioners either graduate to becoming systems thinkers or become too jaded by failed aid projects to go on.

▪ ▪ ▪ ▪ ▪

I remember sitting in the audience at a meeting of the Clinton Global Initiative in New York just after the Haiti earthquake in 2010. On stage, Google's then-CEO, Eric Schmidt, made a compelling case about what should be done for Haiti's students. Don't rebuild the same, textbook-based model of education, he insisted. The earthquake created a blank-slate opportunity (to borrow one of aid critic Bill Easterly's favorite terms) to start over. Get every school "wired with a simple enough connection that they can have a proper computer, and let the kids run it." The weak results of the One Laptop Per Child initiative were not yet so clear.

The idea intrigued me. There was so much discussion about education operating with an old-fashioned model, even in rich countries like our own. No Child Left Behind's standardized testing and the so-called Common Core curriculum, and the emergence of charter schools all over the United States, were part of a broader school reform movement that was captivating our country. So what about revolutionizing education in the poorest places in the world? Could we "hack" global education and, in the process, educate millions of kids?

On the same visit to Ethiopia I referenced earlier, I spoke with Jimmy Leak, who led Nuru International's education work and who has a PhD in education. I told him about Eric Schmidt's proposal and asked if he had considered using tablets to underpin the educational model he was building in rural Ethiopia. He'd looked at it, he said, but the math didn't work: the costs of maintenance, power, internet connectivity, and train-ing—not to mention the tablets themselves—meant that it just wasn't re-alistic to digitize the educational approach in such a low-resource setting.

Since then, I've met many other education experts working to im-prove literacy and learning in the poorest places on earth. The answers I get are similar: there's enormous potential, but it's not as simple as just dropping some laptops or tablets into classrooms. You need to change the entire model—the entire education system—and that's truly hard.

Schmidt wasn't necessarily wrong that tablets could be an important part of a new education system in Haiti. But technology, while neces-sary, isn't the big innovation: it's new business models. The right model can leverage attractive technologies like tablets to improve learning out-comes, but the tablets alone are almost certain to fail.

Bridge International Academies, the most ambitious social enterprise working in global education, is doing just that. It gives tablet computers to teachers, who use them to present their curricula to students in class, but, while the technology is an essential part of the initiative, what sets Bridge apart is its business model. This is not a small nonprofit hoping to improve educational outcomes in a few schools with new technology. Like Kiva before, it's a social enterprise on a mission to become a billion-dollar organization and to revolutionize an entire sector in the process.

Bridge's model is straightforward. It goes to some of the poorest settings in the world where public education exists but is weak and inconsistent. Poorly paid teachers don't always show up; school facilities are often dilapidated; parents need to pay for uniforms and books even if the tuition is free. In such places, Bridge offers a sales pitch to parents: pay around six dollars a month in tuition and your kids will get a better education.[20] Parents have responded to such a degree that Bridge today operates over five hundred schools in five countries: Kenya, Uganda, Nigeria, India, and Liberia.[21] There are more than 100,000 Bridge students, and the social enterprise plans to have ten million by 2025 across twelve countries. By comparison, the largest public school system in the world is New York City's, with 1.1 million students.[22]

The model will fail without scale. Bridge can achieve sustainability only by operating hundreds, or more likely thousands, of schools, so that it can offer a consistent product at a rock-bottom price. With that many schools, the small fees add up, providing enough revenue so that Bridge can invest in the world's best teachers to develop world-class curricula that can be piped into all those schools through tablets. With hundreds of thousands or even millions of students, it's possible to gather data that shows what really works and what doesn't—to measure, learn, and iterate.

A model like this, not surprisingly, has been attractive to Silicon Valley and its most successful denizens. Bridge has raised over $100 million in investments from the likes of Bill Gates, Mark Zuckerberg, and the Omidyar Network, eBay founder Pierre Omidyar's foundation.

Even so, it's far from certain that Bridge will reach its ambitious targets. Bridge operates in the highly regulated education industry, with strong political forces that oppose its model. Some teachers in these countries, like some in the United States when it comes to charter schools, chafe at the idea that their schools are somehow broken or failing and in need of a wealthy savior. They argue that public schools deserve attention, rather than private schools that will never be able to serve more than a small percentage of the students in need. They worry that Bridge is preying on poor families who are spending precious resources they can't afford on a for-profit institution with billionaire backers.

Education leaders outside these countries, including international NGO and union leaders in the US and Europe, see Bridge as accepting low standards of education for poor kids. All these kids get is a minimally trained adult at the front of the room reading from a tablet? Would we accept that for our own kids?

In Liberia, where Bridge faced controversy for operating public schools under the government's PSL plan mentioned earlier, work continues. Even after elections led to a change in government and a new education minister, the PSL program was maintained under a new name: Liberia Education Advancement Program (LEAP). The government wants every public school in Liberia to have great teachers who show up every day but acknowledges that's not today's reality. In fact, it was the country's own president, Ellen Johnson Sirleaf, who declared the education system "a mess" after *all* twenty-five thousand high school students failed the entrance exam for the University of Liberia in 2013.[23]

Bridge and its Silicon Valley backers are running the numbers, using cost-benefit analysis to prove that their kind of model actually makes people better off than they would have been otherwise. Their numbers may be right, but in a complex system like education, disruptive business models can generate so much controversy that they even backfire.

Bridge is trying to get past this debate. In Edo, a Nigerian state where 60 percent of the population lives in poverty, Bridge is playing an enabling rather than leadership role. It has partnered with the government not to run schools but rather to use its technology to train teachers and enable real-time monitoring of lessons for government teachers in public schools.[24]

▪ ▪ ▪ ▪ ▪

Like many other US cities, Washington, DC, suffers tremendous economic inequality along racial lines, and it offers an interesting window on complex systems—even though it's the rich capital of a rich country. There's a discussion board website in Washington called DC Urban Moms and Dads popular with parents trying to navigate education, childcare, and activities for their kids, which, to me, showcases how multifaceted these issues can be.

One common topic of discussion is trying to determine which school is the best for your child. Lots of factors are considered in the often-heated debates on this site, but one that comes up time and again is the percentage of kids at the school who receive free or reduced-price meals based on the economic situations of their families. This data point is used as a proxy for determining the percentage of kids at the school living in poverty. That too serves as a benchmark for how many of your children's classmates might arrive at school with fewer advantages and more challenges and needs.

Sparks fly as commenters on the site—who seem more heavily represented by whiter and more affluent residents of the city—express their concern over what to do with their own children, who don't need the free lunch. Should they put them in the school that is perhaps closer to their own home but has more kids living in poverty? Does that high-poverty statistic necessarily mean the school won't prepare their own child as well as would another school in a more affluent part of the city? If they send their child to another school because of that, won't the average poverty rate at their neighborhood school just go up, up, and up, as they and parents like them all do the same thing?

A single decision, like which school to choose, feels like it could have big implications on your child's life. But also, perhaps, on the lives of other children.

Studies have been done to understand the relationship between poverty and learning outcomes, and the takeaway is that schools where most students live in poverty face challenges that consistently lead to poor academic performance overall.[25] Indeed, as income inequality has grown in the US over the past five decades, the achievement gap between rich and poor students has grown by 30 to 40 percent.[26] This suggests that children in poorer school districts typically end up with weaker academic performance.

A 2016 analysis of federal data by the *Atlantic* found that in nearly every major American city, most African American and Latino students attended a school where most kids were poor—in other words, American poverty is increasingly concentrated and segregated. But what to do about it?[27]

What's at play here is a complex dynamic: parents desperate to do the right thing for their children; community members eager to at least not harm their neighbors and their kids; teachers and their unions, who want to provide quality education to every kid and see demanding respect for their own profession as key to that; and a government with fiscal constraints and voters demanding better schools for their children and lower taxes all at the same time. And all that is itself a massive oversimplification.

Knowledge about a particular intervention—school hours, class size, teacher preparation, or free lunches for that matter—might appear useful on its own but is unlikely to actually matter in the real world, given such a politicized, emotional, dynamic situation, which is perhaps why technocratic approaches to education reform in the United States have so far made limited progress.

What we have here is a complex system that requires systems thinking to improve it. It's a system made up not of molecules, but of human beings, so an understanding of human behavior is essential. These human beings might well want a say in that approach too, so including them in any imagined intervention would likely be quite important. That may be easier to see in the case of a city like Washington, DC, but too often economists and aid donors have caricatured poorer societies, assuming complex problems like education were really just simple problems of a lack of resources. They're not. That's why three threads—systems thinking, behavioral science, and human-centered design—are today at the forefront of a new approach to global development challenges like education.

As a burgeoning "ed tech" market offers virtual learning and gamification, and social entrepreneurs like Bridge offer disruptive models to the education landscape, taking a new approach will be even more important. If we think of education as a complex system and not a market, there's an opportunity to transform learning outcomes faster than we can today predict.

GOVERNANCE REALITIES

Should aid be directed to countries that are less than democratic, such as the "donor darlings," Ethiopia and Rwanda, to build roads or increase agricultural yields? Investments in these countries could eventually have a huge impact on millions of people living in extreme poverty, but the money might also support governments that become authoritarian. What about countries like Myanmar and the Philippines, where aid funds are desperately needed, but donors have huge doubts about the political leadership? A systems-thinking approach to global development must consider the trade-offs inherent in working with governments.

The current president of the Philippines, Rodrigo Duterte, is proudly brutal. He has admitted to personally committing murder while ruling over Davao City as its heavy-handed mayor earlier in his political career, and since becoming the country's president has directed a "war on drugs" that has left several thousand people dead in the streets.[28] He fits the pattern of candidates (some ultimately elected, some not) who have raised popular passions and generated millions of rabid supporters in that country over decades. Some of these leaders have been widely known for their flagrant corruption but were supported nonetheless by those who see politics more like a clan war than a way to preserve individual rights and democratic principles.

For the Philippines, massive "people power" marches, armed rebellions, corruption cases against presidents and presidential candidates, and massacres by political groups against their rivals using private militias are tragically all part of the regular rough-and-tumble of politics. Add to that the current president's antidrug campaign, which has led to thousands of assassinations, and an ISIS-inspired five-month takeover of the major city of Marawi in Mindanao in 2017 that left over a thousand people dead, and it's hard to see how the country could come together around a solution to the extreme poverty that claims so many more lives than conflict.[29]

In fact, the same strange dichotomy obtains in much of the world: seemingly sound interventions to save people from disease and malnutrition appear totally out of tune with a political context of war, kleptocracy, forced migration, and human rights abuses. How can we talk of ending extreme poverty when rival factions in places like South Sudan or Northern Nigeria are carving up the land and the people? Where does the new aid industry thinking fit into the real world?

In a time of numerous funding sources and innovative approaches, doing nothing doesn't have to be the default option. The idea of paying for performance is beginning to catch on as one way to really target aid dollars to a specific result without necessarily propping up a corrupt government or unwittingly taking sides in an ethnic conflict. An example is the concept of development impact bonds that we've already discussed.

These arrangements are not easy to pull off—a recent development impact bond in Rajasthan, India, aimed at reducing the number of women who die in childbirth took two years just to organize—but they will get easier as they become more common. And the advantage is that governmental foreign aid agencies won't need to pick between two awful choices in many places: between funding corrupt and undemocratic governments or sitting on their hands and watching people there suffer.[30] Instead, what's called for and what's beginning to happen, albeit too slowly, are approaches that reward results—by working with good governments where possible and working around them where not.

The Millennium Challenge Corporation (MCC), a relatively new foreign aid institution, is designed to address this issue head-on. It's an example of a government aid agency using market principles to achieve results, in this case on economic growth and poverty reduction. Founded in 2004, this US government agency dispenses aid—primarily for infrastructure projects—to countries that score well on basic measures like fighting corruption and investing in the health and education of their people. They are not conducting a purity test, so it's likely that some of their well-intentioned efforts are tangentially supporting imperfect leaders and regimes, but they are taking a thoughtful, data-driven approach to prioritizing good government and human freedom.

Not only does the MCC carefully select its countries, it delivers aid via local institutions that it carefully monitors. This helps build local capabilities in procurement and implementation and avoids the risks associated with writing a check directly to a foreign government. MCC appeals especially to conservatives who worry that typical development institutions don't incentivize good behavior by governments and might actually reward bad behavior.

MCC began in the George W. Bush administration as a counterpoint to USAID: where USAID was seen as a traditional, project-oriented aid agency, MCC would be a modern, systems-oriented aid agency. President Bush declared the agency would eventually have $5 billion to spend each year, which would make it a major global force.

Expectations were high, but MCC was slow getting started. It wanted countries to drive the process, and waited for governments to propose what they would spend the money on. Almost invariably, the answer came back "roads." Not that there's anything wrong with the US government building free roads, bridges, and other infrastructure around the world, but you could argue this isn't the most efficient use of limited American aid. Some of these countries might have been able to get World Bank loans to build this infrastructure themselves. But free roads are a tangible win for political leaders—palpable results they can show their voters.

Just a year after its founding, MCC came under scrutiny from the *Economist* magazine.

> The MCC is unloved by both left and right. A Republican-led House of Representatives sub-committee has just recommended nearly halving its budget, to $1.75 billion next year. American liberals suspect it is part of Mr. Bush's conspiracy to conservatise the world. And Europeans mock the MCC as slower, meaner and more ideological than their own aid programmes. Some of this criticism is fair, but much is not.[31]

One key issue for MCC was that it had an almost slavish devotion to its model, so much so that others were able to game the system. For example, since MCC wanted to have the most efficient open market for project implementation, it allowed anyone to bid on those roads projects. Chinese state-owned companies got in the game and outbid others for some MCC funded infrastructure projects. Eventually, MCC had to close that loophole, putting a ban on funding state-owned enterprises no matter how inexpensively they would do the work.

Because the model allowed MCC to work only with countries that met a strict set of data-driven indicators—like how much they were investing in their people or their score on various good governance, economic freedom, and anticorruption measures—the pool of countries MCC could work with was limited. So far, just twenty-nine countries have received MCC funding since 2004.[32] To address that limited-pool problem, MCC began giving another bite at the apple to countries that had already received funding once—so called "second compacts"—so that countries that had just received and spent large amounts of MCC grant money could get another tranche. There's nothing inherently wrong with this, either, but MCC's potential scope has been limited by these constraints.

That selectivity was supposed to drive an "MCC effect"—in other words, countries would be desperate to gain eligibility in order to access MCC money, so they would increase their spending on health and education, reduce corruption, or pursue other initiatives to make themselves eligible. But spending did not reach the $5 billion annual expenditure that President Bush had called for. It ended up at under $1 billion per year. As MCC's budget has shrunken, there has been less incentive for countries to practice good behavior.

All those caveats and mistakes aside, MCC is widely seen as an important institution with a thoughtful systems-oriented approach to foreign aid. It is evidence-driven in which countries it selects (rather than operating on the whims of political leaders, like the secretary of state), it pushes countries to prove they are ready to handle a large grant, it funds priorities of the country themselves, it helps to build up the capacity of the government to handle these large grants, it ensures civil society is included in the process, and it opens the bidding process for project implementation to anyone, without regard to citizenship, creating opportunities for companies from the countries where the grants are given.

And, recently, MCC has begun ensuring it doesn't just give away free roads but ties those grants to deep reforms within the government. While MCC works only in a relatively small number of countries, many are of important strategic interest to the US and the world—such as relatively vulnerable countries teetering on the edge of stability like Liberia, Mali, Malawi, and Moldova.[33]

MCC has so far stuck to its good-governance principles. When some countries receiving MCC funds lapsed—for example, by failing to ensure free and open elections—the organization stopped the aid.[34] This has happened in Honduras, Armenia, and Tanzania. And, due to new legislation passed in 2018, MCC can now work at the regional level, not just within a specific country. In cases where the system at play touches multiple countries in a region—for example, transportation and trade networks in Central America—MCC can now take a broader approach.

MCC is an important model for how systems-thinking can be used even at the level of an official foreign aid agency. Nonetheless, it's small and has limited influence. Its approach has not yet been widely adopted.

But the World Bank, which loaned $65 billion in 2016, compared to MCC's $800 million in grants that year, has recently announced a Human Capital Index that has echoes of the MCC model.[35] Though the index is presented as a technocratic tool, it's actually deeply political. It's both a carrot and a stick: countries that score well because they are investing in the health and education of their people might get financial benefits, like cheaper loans; those who are governing poorly could pay more.

Fostering good governance will be needed especially as we get closer to the deadline of the Sustainable Development Goals in 2030. That's because the places likely to lag behind, including on critical objectives like ending extreme poverty, are those with little or no functioning government at all.

9. ENDING EXTREME POVERTY

Getting to Absolute Zero by 2030

AROUND THE TIME I WAS BORN, a drought struck Andhra Pradesh, a state in South India. My father's eldest sister, Radha, and her husband, Gopal, were at the time living in Hyderabad, then the capital of that state, where he was managing a local branch of the State Bank of Travancore. One day a man arrived in their neighborhood riding a bicycle, with a small boy, perhaps seven years old, sitting on the handlebars. I came to know him as Chandra.

Chandra was not an orphan. The man riding the bicycle, I'm told by my relatives, was his uncle. Chandra's parents didn't have enough money to feed all their children. They made the unimaginable decision to send Chandra away to a family for whom he could work in exchange for food and a roof over his head. Perhaps because my aunt and uncle were childless, and because my uncle's role at the bank made him someone known around town, Chandra was brought to them.

I grew up around Chandra. To me he was like an older cousin, just a part of the family. It's only now, as a father of two young kids reflecting back on those days, that the insanity of the circumstances comes through to me: the idea that people could be so poor as to give up their seven-year-old boy is a torture too difficult to contemplate.

Humans face many challenges, plenty of which you can find in your own neighborhood or community. But extreme poverty is something different. It challenges the fundamental idea of humanity. Are all people really equal? Or, as the Bill & Melinda Gates Foundation says in its motto, do "all lives have equal value"? Can we credibly say that we believe in that idea when we tolerate a world in which one in ten families are forced to seriously consider offering up their own children to labor or prostitution or early marriage?

In 2015, the General Assembly of the United Nations endorsed seventeen Sustainable Development Goals for the year 2030, the first of which is stated simply: no poverty. Most of the other goals are closely related to the issue of poverty, especially the next two: zero hunger, and good health and well-being.

The earth is populated by about 7.6 billion people, and about 10 percent of us—746 million is the current estimate—are categorized by the World Bank as living in "extreme poverty." Although one tenth is a small fraction, it equates to the entire population of Europe (about 750 million people)[1] and approaches the combined population of the United States, Canada, Mexico, and South America (a total of about 900 million).[2] It's a staggering number of people. Imagine nearly the entire population of two massive continents as ultrapoor.

How is "extreme poverty" defined? The current metric is an individual consuming less than about two dollars a day worth of food, clothing, shelter, and other necessities.[3] (Technically it's $1.90 per day, calculated based on the purchasing power of a US dollar in 2011.) That two-dollars-a-day definition is somewhat arbitrary in that it comes from what fifteen mostly sub-Saharan African countries happen to have set as their absolute poverty line. Even still, we have to draw a line somewhere, and it's the best metric we have for separating absolute destitution from everyone else living in poverty. As a result, it's become a standard definition across the aid industry.

What is particularly alarming about extreme poverty is that half of the world's ultrapoor are children. For them, just surviving is a struggle. And if they do survive, it's likely their brain development will have been slowed by undernutrition, they will not have achieved full physical growth, and they'll have had little access to quality education. In India, for example, according to UNICEF's data from 2017, 38 percent of all kids do not grow to their full height or weight or mental capacity, all for lack of basic nutrition and clean water.[4]

If a child cheats death and survives into adulthood under these conditions, it's almost impossible for him or her to break this cycle of poverty. This is hard to fathom for people who have not experienced it themselves.

I've met many accomplished people who say, "I grew up poor," or, "I came up the hard way." They take great pride, as they should, that they started from nothing and through hard work and perseverance have achieved financial security and prestige.

My own country is full of stories of people who have realized what we often call the American Dream. Americans especially might think anybody is capable of rising above their circumstances and making a better life for themselves and their family. But that presupposes having access from birth to basic things, like clean water, or the micronutrients needed to avoid blindness, or treatments for the most minor ailments, like diarrhea. When you meet someone who escaped extreme poverty, it's a different thing: it's impressive they even survived.

The danger in pointing out the stark distinctions between poverty here and extreme poverty there is that it can lead to writing off whole portions of the earth as a lost cause. In many ways, we already do. We even have a name for such places: the Third World.

THE THIRD WORLD

It was a French anthropologist and demographer, Alfred Sauvy, who coined the phrase Third World in a 1952 article published in *L'Observateur*. It was the time of the Cold War, and Sauvy was actually trying to categorize those countries that were unaligned with either Soviet bloc countries or NATO countries. But Sauvy's term took on a life of its own and became a shorthand descriptor for the world's poorer, "undeveloped," and "left behind" places. For the past six decades, this neat binary view has informed our thinking.

Even in Sauvy's time, that binary view wasn't truly accurate, but today it's downright false. We need to take a fresh look at the map of the world to get a better sense of exactly where extreme poverty is a real problem.

There is no definable Third World, but rather a complex array of countries at many levels of development and income. The majority of people living in extreme poverty are in relatively large economies that will soon likely have the funds to support them. Chief among them are India, with 27 percent of the world's extremely poor, and Nigeria, with 11 percent. Just in those two countries that's nearly four in ten of the world's ultrapoor.

India and Nigeria are classified by the World Bank as lower-middle-income countries. (Insiders refer to lower-income countries as "licks," and middle-income ones as "micks.") One in five Kenyans live in extreme poverty, even in a fast-growing economy with gorgeous landscapes ripe for ecotourism and a dynamic technology sector. I've experienced high-end restaurants in the rich districts of the capital city of Nairobi but have also witnessed vast slum areas, too—the most famous one is called Kibera, the largest urban slum in Africa. Brazil is an upper-middle-income country and the world's eighth-largest economy—home to 150 billionaires—but also accounts for about 1 percent of the world's ultrapoor.[5]

Nearly every middle-income country is in the midst of political upheaval, as growing middle-class populations challenge entrenched corruption. Malaysia, Mexico, Chile, Colombia, Kenya, Argentina, Peru, Brazil, the Philippines, and South Africa are in similar situations. It's hard to name any middle-income country that has not had a major corruption scandal shake its political establishment in the past few years.[6]

Not all middle-income countries have citizens living in extreme poverty. For those that do, it's easy to say they ought to be able to end extreme poverty on their own given their level of wealth. But they still face many challenges. Money is just one aspect of the problem. Governments that are ineffective or outright corrupt stand in the way of building the kinds of social safety nets, health systems, and schools needed to give the poorest children a shot at upward mobility.

In South Africa, a large upper-middle-income economy that recently ousted its longtime president on corruption charges, the number of people living in extreme poverty has actually gone up by around 25 percent in the past few years.[7]

Other middle-income countries face enormous fiscal challenges to move spending toward poverty reduction. In India, where just 1.5 percent of GDP went to social safety net programs in 2016, the government announced in 2018 that it would institute free healthcare for all.[8] That sounds like a real advancement, but generating the needed tax revenue and training-up and certifying quality healthcare providers will be no small task.

Ending extreme poverty in relatively stable middle-income countries like these will still require an engaged aid industry to hold governments accountable, to partner with them to do the right things, and to support their efforts.

Then there are several low-income countries that are chronically or "structurally" poor and don't have the advantage of a large economy. These include Cambodia, Ethiopia, Haiti, Rwanda, Nepal, Tanzania, Chad, and Malawi. While these are relatively peaceful places, wiping out extreme poverty in countries where nearly everything is underdeveloped—the roads, school system, health clinics, government agencies—will not be a simple undertaking.

An added challenge is that so many of the ultrapoor in these countries are not near the $1.90 per day line but rather far below it.[9] The "poverty-intensity" in these places is much higher than in the middle-income countries, and thus much more needs to be done to bring people up to the poverty line.

These are countries that rely so heavily on foreign aid that they do not have the funding to simply create social safety nets that would bring their people out of poverty. Ethiopia, for example, is a large country of over 100 million people, but it relies on foreign aid for half its budget. In these places, the aid industry's effectiveness will be a critical factor in ending extreme poverty.

Finally, around one in four of the ultrapoor live in countries violently divided by religious extremism, ethnic and tribal affiliations, or geopolitical machinations—including Somalia, Yemen, Afghanistan, Central African Republic, Democratic Republic of Congo, Myanmar, and Burundi.

In these countries—and perhaps in unstable zones of some of the middle-income countries, like some parts of Northern Nigeria—ending extreme poverty will be a herculean effort. Democratic Republic of Congo, for example, has around 7 percent of the world's ultrapoor among its citizens but is ill-equipped to take on this challenge alone.[10]

It's in these countries more than anywhere else that the fight to end extreme poverty by 2030 is likely to stumble. The combination of corrupt, weak governments, conflict and insecurity, and insufficient funding make it hard to see a path toward a hopeful future that doesn't entail getting on a creaky fishing boat to cross the sea to Europe.

As an example, about half the children who die from malaria—an easily curable disease—are in Nigeria and Democratic Republic of Congo, two big countries whose people are suffering from conflict and instability. Solid data is hard to come by, but my estimates from WHO and UNICEF data—confirmed by a technical expert with the Global Fund to Fight AIDS, Tuberculosis, and Malaria—suggest that approximately 45 percent of all children in the world under five years old who die of malaria come from just these two countries.[11]

We have made tremendous progress in reducing poverty worldwide. When I was the age my daughter is now—five years old, which is a standard milestone used to determine child survival statistics—more than four out of every ten human beings on the planet lived in extreme poverty. Today, only one in ten do.[12] That's an improvement at least in part accomplished through the steady, persistent work of the aid industry.

For the first time in modern human civilization since the dawn of the agricultural revolution, we may soon reach a tipping point in which the world remains fundamentally unequal—with billionaires and people just making ends meet living side by side—but where almost no one is born without their basic human needs being met.

The last 10 percent of humanity suffering in extreme poverty will be the most challenging to address. According to an analysis by the Brookings Institution, we could push every poor person across the poverty line by transferring $66 billion per year into their pockets.[13] That's less than a tenth of one percent of the global economy, so in one sense it should be eminently achievable. Still, who would write such a check, year after year, and how would we deliver it? And what about the health systems, schools, water and sanitation infrastructure, and so much more that would be essential to ending poverty? There's no quick fix for extreme poverty.

THE DEBATE ABOUT HOW

In the aid industry there is a raging debate about the *how* of ending poverty. The most prominent one is between the pro-aid camp, most associated with Jeffrey Sachs, who argues that we know what works and we just need a relatively small amount of money in a world awash in riches to fund the end of poverty. The anti-aid camp is most associated with Bill Easterly, who says that aid itself is the problem because it undermines markets and representative government. What's needed instead is a more bottom-up approach—local people finding their own solutions, not big aid coming in from overseas.

Easterly and Sachs are hardly the only economists who seek to analyze and explain the causes of poverty and what to do about it. In fact, there is a long tradition of celebrated economists weighing in on these issues (some are so celebrated they have become celebrities in their own right). The books that sell well and influence public debate and major institutions like the World Bank and USAID are perhaps not surprisingly written primarily by men from the United States and the United Kingdom.

There is a big gap: few women and fewer thinkers from the Global South have broken through into the public debate that dominates the major development-funding institutions. This likely reflects existing power brokers in global development—such as major US and UK university economics departments—and the biases that plague even mission-driven institutions. As Alice Evans, a lecturer at King's College in the UK, has pointed out, there are, in fact, many important books and big-thinking economists from the Global South, including many women.[14] Still, with notable exceptions, such as the widely respected Ngozi Okonjo-Iweala, Sri Mulyani Indrawati, Yuen Yuen Ang, Dina Pomeranz, and Nancy Birdsall (this is by no means an exhaustive list), in my experience the celebrity economists take up most of the oxygen.

Stefan Dercon, the former chief economist of DFID and now an Oxford professor, has a useful shorthand for understanding the main points of celebrity development economists. Borrowing from Dercon[15] and adding my own interpretation, they include the following:

ESTHER DUFLO and ABHIJIT BANERJEE (authors of *Poor Economics*): We assume we know what works at our peril; instead, we need to rigorously experiment in order to find the policies that work, like deworming pills and insecticide-treated bed nets, and then scale those up carefully.

AMARTYA SEN (Nobel Prize–winning economist and author of *Development as Freedom*): Poverty is really driven by inequalities that persist because they benefit some at the expense of others, and if we understand that perhaps we can make progress against it. His early work includes analysis that the three million people who died in the Bengal famine of 1943—which he witnessed as a nine-year-old boy—did not perish because food production was down (there was enough food) but rather because war in the area led to hoarding, panic buying, and price gouging.[16] Those with money, like the urban dwellers and the British military, could afford to survive under those circumstances, but the rural poor starved to death as food prices rose.

DAMBISA MOYA (author of *Dead Aid*): Aid breeds corruption and dependence and should be stopped in favor of a more market-driven approach. Business, not aid, will save Africa.

ANGUS DEATON (Nobel Prize-winning economist and author of *The Great Escape*): It's clear that aid doesn't generate economic growth or reduce poverty. And perhaps it undermines representative government and thus prolongs the agony—delaying the date when poorly governed people rise up. So best to stop the aid.

JOE STIGLITZ (Nobel Prize-winning economist and author of *Making Globalization Work*): Focus on reforming international institutions like the World Bank and IMF, which themselves perpetuate an unequal system because they are unfairly controlled by the richest countries and force Wall Street finance priorities (like budget cuts and pro-business policies) over a pro-poor agenda.

PAUL COLLIER (author of *The Bottom Billion*): Countries in conflict face an almost insurmountable task in trying to defeat poverty.[17] Failing and fragile states really are the most important places for the world to focus, as they're where the "bottom billion" will remain trapped in poverty. The focus must be on making those countries stable and well governed. That means pushing for an international rules-based system that creates transparency around corruption and natural resource exploitation, promoting an open press, and stopping corrupt leaders from amassing their wealth in offshore accounts.

DARON ACEMOGLU and JAMES A. ROBINSON (authors of *Why Nations Fail*): Focus on "extractive institutions" as the key driver of poverty.[18] Examples are South African apartheid and Middle Eastern countries, where only a small elite dominates the economy, and kleptocratic regimes, especially in places like Angola, where the recently deposed leader and his family have stolen massive oil and natural resource wealth.[19] Their prescription is for rich countries to use not just aid but also diplomatic pressure and sanctions to push for reforms in those extractive institutions.

In the end, understanding the big ideas of global thinkers and celebrity economists, especially regarding the poverty problem, is a helpful exercise. So long as it doesn't slow us down from actually taking action but rather propels us to improve the actions we take. Too often, the dialogue devolves into never-ending arguments about the overall economic impact of aid, with aid opponents saying there's little evidence of economic growth or poverty reduction caused by foreign aid and with aid proponents saying the weak results are out of context and the averages mask real success stories.

DATA, ACCOUNTABILITY, RESULTS

With this philosophical background, what's actually required to achieve the goal of zero absolute poverty?

First, we need to quickly and forcefully move to the era of open source aid, in which data about who is doing what and what's working and failing is public and in real time. We know that real-time data can further development work in many positive ways.

For example, thanks to the use of real-time data, there has been a 93 percent reduction in malaria cases in Zambia over just the 2015 and 2016 rainy seasons.[20] Cell phones were used to track reported cases in real time. When a case was called in, antimalarial drugs were then immediately administered to everyone living within a hundred-meter radius of that case. (Although there's a lot of variation, mosquitos swarm at a much higher rate within a hundred-meter radius).[21] Even those who didn't show symptoms were given the drugs because malaria can be transmitted by asymptomatic people. By mapping the real-time data over rainfall patterns and topographical information, the health workers could see where to target their efforts. The result has been a major success that's being replicated around the world.

As with the prevention and treatment of malaria and other infectious diseases, real-time data will become critical for all sorts of development work, from education to job creation to water and sanitation. Aid agencies will soon operate using dashboards where they can see the real-time results of their projects around the world, zeroing in on those that are not reaching the planned targets to find out why and to make changes.

Like the malaria example, efforts can be targeted and assumptions questioned when interventions aren't working as intended.

Real-time data is essential to a results-based aid industry. Broadreach, a South African social enterprise founded by two medical doctors, is building and deploying real-time data dashboards around the world so aid agencies can fundamentally change the way they work to be more results- and data-driven.[22] They've even built a kind of development war room in the South African presidential offices. It's a bit like the Situation Room, except that instead of flat-panel monitors showing troop movements and missile launches, there are graphs and tables showing disease outbreaks and health metrics.

Another real-world example of how real-time information is transforming global development is a San Francisco-based, venture-backed startup called Premise. This company has not only built an app, it's amassed an army of people around the world who can use the app to provide real-time information in exchange for a small payment. In Kenya, for example, Premise might task its local users to take photos of open-air food markets, capture prices, and provide commentary on how busy or quiet the scene feels. This kind of information is then used by the likes of the World Bank, Gates Foundation, USAID, and others to find out what's really happening on the ground around the world. Premise is just a startup, but it's already being used by aid agencies who want to see in real time how their projects are working and to better understand what local people are experiencing. It's a great example of the kind of immediate feedback—positive and negative—so critical to an open source aid culture.

Real-time data will ultimately unlock a systemic change that lets us evaluate development effectiveness at the microlevel. That in turn will allow market forces to encourage the most cost-effective results. For example, pay-for-performance financing instruments like development impact bonds are an exciting current innovation. But they're not like true bonds, in part because it's not easy to adjust their prices over time. That's due to the lack of data about how the projects they fund are performing. Real-time data will allow a secondary market to develop. That would mean a private funder could create a bond that pays out when a development project succeeds and then sell that bond before the project is completed. The pricing would be based on how the project is going. This opening up of a larger secondary market for development impact bonds (and other kinds of impact investments) will ultimately attract more money to global development and help to fill the financing gap required to achieve the Sustainable Development Goals.

No marketplace can function without data, and a lack of sufficient real-time data is a huge stumbling block for the aid industry today. As drones, sensors, and satellites get cheaper and more powerful, there will no longer be any practical excuses for not using real-time data to make decisions. That's why all of us need to make real-time data provision the industry standard. That's not going to happen organically: donors need to demand it and we all need to push for it.

A second, and related, step in the quest to end extreme poverty: we'll need to begin holding billionaires accountable. Those who aren't giving today need to be called out, and those who are giving need to be held to a higher standard, which includes far greater transparency around what they're doing and what results they're achieving. If billionaires—who are the likely source of a major part of the funding that will end extreme poverty and achieve the other Sustainable Development Goals—aren't pushed to join a market where results, not good intentions, matter, we could drag out the old era of charitable giving. We can still congratulate someone for signing the Giving Pledge, but let's not go overboard: journalists, think tanks, and the public should reserve real praise until we see what results are really being achieved.

If billionaire donors operate in secret—largely the norm today—they'll need to be called out for it and lose some of their social license to operate. Want to partner with credible NGOs, UN agencies, and others? In this new era, we'll need to insist that it takes more than just a big checkbook. They'll need to earn that credibility by being more transparent about what their philanthropy hopes to achieve and how it's operating, even if it's organized as a limited liability corporation and not a nonprofit foundation (as is increasingly common).

This accountability must also apply to traditional foundations, many of which have grown to spend too much on overhead and support too many disparate issue areas because of relationships and tradition. These foundations will need to compete in this new era, homing in on fewer areas of real comparative advantage and becoming much leaner and meaner—more like fast-paced businesses and less like sleepy academic institutions. They'll also need to invest in building up the organizations actually doing the work around the world, dedicating more funding to core grants and using their expertise to prepare NGOs to take on the coming wave of billionaire philanthropy. Traditional foundations will need to be rated and ranked by their results, called out for failures, and held to high standards by independent boards.

Finally, government aid agencies will need to move beyond their usual procurement processes to move us closer to a market based on results. They'll need to dramatically ramp up funding for pay-for-performance initiatives, tiered innovation grants, impact investments, and blended finance projects, and significantly reduce their spending on traditional grants and contracts. At the same time, they'll have to support their traditional implementation partners through core grants to build out data systems and evidence-gathering capabilities in order to not lose the value of all the funding that's come before.

Government aid agencies will need to realize their true mission is not to determine the problem, design the solution, and then pay someone to deliver it. Instead, they'll need to be more like financial engineers, incentivizing innovation and investment and providing the capital needed to scale-up and de-risk big ideas. They can do so by tapping into think tanks, like the Copenhagen Consensus Center, Center for Global Development, and Overseas Development Institute, and similar groups in the Global South, to help determine the most impactful places to invest and to avoid being caught up in the latest whims of their political leaders or trends in mainstream thinking.

Certainly there will be areas of work that don't lend themselves to this kind of financial engineering—leadership development or democracy promotion might be examples—so there will still be room for USAID, DFID, and their peers to offer grants and contracts according to the old model. But the ethos around paying for results is important even in these areas: funders should develop an investment thesis, not the complete business model. Too often government aid donors equate financial stewardship with operational direction: like venture capitalists, they should invest in for-profit and nonprofit organizations they trust and then leave most of the decisions up to them, holding them accountable for the results, not how they got there. If we're to end extreme poverty by 2030, these aid agencies themselves will need to fundamentally transform to be less like domestic government agencies and more like global investment funds.

BEYOND PHILANTHROPY

The open source model will be critical to driving us closer to the goal of ending extreme poverty, but it's unlikely to get us all the way there. There are too many countries in conflict and too many deeply entrenched human rights problems to solve this global challenge entirely with a more efficient system of service provision.

For the toughest cases, in places like Somalia and Syria and so many more, we'll need a combination of tools in our belt. One will remain the domain of governments, but advocates will need to push governments to do the right thing. This includes ramping up humanitarian response capabilities, especially for conflict zones. Much of this will require collaboration with the military and use of military assets, as was the case during the 2014 Ebola response.

More collaboration with faith communities and the many frontline faith-based humanitarian agencies that operate at tremendous scale, and in some of the most challenging locations, will be critical too. Engaging citizen volunteers also has tremendous scaling potential. One open collaboration network, the Humanitarian OpenStreetMap Team, engages citizens around the world to populate maps with critical health, humanitarian, and development information. For example, volunteers in Guatemala are currently creating maps to identify malaria hotspots as part of the national malaria elimination plan.

In this new era of results, architects, engineers, product designers, and even filmmakers are adding an "impact lens" to their work. A good example is Participant Media, the Hollywood studio that makes films designed to be both commercially successful and tell stories with social impact. Engaging professionals like these to do what they already do but also add a focus on results for the world's poorest is another way to extend beyond the traditional aid community.

Another way to make an impact beyond aid is in the area of migration. The scholar Michael Clemens and others have shown that labor mobility can be the most effective way to reduce poverty, sometimes even just helping people to move within their own country to where the jobs are located. Due to the economic and political crises there, over two million Venezuelans have moved abroad, earning money with their skills overseas and sending funds home to their struggling families.[23] (In Colombia recently, I met a young Venezuelan man selling beer and bottled water on the street. He told me how, before migrating, he had to remove the tires from his pickup truck—his most valuable possession—and then bury the entire truck in a hole he dug near his house. He's hoping to unearth it if he can return one day, but for now he's putting food on the table for his young kids.)

Migration may be a sensible tool to fight poverty in the most challenging situations, but politics globally is moving in the opposite direction. Walls and fences are ascendant as political tools in the West, and clan identity is on the upswing among Buddhists in Myanmar, Hindus in India, Muslims in Indonesia, and Christians in many African countries. Marriage equality has enshrined the rights of LGBTQ people in law in twenty-six countries, but in seventy-three others homosexual sex is illegal and gay rights is often used as a wedge issue to divide the public.[24] While many technical solutions to extreme poverty are working, from vaccines to school feeding programs, we can't ignore these broader political forces as they could well upend any hope of ending extreme poverty by 2030.

Yes, the coming decade will almost certainly be one of dramatic technological change that will fundamentally alter the way we live and work, and create new opportunities to end poverty, control disease, and educate children everywhere. But those same forces could unleash further social marginalization and polarization, dividing countries and ethnic and religious groups, taking poverty eradication off the agenda in favor of "extreme vetting" and counterterrorism.

In a decade that could see more terrorism in the West, more geopolitical instability, more uncontrolled mass migration, more infighting in countries with the biggest remaining pockets of extreme poverty, we will need to push governments to hold fast on the upward momentum around foreign aid spending. It's easy to imagine the current populist wave getting stronger under these circumstances and political leaders wavering. Staying the course will be particularly hard as poverty goes down and political leaders talk of ending aid as a kind of success. Much like Bill and Melinda Gates's commitment to funding polio eradication, even when few cases remain, funding for foreign aid must continue even as private philanthropy rises and antipoverty efforts find initial success.

The division between two worlds—one with shorter life spans and high birth rates, and the other with longer life spans and low birth rates—will become even more stark in the next decade. For example, Nigeria has around half the population of the US today, and is expected to surpass us by 2050. Fully half of the coming population growth in the world is expected to take place in Africa.

As much as some people in the West might like to close their borders and focus on their own problems, this is one small planet and it will feel even smaller in the decade to come. Sensible migration policies, more foreign aid and philanthropy, and a deeper commitment to stamping out extreme poverty wherever it remains will be essential to ensuring the next phase of human history is one of peace and prosperity.

▪ ▪ ▪ ▪ ▪

Recently, I think a lot—more than I have in years—about Chandra, the little boy who came to live with my relatives so long ago.

Although my sister and I stopped visiting India so frequently after high school, my family members stayed in touch with Chandra. We knew that when he was around eighteen he went home to Hyderabad to live with his parents. I subsequently learned that he returned there in part because his main job for our family was taking care of my grandparents, and when they died he was no longer needed. I recall seeing Chandra at my grandmother's funeral in 1986 when I was ten years old, and shortly after that he went back to his family in Hyderabad.

When Chandra was around twenty he went to Bombay, where he lived with another aunt and uncle of mine. There he opened a small outdoor stall selling snacks right in front of the US consulate. It was a short-lived; he was threatened and pushed out of this prime location by other street vendors. Back in Hyderabad, he set up shop as a *chaiwala* (tea vendor) in front of a bank.

The last time I saw Chandra was in the year 2000, at the Bangalore funeral of the very same aunt who had taken him in when he was just a boy. By then he must have been around thirty and I was in my early twenties, just before I began work on Devex. Chandra seemed to be doing fine.

One thing was clear: he and his children had escaped the extreme poverty that his parents had experienced.

Thinking about all that Chandra went through in one lifetime—being given away to another family, and then eventually coming home as an adult and building his own family—makes me realize how much is possible in such a relatively short time. I struggle to reconcile how human progress can seem both glacially slow and mystifyingly fast at the same time.

Technological change is certainly moving at an unprecedented pace. The smartphone was born just a decade ago, and now it's at the center of our social and work lives. In some ways, 2030 seems just around the corner, but perhaps a decade in this fast-moving era is enough time to radically change the world for the better.

For example, it's quite possible to imagine that by 2030 many of the poorest countries become largely cashless economies, using mobile money and perhaps even virtual currencies almost exclusively. My view is that these lower-income societies are more likely to leapfrog rich countries in this way: already people in places like Kenya and the Philippines are ahead of Americans in terms of using mobile banking and virtual payment platforms. They may end up with credit scores and advanced financial services like insurance products more quickly than we can imagine too.

In that vision of the world, I can see internet connectivity reaching nearly every person on the planet, often through smart devices like health trackers and smartphones. True, the poorest people may not be able to afford these things, but aid agencies, philanthropies, and governments may well find it more efficient to provide devices and connectivity in an era when facilitating electronic cash transfers and getting feedback direct from recipients will be so critical. One example that already exists is Khushi Baby, a wearable necklace that stores medical history information for mothers and babies so community health workers in India can maintain continuity of care—knowing, for example, which vaccines have been given and which expectant moms might face pregnancy complications. And all of this will be further enabled by the movement to identify the remaining 1.1 billion people who don't exist on the official rolls.

Healthcare provision to the poorest people is also likely to be radically different because of technology. In parts of the world with so few doctors, the focus must be on training up more community healthcare workers and equipping them with technology that makes them more effective. This will almost certainly include the ability to conduct sophisticated diagnostic testing on site using a smartphone and using AI tools to prescribe medicine based on the results and reported symptoms. Already it's possible for community healthcare workers to take a picture of a drop of blood, send it to a service in the cloud, and receive a diagnosis. While the reality today is that the most exciting innovations for community healthcare workers still have important low-tech components (like color-coded paper strips that can be wrapped around a baby's arm to determine whether the child is underweight and needs medical attention), by 2030 what seems high-tech today will almost certainly be ubiquitous, cheap, and possible even in the lowest-resource settings.

THERE IS NO END TO THE JOB

There's a refrain of the old aid worldview—the fortunate "us" displaying generosity toward the needy "them"—that remains strong in the politics of the old aid industry. Both President Obama's and President Trump's USAID administrators have repeated it regularly, as do aid ministers in the UK, Australia, and around the world. It goes something like this: "We need to work ourselves out of a job."

The idea that global development work can have a fixed end, that once people have graduated from poverty they can stay that way and countries can take care of themselves, has a strong political appeal. The implication is that the spigot will eventually be shut off. That generosity will not be open-ended.

This message is also appealing because of its tough love undercurrent: it says to foreign leaders that they can't assume the US and other major donor nations will just keep funding their people forever. They need to increase their own budgets for health and education, for example.

What's wrong with aiming toward a day when foreign aid won't be needed?

For one thing, it's ahistorical. The poorest countries in the world got that way for many reasons, but a big one is their multigenerational history of colonialism, slavery, and indentured servitude—and the global system that has been built around their poverty to the great benefit of what today are the richest countries in the world. To dangle foreign aid over their heads as a time-limited gesture of generosity sends the wrong message to them and to us: that it's something optional we choose to do because we're good, humanitarian people. That we're like parents giving out allowances so long as our kids get on track toward earning their own money. It promotes a misleading mind-set that ending all poverty is something that will happen quite quickly, when we know from the experience of even the richest countries that it will take generations.

For another, it's disingenuous. Somalia's per capita income, adjusted for purchasing power to make it comparable, is around $600;[25] in the United States—where there are still plenty of problems and a much-needed and large charity and nonprofit sector—it is around $59,000.[26] Countries like Venezuela and South Africa are backsliding. To suggest that NGOs and aid agencies are anywhere near the point where they can close up shop isn't realistic, and we all know it. In fact, one statistic often bandied about as part to this line of argumentation is that foreign direct investment is now many multiples of aid to "developing countries." That may be true when countries such as China and India are included, but for the least-developed countries foreign aid still accounts for around three-quarters of all funds coming from abroad.[27]

Our goal should not be "working ourselves out of a job." That's the vision of the miser, not the true altruist. Our first goal instead should be quite simply ending extreme poverty—just as it's the first of the Sustainable Development Goals. We should be laser-focused on that goal and do whatever it takes to get there, including expanding our "business" and creating more "jobs," if that's what it takes.

Once extreme poverty is ended, it's not as though all will be well in the world. We'll still live in a deeply unequal global society in which those at the lower end of the income scale aren't seeing their human potential fulfilled. There will remain much to do for generations, just as there remains so much to do even in the richest countries in the world like the United States. When a remarkable coalition including the Gates Foundation and Rotary International eradicates polio entirely in the next few years, that won't be a chance to reduce global health spending but rather to redirect it to the next urgent need.

Let's not forget that rich countries are not yet even meeting their own targets for foreign aid spending, so talk of ending aid is far too premature. The agreed-upon funding level is meant to be 0.7 percent of the total economy of each donor country, but only a few actually hit that mark.[28] For example, though the UK has reached that target, the US is less than one-third of the way there. Many others, like France and Germany, take advantage of loopholes in the way aid is officially calculated to make their aid budgets, fat with loans but low on grants, appear bigger than they are.

It is because of the magnanimity of so many people, the diversity of ways to give, and the encouraging results we have achieved over the years—despite the many challenges I've outlined—that I believe that this transformation has so much potential. We truly can make great strides toward some audacious-sounding goals, from achieving equality, to saving the planet, to eradicating hunger and disease.

It's entirely possible, for example, that we could completely eliminate not one but several diseases in the next couple of decades: polio, guinea worm, malaria, elephantiasis, river blindness, measles, yaws, rubella, rabies, syphilis, hookworm, and variant Creutzfeldt-Jakob are all predicted by experts to be close to global eradication. There's even a fund set up specifically to entirely eradicate "neglected tropical diseases," the diseases most people in advanced countries have never heard of, that are really cheap to address, but nonetheless continue to plague millions of poor people. The fund is called, appropriately, the END Fund, and it shows how eradication is both a priority and a real possibility.

It's estimated that the last case of polio will cost $200 million to stamp out. Nonetheless, once polio is gone (as with the other diseases that health experts hope to eradicate), all the ongoing costs of vaccinations and treatment go away.

Imagining a world with no hunger, no disease, no poverty is, at one level, hopelessly utopian. But tremendous progress never before experienced at the level of our species actually is possible in our time.

10. USHERING IN A NEW ERA
What We Can Do

WHEN THE NEW YORK FINANCIER John Paulson donated $400 million to Harvard's engineering school (and got his name permanently affixed to it), he probably expected praise. What he got instead was a firestorm on Twitter, especially from the author Malcolm Gladwell, questioning whether the world's richest university really needed more money when so many urgent issues are underfunded. It happened again when the music mogul David Geffen donated $100 million to renovate Avery Fisher Hall at Lincoln Center in New York, which was swiftly renamed David Geffen Hall. Some argue that in a world where you can avert a human death for $4,000, these kinds of donations to elite institutions are more about social status than they are about actually doing the most good possible in a world with so much need.

There was a time when a big donation like Paulson's or Geffen's earned instant respect. Today people are questioning the cost-effectiveness of naming a concert hall, museum exhibit, or university building, and they are calling out donors who seem to be trying to buy credibility rather than making an actual dent in the universe. This broad push for effectiveness and results is part of what's driving change in the global aid industry, too. Here, the cynicism of aid workers and skepticism of aid critics has a big upside, it turns out: it is creating a market dynamic in which billionaires and social entrepreneurs with the next big idea for saving the world are beginning to realize they need to show results before people will shower them in praise.

I'm always struck by how difficult it is to give away large sums of money effectively. Consider that CARE, the massive and respected global NGO that's been around for nearly seventy-five years, has revenues of slightly under $1 billion per year. They've taken that long to reach this stage, and one billionaire philanthropist could double those revenues with a single check. Imagine how challenging it would be to hire around double the staff, to double the scale of the programs, and to enter so many new countries and sectors in order to use that funding effectively? People like Bill and Melinda Gates, who have to find an effective way to spend around $5 billion per year, know this. Warren Buffett understood it so well that he just gave most of his money to Bill and Melinda, to let them figure it out.

The "how" of philanthropy may not seem that complicated. Many aid organizations focus on specific initiatives such as helping farmers increase their yields and ensuring that mothers survive childbirth. How difficult can it be to get a farmer some drought-resistant seeds and teach them to use fertilizer? How much could it cost to train local nurses in a procedure for sterilizing equipment and to provide basic medical gear like gloves?

Trying to answer the "how" question is the fundamental driver of the current transformation of the aid industry. That's what has propelled so much of what's happening now: a dramatic revolution in the way the aid industry is organized, how it works, and what it measures. Get the "how" right and you get results that can lead to the end of extreme poverty. Get results, and philanthropists and taxpayers alike will be ready to open their wallets further.

WHAT INDIVIDUALS CAN DO

If everything we were taught about aid based on good intentions is becoming obsolete and massive technological and market forces are fundamentally transforming the $200 billion global aid and development industry, what should we be doing differently today? It's not as simple as just avoiding the urge to think of Ethiopian farmers as helplessly, irrevocably poor. Once you do that, there are a number of things you can personally and proactively do to ensure that you're part of the new era of good results, not the old one of good intentions.

For the average individual, the first thing is to make donations only to organizations that either show you rigorous data that prove their interventions work or that can make strong, logical cases for their expected impacts. The era of glossy brochures may not be entirely over, but if the nonprofit can't make a clear case for how it is achieving results—and ideally back it up with data—no matter how compelling its photography or testimonials, stay away.

Individual donors should also punish organizations that exploit images of children as victims. Don't fund a sponsor-a-child group that tries to make you pity others when we should be thinking about empowering them.

On the other hand, we should also stop punishing organizations that talk about their failures. Instead, actively seek them out! Anyone working on issues as tough as reducing maternal mortality or stopping kids from dying of malaria ought to be able to admit to some failures. If they're not learning from their mistakes, don't make the mistake of funding them.

In my view it's OK to support causes you believe in out of personal interest or experience (say, a cure for Alzheimer's because your grandfather suffered from it), but don't let your passion blind you to the need to ask tough questions about the results the organization is achieving. If you find yourself feeling good just because you made that donation, ask if there's any evidence of progress.

It can be hard to find small local organizations doing great work around the world. It's getting easier because of crowdfunding platforms and competition grants. If you have the interest, take some time to explore the opportunities to get your money directly to the organizations that need it and might be able to use it most cost-effectively because their overhead is so low and they're closer to the problem.

Supporting credible, big, global brand-name charities can make good sense. But let's use our voices to push those big NGOs to find and support the most effective local organizations. Many already do so, but they need to hear that their donors support the idea of pushing more money to the local level, even though it can entail more risk. Building organizational infrastructure on the national and local level is how long-term change happens.

As we focus more on results, organizations that can more easily demonstrate success will become more attractive to donors. That's a good thing. But never forget that what underpins nearly every global development challenge is human rights. Poverty is not incidental. It's directly linked to stories like Jaha Dukureh's, with which I began this book. A girl who

marries against her will, unsurprisingly, is more likely to miss out on education, have more children than she can support, lack sufficient income-
generating opportunities, and perhaps even die in childbirth. Look to
fund organizations, even small ones, that are campaigning for human
rights, including women's rights, LGBTQ rights, and the rights of people
living with disabilities around the world.

Finally, consider supporting organizations—they can be nonprofit
or for-profit—that are using technology and market mechanisms to empower people. As I detail in this book, there is enormous potential to
change people's lives at scale, and the organizations attempting it deserve
your consideration.

We can also utilize our small-scale giving in a way much like the
Gates Foundation does its larger grants: to create leverage. Even as a
small donor to a big global NGO, you can move the needle. Fund the infrastructure it needs for the future. Demand to have access to more real-
time and raw results, and target your donations to building out those
kinds of information-collection and sharing systems specifically. If you're
writing larger checks, ask to speak to the NGO's executives and see what
kinds of systems the organization needs to take its effectiveness to the
next level. Above all, ask tough questions and demand metrics about how
much funding is applied based on programs designed by the people in
need themselves, and about the degree to which decision-making is made
at the national level and not at headquarters.

As voters in rich countries, we have obligations in this new era too.
People who care about the world have long pushed their representatives
in Washington and elsewhere to support foreign aid. That's still vitally
important. But at the same time we push for more aid, we should also be
pushing for better aid.

That means encouraging some innovation and risk-taking with our
tax dollars. Politicians are so afraid of the front-page story of foreign aid
corruption that they tie the hands of the people whose job it is to solve
tough problems in the world's most difficult places. We need to loosen
the reins and give aid agencies the opportunity to take more measured,
calculated risks, including by investing more in start-up funds, tiered
funding and challenge grants, development impact bonds, and early-
stage research and development.

It also means demanding that we measure the success of our foreign aid by the results it achieves for people, not for American businesses or, for that matter, businesses in other major donor countries like the UK or Germany. It's ridiculous that half our food aid must be purchased in the US and shipped overseas on expensive US-flagged vessels all because there's a lobby for those commercial interests. The amounts of money involved are tiny for American businesses and farmers but they could buy mountains of additional food for people facing the prospect of famine in places like Yemen and Somalia.

In the United States, the US Global Leadership Coalition (USGLC) has been the essential ingredient in building and maintaining congressional support for foreign aid, even as populist and isolationist sentiments have roiled our politics. The coalition has brought together unlikely allies representing the military, corporations, and NGOs. Together, they argue for foreign aid as critical to our national security (peace and stability overseas means less military intervention), economic growth (more prosperity overseas means more markets for American businesses), and humanitarian values (saving lives overseas is who we are). Importantly, the coalition has not resorted to connecting specific foreign aid investments with specific US constituencies, avoiding the kinds of linkages that created the Haiti rice disaster.

At a time of tremendous political division, US voters can take a page from USGLC—ensuring that foreign aid remains a nonpartisan national priority and avoiding the aid budget politicization that has befallen the UK. The important political debate should be about *how* we spend our aid dollars, not whether we should be engaged in the biggest global challenges of our time.

Global development work is hard, and as I express to our reporters at Devex all the time, we're not out to get anyone. Getting the "how" right is no small feat. Nonetheless, there must be a sense of accountability to the mission that ought to be driving everyone.

BUILDING A CAREER IN AID

For some, that sense of mission will lead to a career in the aid industry. That, too, has changed as the industry has evolved.

Ten years ago, I met a young Italian guy who told me how he got his start in global development after graduating from college. It was simple: he took a flight to East Timor in the early 2000s, shortly after the UN peacekeepers had arrived, and, as soon as he got there, started knocking on the doors of NGOs and UN agencies asking for a job. He didn't know much about the aid industry and didn't have experience, but he could type, knew how to use a computer, and spoke English. After a few weeks, he got hired to do administrative work. He fit the stereotype of the aid worker of the day: adventurous, backpack at the ready, eager to rush to the next emergency or conflict zone. Development work was a bit like joining the French Foreign Legion—a chance for adventure in a faraway land.

No longer. Devex has a membership of around one million people working in the field of development, and we estimate there are another million or so working there. The vast majority are not inexperienced. They're not young Europeans dashing off to East Timor, or even experienced aid workers parachuting into "D-rock" (what expat aid workers call the Democratic Republic of Congo; Tanzania is "T-zed"). Rather, they hail from lower-and-middle-income countries and work in the countries where they live.

One example: the Peace Corps sends around seven thousand American volunteers overseas every year; in the '60s there were twice as many.[1] Voluntary Service Overseas (VSO), the UK's version of the Peace Corps, has gone even further. Once reserved for British citizens looking to do good overseas, VSO now accepts "volunteers" from developing countries. They are paid a nominal amount (by UK standards) and do their service in their own communities. Today 30 percent of VSO volunteers are nationals of the country in which they serve.[2]

In today's aid industry, landing a job in global development is becoming more and more competitive. Knowing how to use a computer and having English language skills is far from enough. Even graduates from top universities find it extremely hard to get a posting, particularly if they want to get out of headquarters and into what is still quaintly referred to as "the field."

Most Americans and Europeans get their start doing administrative work at the rich-country offices of an international NGO or development consulting company. Their jobs involve processing visas, filing expense reports, recruiting expert consultants, and drafting funding proposals to aid agencies. A few of those who pursue graduate studies or find a way to learn technical skills on the job may, eventually, find opportunities to travel overseas and earn that coveted international posting, but many won't.

There are a couple of reasons for that. One is that there's more talent available than ever before in the countries where the aid work is done. Why fly in an expensive Brit when there's a Kenyan professional with the finance skills needed to set up a cooperative for former fishermen in Kisumu? Another reason is that many of the countries where aid work is most urgent are in conflict. The physical security risks are just too high to send Westerners who will stick out like sore thumbs and require expensive security teams. That has created opportunities for Americans, UK-citizens, and others who are members of the diaspora. For example, Somali Americans may be better suited to doing aid work in Somalia than other Americans because they know the language and culture and can blend in.

This kind of role has grown to such a degree that there's now a name for it: "inpats"—as opposed to expats. These inpats jobs can be for citizens of Western countries who are members of the diaspora willing to go back to the country of their heritage or birth. Or they can be for citizens of a poor country who studied in Europe and are now living and working in Paris and are willing to go home to help their country develop. Inpats can earn the same international salaries as expats or, often, one level below, especially when they are not citizens of a Western country. Some of the same inequalities that persist in the world can be found within the aid industry.

Many of the people you meet running big NGOs or companies that implement development projects today cut their teeth in the Peace Corps or a similar organization. They backpacked and volunteered in countries that are now too rich to be aid priorities or too dangerous to travel around. That path to a high-level aid job isn't closed, but it's more difficult and competitive to navigate. One reason is that trained aid professionals from poor countries are slowly beginning to take on executive roles at these organizations, sometimes as a result of campaigning by donors and employees.

On the other hand, many of the top jobs at the UN and multilateral development banks are still tied to nationality by tradition. They include the heads of the UN's humanitarian agency (always British), the Asian Development Bank (always Japanese), the IMF (always European), UNICEF, the World Bank, and the World Food Programme (always American). There are still far too many Americans and Europeans leading international aid agencies at a time when there are so many talented Africans, Asians, and Latin Americans who can be making change in their own countries. Leaders should be grooming their replacements by looking to the places where their organizations work.

Changing these kinds of nationality requirements will require a groundswell that is hopefully coming soon. In fact, until 2018, the International Organization for Migration, a UN agency, had for fifty years always had an American at the helm. But after President Trump put forward an American candidate who was accused of making anti-Muslim statements, a Portuguese candidate was elected to the role.

For would-be aid workers just starting out in such a competitive job market, one way in is taking a job in a riskier location. There is a growing role for aid workers in countries that are experiencing prolonged fragility, violence, and terrorism. Offering to be "Birkenstocks on the ground" in places like Afghanistan and South Sudan can be easier because the demand often outstrips the supply. With the number and severity of crises growing due to a combination of extremism, ethnic conflict, geopolitical machinations, and climate change, there are likely to be more of these roles in the future. That said, even in these places technical skills can be important, including expertise in transitional justice, formal conflict management systems, peace-building programs for young people, and local governance.

It may seem paradoxical that getting a job in global development is hard. You would think that the low pay and potentially dangerous circumstances would mean few people would apply to places like CARE or Oxfam, but the opposite is true. Recruiters we work with at Devex have told us demand for these jobs has never been stronger, yet professionals with the right skills are hard to find. In fact, our online job board typically has four thousand to five thousand open positions at any one time, often with daunting requirements. Many require graduate degrees, international experience, proficiency in multiple languages, familiarity with specific funding agencies, and highly specialized technical skills. Just wanting to do good in the world won't cut it. Our online job board typically has four thousand to five thousand open positions at any one time.[3]

As I've said, people—especially younger people—are eager for a career built on purpose. Most have student loans to pay and want a comfortable life, but they're willing to make some financial sacrifices for a chance to do some good in the little time we all have on this earth. Many people are attracted to the challenge of huge, seemingly intractable problems like global poverty, as well as the rich cultural experiences to be had in some of the poorest and most traditional societies on earth.

Because there's so much interest in these kinds of careers, I'm sometimes invited to speak at universities to help students there better understand their job opportunities in global development. I'm always surprised to see more students attending these sessions year by year from university programs you might not expect, like business, engineering, and law schools. Academic interest in the area is growing; our internal list at Devex shows there are now 513 degree programs around the world directly or indirectly preparing students for careers in global development. Within that broad group are thirty-six master's programs specifically targeting "development practice."[4]

Will there be jobs for all those students and the many others seeking a career in the aid industry? Although the competition has never been stronger—especially from professionals who hail from poor countries— in a sense there's more opportunity than ever before. As I've argued in this book, the very definition of the aid industry is changing. Some huge corporations may become social enterprises, and they'll need the kinds of professionals who previously may have only worked at places like the Rockefeller Foundation or World Vision. They'll seek talent for social, environmental, and governance assessments; experts in sustainable supply chains; and business developers who intimately understand bottom-of-the-pyramid customers.

Beyond corporations, there are more social enterprise startups than ever before. These create opportunities for aid professionals of all kinds with skills in finance, grant management, mobile money, connectivity, and impact measurement. The growing number of foundations means many more jobs helping all those billionaires figure out how to effectively make their contributions to the world.

There are still many opportunities for international experts who want to help solve problems far from home, but the kinds of roles are changing. Whereas expat civil engineers were once in demand to build water and sanitation systems for poor countries, those skills now exist domestically in most countries. What's in more demand are financial engineers and technologists. The aid industry needs more people who can structure complex blended finance deals that bring together philanthropic and investment capital, or help design data privacy regulations to ensure even the poorest people are protected as they get rapidly connected online.

WHAT LEADERS AND PROFESSIONALS CAN DO

Leaders of nonprofits and socially responsible businesses can make enormous contributions to the new aid industry too, but they may need to operate differently than they do now. Whether you're one of them or can influence them—perhaps as an employee, a shareholder, or a donor—know that business as usual is ending fast.

Organizations need to work quickly to distribute authority to the national and even local level and empower people on the ground to make decisions and to have real budget authority. That can mean turning national offices into full-fledged, legally separate entities with their own boards and executives.

Corporations also need to find ways for people who want to make a social contribution to do so—even if that is not currently the core mission of the company. A good example of a traditional business that has found a way to enable its people to make a social contribution is Accenture Development Partnerships (ADP). This is essentially a nonprofit unit within a for-profit company, the massive consulting firm Accenture. ADP creates an opportunity for Accenture's management consultants to put their skills to work for social benefit. A few hundred of them work on projects for organizations like UNICEF or the Gates Foundation, and Accenture Development Partners charges much lower fees to those not-for-profit clients than it does to profit-making ones. The Accenture employees who do this work have to agree to a big pay cut: they get less than half their normal salary while they engage in these projects. Accenture uses the idea that you can take a pay cut and work on social good projects as a recruitment tool, and there's an enormous waiting list of forty thousand people, meaning 10 percent of Accenture's workforce wants to do this work so badly they're ready to take a pay cut. Something clearly has changed in corporate America.

Gib Bulloch, who founded ADP, recently published a book on social entrepreneurism within corporations. In it, he envisions a corporate CEO receiving the Nobel Peace Prize. It's an out-there idea, the sort of notion that would be anathema to the activists who chained themselves to trees or exposed inhumane working conditions with secret cameras. But it would also be their victory, the ultimate culmination of all the decades of efforts made to compel corporations to serve not just shareholders but everyone.

Above all, leaders of mission-driven organizations need to become much more transparent in publishing data on what's working and what's not, while showing their thought processes and how they're learning from their mistakes.

This is happening but remains in its nascent stages. Nonprofits have some funders who appreciate their honesty when they point to failures, but many others who do not. Many of them rightly fear that transparency could hurt their organization and punish the people they're trying to help. As major funders adopt an open source aid mind-set, this practice is beginning to change, but there's a long way to go.

To get an idea just how far we have yet to go, consider the Publish What You Fund campaign. This advocacy initiative, born at an international aid conference in 2008, has a straightforward ask of major donors like USAID and the World Bank: openly share data on what you're funding, do it regularly and in a format that others can read and use, and try to tell everyone in advance about what you'll be funding down the road. Since these are taxpayer dollars being spent in other countries, it seems pretty reasonable to ask that we can see, for example, that UNICEF will be launching a school feeding program in Tanzania next year.

One reason that kind of information can be so important is to avoid duplication. The proverbial example among aid workers is that of an NGO arriving in a village to launch a project only to find three other NGOs already doing the same thing. One of the world's largest foundations once showed me a map it commissioned that pinpointed where its grantees were working in a particular country. It was fascinating to see which areas were overrepresented with grant-funded services and which were barren. Even more interesting was that it had taken them until 2017 to start the relatively simple practice of mapping these activities.

A decade after its launch, Publish What You Fund says that a majority of the biggest donors in the world still do not comply with even the basic elements of aid transparency. Why not?

There are only weak incentives to share information and strong ones not to. Sure, not sharing will get you called out by Publish What You Fund in its annual ranking, but how many voters even know the organization exists or care about its mission?

That's where the disincentive comes in: big donors like USAID and DFID—as well as traditional foundations like Ford and Rockefeller—want to do what they want to do. They have their own ideas for the issues that matter most and the projects that should be funded to tackle them. Sometimes their rationale has more to do with politics than sound development theory; other times relationships and a history of giving to a certain region or nonprofit come into play. Whatever the reason, telegraphing what they intend to give and sharing timely information on what they have given doesn't help their autonomy, it weakens it. It makes them subject to criticism and second guessing. Recipient governments, other donors, and advocacy groups can call them and make a case to change their plans. All this, and it takes some work to set up a process for collecting and sharing this data.

Sharing data on development funding is relatively easy and there's an accepted standard known as the International Aid Transparency Initiative—basically a way to categorize your giving so it's possible to separate out education projects from healthcare interventions. But results are the most important information about aid funding: what worked, what didn't. And unlike computer code, data about global development results can be challenging to share because there are few standards.

Much of the data shared today is based on inputs—how much money was spent—and outputs—for example, perhaps how many children attended an after-school program. What's required is being able to assess return on investment: just how much result does every dollar of aid create? That is a high bar, and the global development community is unlikely to reach it soon. Nonetheless, there are many possible interim steps that would still provide tremendous value in terms of learning what's working and what's not.

Those steps include publishing real-time and raw granular data directly from a project to the web. Of course some projects have security concerns (when work takes place in conflict zones, for example), but those are a minority of cases and data can always be anonymized. Raw data could allow a broader community of practitioners to offer advice on how to analyze return on investment, as well as course correction input, in real time. The process for most aid work today—collecting data over time and analyzing that data, polishing the results through communications professionals and lawyers, followed by publication—is antithetical to the principle of open collaboration. An even playing field of information is essential, and that can only happen if results are published with all their imperfections.

Sharing results feels risky, which is why so little of it takes place today. I can't think of a single global development leader who was fired or held accountable in some other way for poor results. There have been plenty of scandals, from corruption to sexual improprieties, that have felled NGO executives and aid agency chiefs. But while CEOs of for-profit companies are routinely fired for poor financial results and stock-price downturns, no such mechanism exists in the world of global aid. What I'm advocating—radical transparency of results as part of an open source aid era—puts all of us who purport to be doing good on the spot.

CAN WE GET THERE?

What's really begun to shift the discussion around development results is competitive pressure. It's no coincidence that Bill Gates, who disrupted an entire industry to make his fortune, would be asking the questions that disrupt this one. His foundation is relentlessly chasing "big bets" and "zero goals." That demand for results, with a huge checkbook behind it, has been a major part of the shift in attitude in the aid industry.

When I sat down for an interview with Gates in January 2018, I wanted to know how he saw the prospects for achieving the First Sustainable Development Goal by 2030—ending extreme poverty. With all the new money and technology available, and the growing results focus of the aid industry, I wondered if Gates thought we could get there.

He was cheeky about the goal itself:

Well, the end of extreme poverty—I mean, let's say I'm schizophrenic and I'm wandering the streets, and somebody does or doesn't stuff a hundred dollar bill in my pocket, I'm still a schizophrenic wandering the streets.

And somebody says, Well you're not in extreme poverty. But hey, I'm crazy, come on!

Gates went on to flesh out his argument that the end of extreme poverty is itself a kind of arbitrary goal. He explained that even the World Bank's technical definition of ending extreme poverty allows for 3 percent of a country's population to still be living under the poverty line—a measure that is itself changeable. And he pointed out that the important success in so many countries of reducing childhood death has meant more kids surviving only to end up living in poverty and suffering from a lack of nutrition. Those kids are likely to be underweight, under their normal height, and cognitively deficient. As we've seen, that fuels the continuing cycle of poverty.

Gates isn't optimistic that we'll end extreme poverty by 2030, "but we're making incredible progress," he told me. His prediction is almost certainly right, and yet, in that word "progress" we can take great hope.

■　■　■　■　■

I was ten years old when my grandmother died. I remember the funeral in the Indian state of Kerala where she lived, where my dad was born and raised, and where I spent part of my childhood. Banana leaves were arranged on the concrete floor of the house's sitting room. Once the women in saris and men in sarongs sat cross-legged and barefoot in front of them, servers bearing steaming cauldrons of food appeared. Heaping portions of rice and curries rich with fresh coconut were quickly ladled onto each leaf. People ate fast with their hands and, when they finished, a new group would arrive to sit and be fed. A framed photo of my grandmother with a garland of orange flowers around it and a swipe of red powder on the glass above her forehead signified that this was a solemn send-off. A few days later, my uncle traveled 1,500 miles north by train to scatter her ashes in the Ganges River.

Some of these people who attended the dinner were my relatives and friends of the family. But many were people who didn't normally get a full meal like this. It felt good to know that my family was generous, that to honor my grandmother we were being charitable in this way. I was told those who were not relatives and friends were "poor people," and some might have been the parents of the neighborhood kids with whom I used to play soccer, kids who ran full tilt on the gravel field without shoes. I was the only player who owned sneakers.

I didn't know until years later that feeding the poor at a funeral is an ancient tradition. It was even practiced in medieval Europe, with the food provided in exchange for prayers for the deceased. "Poverty" and "charity" are two old ideas that have been integral parts of the human experience for millennia. "Progress" is a relatively new one. It contains within it the sense that what has come before can be changed. That we are not consigned to our present circumstances. That even as we pass milestones and achieve goals, there will remain more to do.

ACKNOWLEDGMENTS

WRITING MY FIRST BOOK turned out to be much harder than I expected, but not in the ways I might have assumed. I was quick to put my thoughts on paper, including one intense week of writing during the Christmas holidays of 2017. Nonetheless, I soon learned that the muscles trained writing and editing articles were different than the ones needed to write a book. The finality of putting thoughts I might have casually shared in a public talk into printed words on paper became daunting as I progressed. I simply couldn't have done it without the support of many friends and colleagues.

Pontificating on weighty issues from climate change to human rights was especially hard, since in my day job I get to meet true experts and courageous pioneers on these topics, including many who are rolling up their sleeves in the communities where they live. First, I want to acknowledge them. Whatever insights you may appreciate in these pages were gleaned by me from the many thousands of aid workers and leaders I've had the privilege of getting to know over the past two decades. I still can't believe my luck to have a job that allows and even requires me to spend time with and learn from people I so deeply respect.

That job only exists because of true friendships. Kami Dar was my best friend in college since early in our freshman year in 1993. We both came from immigrant families and had experiences that made us think about what life was like far from home. One of our common topics of conversation was social enterprise, even though the term wasn't in use in those days. We batted around concepts for years until finally settling on the idea for Devex in 2000. At that point I was a student at the Harvard Kennedy School, and Kami had just been accepted there for the following semester as a Dean's Fellow, which is a prestigious free ride plus a stipend. I imagine there is a very short list of people who have turned down that fellowship, but Kami thankfully did. His analytical mind and faith that there is no problem too hard to solve were essential to getting Devex off the ground. Even two decades later, I still feel there's magic when we put our heads together.

Two of the first calls I made after drafting the original Devex business plan were to Alan Robbins and Jason McNaboe. The four of us (including Michael Karl, who took a different career track) are the four musketeers. We met in pre-school in New Jersey and have been inseparable ever since—more like brothers than friends. Alan and Jason quit their jobs to start Devex with me and Kami, for which I'll forever be grateful. Alan is masterful at business and is a big part of the reason why Devex succeeded where so many other similar enterprises fail. For eighteen years he has brought a business sensibility to a deep understanding of the aid industry, ensuring we earn the revenue to support our vision.

Jason is a creative genius. From our logo and tagline to our mission statement, he's taken a nebulous concept like an online community for aid professionals and infused it with the purpose and energy that propel us to this day. If you're one of the more than one million Devex members, it's Jason who wakes up every morning thinking about how to make your experience on our website and with our content better. He, too, has made us successful as a business, a tall order for media platforms and social enterprises alike.

Devex has had two distinct phases. We were an online community until 2008. Then we expanded our vision to become a media platform. We may have never succeeded at that if not for Kate Warren, who joined us that year. Kate, who is now a member of our executive team and has become a close friend, leads one of the most impactful and rewarding parts of Devex: our recruitment and career services. There is little more gratifying than meeting an aid worker who got their start because of advice they read on Devex or is supporting a major humanitarian agency to find the local talent to respond to an emergency. That Devex has become such a leader in these areas is because of Kate.

Every day I feel honored to work with my colleagues at Devex. It would be hard to find a comparable team so talented, so committed to their organization, and so driven to make a positive impact in the world. I was even more proud as I researched data points and key issues to include in my manuscript: as you can see in the endnotes, so much of what I was looking for I found on our own website.

Two of my closest colleagues at Devex were instrumental to this publication and to helping me somehow, probably badly, juggle so many priorities at once. My chief of staff, Margaret Richardson, did the painstaking work of fact-checking and citing sources. She is a trusted advisor and friend, who somehow keeps the big picture in mind even while we're toiling in the weeds. And Diana Palomares, my personal assistant, keeps the trains of my life running on time and always has a smile on her face. It's a joy to work with both of them, and I could have never tackled this book without their support.

Writing a book was not a lifelong dream. I just felt one needed to be written on what, to me, seems such an important and timely topic. Fortunately, the venerable Beacon Press felt the same way. I cannot thank them enough, especially my editor, Joanna Green, for seeing the aid industry and the fight against extreme poverty as issues worthy of a broad audience.

Joanna is the sort of editor who asks questions that are deceptively innocuous but actually force a writer to rethink everything. This book benefited immensely from her involvement. Assistant editor Ayla Zuraw-Friedland made me see that what I thought was a near final version of the manuscript could be tightened up much further. I'm grateful.

One of the best decisions I made was to work with John Butman on the book proposal and manuscript. He never failed to nudge me toward a clearer description of my ideas or a more compelling example to make my point. His work on structuring the book and making it flow were essential for someone used to working on articles and blogs. I simply couldn't have produced this book without him and his kind but direct feedback.

My agent, the formidable and persistent Tom Miller, willed this book into existence. He always had an opinion, something I deeply appreciate, and never failed to make his case. He forced me to ask myself tough questions about my own arguments, and I think they're stronger for it.

The ultimate source of inspiration for this book is my family. My grandfather John Joseph was a vocal progressive (to put it mildly) who ran and lost a race for Congress on a civil rights and anti–Vietnam War platform. Like so many other Jewish families, he and his parents fled

France just before World War II, ending up in New Jersey. My mom, Jean Kumar, grew up attending civil rights rallies. In a story my mother proudly tells, her mother, Louise, saw "whites only" and "colored only" signs at the restrooms of a gas station in the 1950s and proceeded to throw them in her trunk and drive off. Her side of our family, including to this day my wise and loving grandmother Patricia Joseph, have a social justice worldview that they'll never let me forget.

My father, Mohan Kumar, immigrated to America at a time when there were few Indian immigrants here. He fits many of the immigrant stereotypes, including working immensely hard, sacrificing for his family, never forgetting where he came from, and loving his adopted country. One he doesn't fit: he never pushed my sister or me to take up a specific career. In fact, he supported me even when I eschewed more prestigious work to be an unpaid volunteer on political campaigns. And when I came to him with the idea for Devex, he wrote me a $50,000 check of very hard-earned money without a question.

My dad is different in another way too: his love of all cultures. On our regular trips back to India as kids, he would organize week-long lay-overs in different countries. After a career working in New York's electric company Con Edison with immigrants from all over the world, he had friends everywhere, and we would stay with them. He even brought us on a family vacation to the Soviet Union as it was collapsing in December 1991: the tickets and hotels were impossibly cheap, and we watched the tanks surrounding the Kremlin.

My dad's late sister Geeta was also a bit of a rebel and ended up leaving India too. Coming from a small-town Hindu family, my dad married a Jewish American and she married a Muslim Indian. Geeta and her husband, A. H. Somjee, created a unique life for themselves, spending half the year traveling across Indian villages and throughout Asia to study human development, and the other half teaching what they learned at universities in the UK, North America, and Japan. They are the reason my sister Sona and I both studied global development at university and that I ultimately pursued this career. I can still remember in my first week at Georgetown University going to the library and typing "Somjee" into the library computer. I found nine books by my uncle and three by my aunt—all on global development topics. It gives me immense satisfaction to think that I can add my modest contribution to that collection.

The best thing that ever happened to me was meeting my wife, Maria Teresa Kumar. She is an inspiration to many people and especially to me. In 2004 Maria Teresa took a fledgling voter registration initiative called Voto Latino and turned it into one of the most effective social impact organizations in the United States. In 2018 she and her colleagues registered a record two hundred thousand voters for the mid-term elections. We have a lot of challenges in American politics these days, but watching Maria Teresa work will give you hope. She's also still a kid at heart, which makes it easy for me to be one too. There's nothing more fun than being with her and laughing our way through life together. I can't thank her enough for tolerating my sometimes insane writing schedule (my preferred writing location is a pinball parlor) with only an occasional side-eye.

We are blessed with two joyous little ones, six-year-old Lucia and four-year-old Eduardo. The kids have been watching their father write for a good part of their childhood so far and are quite familiar with this book. As I worked on the final set of edits, my son asked if this was a second book or if I was still working on the first. And I found my daughter, who couldn't read when I began this work, sounding out the prologue. I hope they will one day gain some perspective from these pages.

There are countless friends to thank, more than I can here. Daniel Lifton and Bradley Honan were kind enough to read an early version of the manuscript and give me candid and valuable feedback. They and others helped me think through the ideas that found their way on these pages. I am grateful, but please know that any mistakes or omissions are mine alone. Where I offered critiques—of organizations or individuals—I do so with true humility. Global development work is hard, and it's easy to poke holes. I hope those who don't agree or don't appreciate what they read accept the spirit with which it is offered.

Finally, I want to thank someone whose name still comes to me frequently, even seventeen years after his death. Micky Theodoridis was one of the earliest investors and thought partners who helped get Devex off the ground. My wife recalls my telling her that he was going to become a lifelong friend, and that's truly how I felt. Tragically, he and his wife, who was seven months pregnant at the time, were in one of the planes that struck the Twin Towers on September 11, 2001. His spirit remains with us.

NOTES

INTRODUCTION: THE END OF CHARITY

1. Michael E. Porter and Jan W. Rivkin, "Industry Transformation," Harvard Business School, Note 9-701-008, July 10, 2000.

2. "The Facts on Child Marriage," International Women's Health Coalition, https://iwhc.org/resources/facts-child-marriage, accessed October 22, 2018.

3. Luisa Kroll and Kerry Dolan, "Meet the Members of the Three-Comma Club," *Forbes*, March 6, 2018, https://www.forbes.com/billionaires/#5f65e96d251c.

4. Max Roser and Esteban Ortiz-Ospina, "Global Extreme Poverty," Our World in Data, last modified March 27, 2017, https://ourworldindata.org/extreme-poverty.

5. "The World Bank in Gambia," World Bank, last updated April 19, 2018, http://www.worldbank.org/en/country/gambia/overview.

6. According to research by the Hudson Institute's Center for Global Prosperity, in 2016 there was $147 billion of official development assistance and $64 billion of private philanthropy to developing countries. Adding in philanthropy not captured in the report, plus domestic resources in developing countries, concessional portions of impact investments and other private sector flows would raise this figure much further. Center for Global Prosperity at the Hudson Institute, *The Index of Global Philanthropy and Remittances 2016*, https://scholarworks.iupui.edu/bitstream/handle/1805/15876/2016%20IGPAR.pdf?sequence=1&isAllowed=y, 4, accessed October 22, 2018.

7. Porter and Rivkin, "Industry Transformation."

8. "Historic New Sustainable Development Agenda Unanimously Adopted by 193 UN Members," UN website, last modified September 25, 2015, https://www.un.org/sustainabledevelopment/blog/2015/09/historic-new-sustainable-development-agenda-unanimously-adopted-by-193-un-members.

9. Stock prices fluctuate, but as of this writing, GM and Tesla had a market value of approximately $50 billion each, and Uber's reported market value is approximately $70 billion.

10. Helen Zhao, "These 21 Major Retailers Are Worth Less Than Amazon . . . Combined," CNBC, September 7, 2018, https://www.cnbc.com/2018/09/06/22-major-retailers-worth-less-than-amazon-amzn-stock-valuation-trillion-market-cap-jeff-bezos-ecommerce-retail-sales.html.

11. USAID, Agency Financial Report 2017 Fiscal Year, 32, https://www.usaid.gov/sites/default/files/documents/1868/USAIDFY2017AFR.pdf.

12. Peter Duffy, "Lessons from Haiti: How Food Aid Can Harm," *Atlantic*, August 31, 2010, https://www.theatlantic.com/health/archive/2010/08/lessons-from-haiti-how-food-aid-can-harm/62252.

13. Ibid.

14. Ibid.

15. Lesley Wroughton and Patricia Zengerle, "Exclusive: White House Weighs Tightening U.S. Food Aid Shipping Rules—Sources," Reuters, June 29, 2017, https://www.reuters.com/article/us-usa-trump-aid-exclusive/exclusive-white-house-weighs-tightening-u-s-food-aid-shipping-rules-sources-idUSKBN19K33S.

16. Ibid.

17. Erin C. Lentz, Stephanie Mercier, and Christopher B. Barrett, "International Food Aid and Food Assistance Programs and the Next Farm Bill," Agricultural Policy in Disarray Series: Reforming the Farm Bill, American Enterprise Institute, 2017, 7.

18. "Ag and Food Sectors and the Economy," Economic Research Service, US Department of Agriculture, last modified May 2, 2018, https://www.ers.usda.gov/data-products/ag-and-food-statistics-charting-the-essentials/ag-and-food-sectors-and-the-economy.

19. Sophie Edwards, "Bob Corker: Food Aid Reform Threatened by 'Nativist' White House Interests," Devex, October 20, 2017, https://www.devex.com/news/bob-corker-food-aid-reform-threatened-by-nativist-white-house-interests-91345.

20. Charles Kenny, "Results Not Receipts: Counting the Right Things in Aid and Corruption," *Brookings*, Center for Global Development, June 20, 2017, 1.

21. Clifford Krauss, "U.S. Cuts Aid to Zaire, Setting Off a Policy Debate," *New York Times*, November 4, 1990, https://www.nytimes.com/1990/11/04/world/us-cuts-aid-to-zaire-setting-off-a-policy-debate.html.

22. Duncan Green, "The Great Nairobi Swimming Pool Dilemma—Cast Your Vote Now," *From Poverty to Power*, Oxfam blog, January 25, 2012, https://oxfamblogs.org/fp2p/the-great-nairobi-guesthouse-swimming-pool-dilemma-cast-your-vote-now.

23. Steve Lewis and Nic Christensen, "How Millions of Australia's Foreign Aid Is Being Wasted on Executive Pay and Costly Contracts," News.com.au, originally published as "Millions in Foreign Aid Blown on Executives," *Daily Telegraph*, May 24, 2010, https://www.news.com.au/national/how-millions-of-our-foreign-aid-is-being-wasted-on-executives/news-story/15c71b2d0bf6fc4093d224dbcccd9d71?sv=2373add886b4737155842bc23744db6.

24. Ibid.

25. Michael Igoe, "Trump Administration Takes Aim at World Bank Salaries," Devex, April 18, 2018, https://www.devex.com/news/trump-administration-takes-aim-at-world-bank-salaries-92566.

26. Scott Weathers, "Don't Judge a Nonprofit by Its CEO Salary," *Huffington Post*, January 2, 2017, https://www.huffingtonpost.com/entry/dont-judge-a-nonprofit-by-its-ceo-salary_us_586a3dd1e4b04d7df167d60f.

27. Molly Anders, "Good News: Tools for Facing Down Anti-Aid Media Attacks," Devex, April 10, 2018, https://www.devex.com/news/good-news-tools-for-facing-down-anti-aid-media-attacks-92439.

28. "Gavi Gets Top Rating in UK Aid Review," Gavi, the Vaccine Alliance, last modified December 1, 2016, https://www.gavi.org/library/news/statements/2016/gavi-gets-top-rating-in-uk-aid-review.

29. Molly Anders, "UK Media and the Great Aid Debate," Devex, February 27, 2018, https://www.devex.com/news/uk-media-and-the-great-aid-debate-92183.

30. Mawuna Remarque Koutonin, "Why Are White People Expats When the Rest of Us Are Immigrants?," *Guardian*, March 13, 2015, https://www.theguardian .com/global-development-professionals-network/2015/mar/13/white-people-expats -immigrants-migration.

31. William Easterly, *The Tyranny of Experts: Economists, Dictators, and the Forgotten Rights of the Poor* (New York: Basic Books, 2014).

32. Yumeka Hirano and Shigeru Otsubo, "Aid Is Good for the Poor," World Bank Group, Policy Research Working Paper 6998, August 2014, 2.

33. Channing Arndt, Sam Jones, and Finn Tarp, "Assessing Foreign Aid's Long-Run Contribution to Growth and Development," United Nations University, UNU-Wider Journal Article, https://www.wider.unu.edu/publication/assessing-foreign-aid%E2%80 %99s-long-run-contribution-growth-and-development, accessed September 17, 2018.

CHAPTER ONE: THE BILLIONAIRE EFFECT

1. Ariana Eunjung Cha, "Cari Tuna and Dustin Moskovitz: Young Silicon Valley Billionaires Pioneer New Approach to Philanthropy," *Washington Post*, December 26, 2014, https://www.washingtonpost.com/business/billionaire-couple-give-plenty-to -charity-but-they-do-quite-a-bit-of-homework/2014/12/26/19fae34c-86d6-11e4-b9b7 -b8632ac73d25_story.html?utm_term=.d89c07b8280a; Ariana Eunjung Cha, "Cari Tuna and Dustin Moskovitz: Young Silicon Valley Billionaires Pioneer New Approach to Philanthropy," *Washington Post*, December 26, 2014, https://www.washingtonpost .com/business/billionaire-couple-give-plenty-to-charity-but-they-do-quite-a-bit-of -homework/2014/12/26/19fae34c-86d6-11e4-b9b7-b8632ae73d25_story.html?utm _term=.b8fbd5869dfe; Cari Tuna, *Yale Daily News*, https://yaledailynews.com/blog /author/carituna/page/7; Ben Gose, "A Facebook Co-Founder and His Wife Use Effective Altruism to Shape Giving," *Chronicle of Philanthropy*, November 3, 2013, https://www.philanthropy.com/article/Young-Technology-Couple-Is/154099; Dustin Moskovitz, "Compelled to Act: We're Committing $20M to Help Democrats in the 2016 Election," Medium, September 8, 2016, https://medium.com/@moskov/compelled -to-act-141393004 1ee; Cari Tuna, "Giving Away a Facebook Fortune," *Financial Times*, video, November 5, 2015, https://www.ft.com/video/ee9b9f1d-4bd1-3417-9e0c -3759298b1683.

2. "Grants Database," Good Ventures, http://www.goodventures.org/our-portfolio /grants-database, accessed September 17, 2018.

3. "Grantmaking Approach," Good Ventures, http://www.goodventures.org/our -portfolio/grantmaking-approach, accessed September 17, 2018.

4. "#66 Aliko Dangote," Forbes, https://www.forbes.com/profile/aliko-dangote /#4203101022fc, accessed September 17, 2018.

5. Sean Kilachand, "Forbes History: The Original 1987 List of International Billionaires," *Forbes*, March 21, 2012, https://www.forbes.com/sites/seankilachand/2012/03/21 /forbes-history-the-original-1987-list-of-international-billionaires/#15462d9e447e.

6. Luisa Kroll and Kerry A. Dolan, "Forbes 2017 Billionaires List: Meet the Richest People on the Planet," *Forbes*, March 20, 2017, https://www.forbes.com/sites /kerryadolan/2017/03/20/forbes-2017-billionaires-list-meet-the-richest-people-on -the-planet/#7b692bcd62ff.

7. Ibid.

8. Tom Metcalf and Jack Witzig, "World's Wealthiest Became $1 Trillion Richer in 2017," *Bloomberg*, December 27, 2017, https://www.bloomberg.com/news/articles /2017–12–27/world-s-wealthiest-gain-1-trillion-in-17-on-market-exuberance.

9. Maria Di Mento, "Buffet, Gates, and Bloomberg Give Largest Share of Wealth to Charity," *Chronicle of Philanthropy*, September 17, 2017, https://www.philanthropy .com/article/Buffett-GatesBloomberg/241235.

10. "Tobacco," World Health Organization, last modified March 9, 2018, http:// www.who.int/news-room/fact-sheets/detail/tobacco.

11. *The Global Tobacco Crisis*, World Health Organization report, 2008, http://www .who.int/tobacco/mpower/mpower_report_tobacco_crisis_2008.pdf.

12. Dipan Bose, "Reducing Road Deaths: An Urgent Development Goal," World Bank Group, Transport & ICT Connections 96253, Note 12, April 2015, https:// openknowledge.worldbank.org/handle/10986/22298.

13. "Tuberculosis," World Health Organization, February 16, 2018, http://www .who.int/news-room/fact-sheets/detail/tuberculosis.

14. "Road Safety: Helping to Save Lives Through Proven Interventions That Reduce Road Traffic Fatalities," Bloomberg Philanthropies, https://www.bloomberg.org /program/public-health/road-safety/#overview, accessed October 22, 2018.

15. *Bloomberg Philanthropies Annual Report*, 2017, https://www.bbhub.io/dotorg /sites/26/2017/05/May_2017_Annual_Report.pdf, 9.

16. "Canada Deep Dive Global Health," Donor Tracker, https://donortracker.org /Canada/globalhealth, accessed September 17, 2018.

17. "John D. Rockefeller," *Wall Street Journal*, http://interactive.wsj.com/public /resources/documents/mill-1-timeline-rockefeller.htm, accessed September 17, 2018.

18. Dileep K. Rohra, "Failure of Polio Eradication in Conflict Areas: Another Perspective," August 27, 2014, response to "WHO Declares Polio a Public Health Emergency," *British Medical Journal* 348 (May 6, 2014): doi: 10.1136/bmj.g3124.

19. Shazia Ghafoor and Nadeem Sheikh, "Eradication and Current Status of Poliomyelitis in Pakistan: Ground Realities," *Journal of Immunology Research* 2016, article ID 6837824, https://doi.org/10.1155/2016/6837824.

20. Taimoor Shah and Mujib Mashal, "In Polio's Worst-Hit District, Vaccinators Strain for Access," *New York Times*, December 19, 2017, https://www.nytimes.com /2017/12/19/world/asia/afghanistan-polio-vaccine.html.

21. "GPEI Budget 2017," GPEI—Global Polio Eradication Initiative, http:// polioeradication.org/financing/financial-needs/financial-resource-requirements-frr /gpei-budget-2017, accessed September 17, 2018.

22. Ibid.

23. "Economic Case for Eradicating Polio," Global Polio Eradication Initiative, http://polioeradication.org/wp-content/uploads/2016/07/EconomicCase.pdf, accessed September 17, 2018.

24. "About—History of the Pledge," Giving Pledge, https://givingpledge.org /About.aspx, accessed September 17, 2018.

25. "Home," Founders Pledge, https://founderspledge.com, accessed September 17, 2018.

26. David Callahan, "Ford Sinks Over $1 Billion a Decade into Overhead. Is That Money Well Spent?," *Inside Philanthropy*, April 10, 2015, https://www.insidephilanthropy .com/home/2015/4/10/ford-sinks-over-1-billion-a-decade-into-overhead-is-that-mon.html.

27. Robert Safian, "The Amazing Ascent of Priscilla Chan," *Quartz*, October 1, 2018, https://qz.com/1402697/the-amazing-ascent-of-priscilla-chan/, accessed October 22, 2018.

28. This is a rough estimate based on the net worth of the Gateses and Warren Buffett and of the pledges made.

29. Laura Stevens, "Jeff Bezos to Create $2 Billion Fund for Homeless, Preschools," *Wall Street Journal*, last updated September 13, 2018, https://www.wsj.com/articles/jeff-bezos-to-create-2-billion-fund-for-homeless-preschools-1536856739.

30. David Gelles, "George Soros Transfers Billions to Open Society Foundations," *New York Times*, October 17, 2017, https://www.nytimes.com/2017/10/17/business/george-soros-open-society-foundations.html.

31. "Grants," Laura and John Arnold Foundation, http://www.arnoldfoundation.org/grants, accessed September 17, 2018.

32. "Who We Are: Financials," Bill & Melinda Gates Foundation, https://www.gatesfoundation.org/Who-We-Are/General-Information/Financials, accessed October 22, 2018.

33. Rough estimate based on $43 billion of net assets currently held by the Bill & Melinda Gates Foundation, and net worth and stated giving plans of Bill and Melinda Gates and Warren Buffet.

34. Safian, "The Amazing Ascent of Priscilla Chan."

35. Rough estimate based on current value of Facebook stake (1.5 percent of shares at current market capitalization of approximately $450 billion) and their stated intention to donate 99 percent of their Facebook shares to CZI. "Bloomberg Billionaires Index," *Bloomberg*, https://www.bloomberg.com/billionaires/profiles/mark-e-zuckerberg/, accessed October 22, 2018.

36. Rough estimate based on reported $33 million grant in 2018 for undocumented students. Peter Kotecki, "Jeff Bezos Is the Richest Man in Modern History—Here's How He Spends on Philanthropy," *Business Insider*, September 13, 2018, https://www.businessinsider.com/jeff-bezos-richest-person-modern-history-spends-on-charity-2018-7.

37. Tom Metcalf, "World's Richest People Just Can't Give Away Their Money Fast Enough," *Bloomberg*, August 30, 2018, https://www.bloomberg.com/news/articles/2018-08-30/world-s-richest-simply-can-t-give-away-their-money-fast-enough.

38. Department for International Development, *Multilateral Aid Review: Ensuring Maximum Value for Money for UK Aid Through Multilateral Organisations*, March 2011, last modified April 28, 2011, 173, https://assets.publishing.service.gov.uk/government/uploads/system/uploads/attachment_data/file/67583/multilateral_aid_review.pdf.

39. "Grantmaking: Awarded Grants," Bill & Melinda Gates Foundation, https://www.gatesfoundation.org/How-We-Work/Quick-Links/Grants-Database, accessed September 17, 2018.

40. "How We Work: Grant," Bill & Melinda Gates Foundation, https://www.gatesfoundation.org/How-We-Work/Quick-Links/Grants-Database/Grants/2007/05/OPP48046, accessed October 22, 2018.

41. Bill & Melinda Gates Foundation, "Bill & Melinda Gates Foundation Boosts Vital Work of the University of Washington's Institute for Health Metrics and Evaluation," press release, January 25, 2017, https://www.gatesfoundation.org/Media-Center/Press-Releases/2017/01/IHME-Announcement, accessed October 22, 2018.

42. Metcalf, "World's Richest People Just Can't Give Away Their Money Fast Enough."

43. These books were reviewed in Elizabeth Kolbert, "Gospels of Giving for the New Gilded Age," *New Yorker*, August 27, 2018, https://www.newyorker.com /magazine/2018/08/27/gospels-of-giving-for-the-new-gilded-age.

44. Michael Igoe, "Q&A: How Hungary Dismantled Its Refugee Asylum System," Devex, April 26, 2018, https://www.devex.com/news/q-a-how-hungary-dismantled -its-refugee-asylum-system-92617.

45. "About Us: Expenditures & Budget," Open Society Foundations, https://www .opensocietyfoundations.org/about/expenditures-budget, accessed September 17, 2018.

46. Michael J. Abramowitz, "Democracy in Crisis," Freedom House, https:// freedomhouse.org/report/freedom-world/freedom-world-2018, accessed September 17, 2018.

47. "People Power Under Attack: Just 3% of People Live in Countries Where Fundamental Civic Freedoms Are Fully Respected," CIVICUS, last modified April 4, 2017, https://www.civicus.org/index.php/media-resources/media-releases/2803-people -power-under-attack-just-three-percent-of-people-live-in-countries-where-fundamental -civic-freedoms-are-fully-respected.

48. Sophie Edwards, "Early Results: Did Private Outsourcing Improve Liberia's Schools?," Devex, September 7, 2017, https://www.devex.com/news/early-results-did -private-outsourcing-improve-liberia-s-schools-90943.

49. Ibid.

50. Molly Anders, "Power of Nutrition: The $1 Billion Startup," Devex, December 9, 2015, https://www.devex.com/news/power-of-nutrition-the-1-billion-startup -87460.

51. Catherine Cheney, "Global Nutrition Summit Sees New Funding, Political Commitments," Devex, November 6, 2017, https://www.devex.com/news/global -nutrition-summit-sees-new-funding-political-commitments-91461.

52. Hans Dembowski, "Praise Individuals, Not the Trend," D+C Development and Cooperation, last modified June 22, 2017, https://www.dandc.eu/en/article /growing-influence-philanthropy-public-affairs-worrisome.

53. Catherine Cheney, "Because Money Alone Cannot Change Systems, These Billionaires Are Trying Something New," *Devex*, November 22, 2018, https://www .devex.com/news/because-money-alone-cannot-change-systems-these-billionaires -are-trying-something-new-91583.

54. James McBride, "How Does the U.S. Spend Its Foreign Aid?," Council on Foreign Relations, April 11, 2017, https://www.cfr.org/backgrounder/how-does-us -spend-its-foreign-aid.

55. Roser and Ortiz-Ospina, "Global Extreme Poverty."

CHAPTER TWO: THE DEMAND FOR RESULTS

1. Namank Shah, "A Blurry Vision: Reconsidering the Failure of the One Laptop Per Child Initiative," *WR: Journal of the CAS Writing Program* 3 (2010–11): 88–98, http://www.bu.edu/writingprogram/journal/past-issues/issue-3/shah.

2. Berk Ozler, "One Laptop Per Child Is Not Improving Reading or Math. But, Are We Learning Enough from These Evaluations?," *Development Impact*, June 14, 2012, http://blogs.worldbank.org/impactevaluations/one-laptop-per-child-is-not -improving-reading-or-math-but-are-we-learning-enough-from-these-evaluati.

3. Ibid.

4. "Background," Second African Road Safety Conference, last modified November 11, 2011, http://www1.uneca.org/Portals/0/CrossArticle/1/Documents/Road SafetyConferenceAnnouncement.pdf, accessed November 14, 2018.

5. James Habyarimana and William Jack, "Heckle and Chide: Results of a Randomized Road Safety Intervention in Kenya," William Jack's Papers: Working Papers, Georgetown University, July 27, 2010, http://faculty.georgetown.edu/wgj/papers /Matatu-paper-July2410.pdf.

6. "Meningitis A Vaccine Support," Gavi, the Vaccine Alliance, https://www.gavi .org/support/nvs/meningitis-a, accessed September 17, 2018.

7. "Meningococcal Meningitis," World Health Organization, last modified February 19, 2018, http://www.who.int/en/news-room/fact-sheets/detail/meningococcal -meningitis.

8. "Putting an End to Epidemic Meningitis in Africa," PATH, April 2017, https:// path.azureedge.net/media/documents/CVIA_mena_fs_2017.pdf.

9. "Meningitis A," Centers for Disease Control and Prevention: Global Health, https://www.cdc.gov/globalhealth/immunization/infographic/meningitis_a_infographic .htm, accessed September 17, 2018.

10. Kara Rogers, "Guinea Worm Disease," *Encyclopedia Britannica*, last modified July 3, 2018, https://www.britannica.com/science/guinea-worm-disease.

11. "Guinea Worm Case Totals," Guinea Worm Eradication Program, Carter Center, https://www.cartercenter.org/health/guinea_worm/case-totals.html, accessed September 17, 2018.

12. Ibid.

13. Ibid.; Adrian Blomfield, "Guinea Worm Outbreak Dashes Hopes of Elimination in South Sudan," *Telegraph*, July 25, 2018, https://www.telegraph.co.uk/news/0 /guinea-worm-outbreak-dashes-hopes-elimination-south-sudan.

14. "South Sudan Inches Closer to Eliminating Guinea Worm Disease," South Sudan, Regional Office for Africa, World Health Organization, https://afro.who.int /news/south-sudan-inches-closer-eliminating-guinea-worm-disease, accessed September 17, 2018.

15. "Going, Going . . .: An Awful Infestation Has Nearly Been Wiped Out," *Economist*, February 6, 2016, https://economist.com/science-and-technology/2016/02/06 /going-going.

16. "History of HIV and AIDS Overview," Avert, https://www.avert.org /professionals/history-hiv-aids/overview, accessed September 17, 2018.

17. Gloria Pallares, "Q&A: How South Sudan Stopped Guinea Worm Disease in Its Tracks," Devex, March 26, 2018, https://www.devex.com/news/q-a-how-south -sudan-stopped-guinea-worm-disease-in-its-tracks-92414.

18. "4 The Burden of HIV/AIDS: Implications for African States and Societies," *Preparing for the Future of HIV/AIDS in Africa: A Shared Responsibility* (Washington, DC: National Academies Press US, 2011), online edition, https://www.ncbi.nlm.nih .gov/books/NBK209743.

19. "Children, HIV and AIDS," Avert, https://www.avert.org/professionals/hiv -social-issues/key-affected-populations/children, accessed September 17, 2018.

20. "Global HIV and AIDS Statistics," Avert, https://www.avert.org/global-hiv -and-aids-statistics, accessed September 17, 2018.

21. "Children, HIV and AIDS," Avert; UNAIDS, "HIV Treatment Now Reaching More Than 6 Million People in Sub-Saharan Africa," press release, July 2, 2012,

http://www.unaids.org/en/resources/presscentre/pressreleaseandstatementarchive/2012/july/20120706prafricatreatment.

22. US President's Emergency Plan for AIDS Relief, "PEPFAR Now Reaches Over 14 Million People Globally with Lifesaving HIV Treatment," press releases, May 16, 2018, https://www.pepfar.gov/press/releases/282136.htm.

23. US President's Emergency Plan for AIDS Relief, *Fourteenth Annual Report to Congress (2018)*, https://www.pepfar.gov/press/2018annualreport/index.htm, accessed September 17, 2018; "2015 Antiretroviral (ARV) CHAI Reference Price List," Clinton Health Access Initiative, November 2015, https://clintonhealthaccess.org/content/uploads/2016/01/2015-CHAI-ARV-Reference-Price-List.pdf; "PEPFAR Funding," U.S. President's Emergency Plan for AIDS Relief, https://www.pepfar.gov/documents/organization/252516.pdf, accessed September 17, 2018; "The Global HIV/AIDS Epidemic," HIV.gov, last modified July 17, 2018, https://www.hiv.gov/hiv-basics/overview/data-and-trends/global-statistics.

24. Laurie Garrett, "Welcome to the Next Deadly AIDS Pandemic," *Foreign Policy*, July 25, 2018, https://foreignpolicy.com/2018/07/25/welcome-to-the-next-deadly-aids-pandemic.

25. Lindsay Bingaman, "Reflecting on 5 Years of Deworming in Kenya for Samu, Valentiyne, and 6 Million of Their Peers," *Evidence Action*, https://www.evidenceaction.org/blog-full/5-years-kenya-deworming, accessed September 17, 2018.

26. "Orphans," UNICEF for Every Child Press Centre, last modified June 16, 2017, https://www.unicef.org/media/media_45279.html.

27. John Williamson and Aaron Greenberg, "Families, Not Orphanages," Better Care Network Working Paper Series, September 2010, 5, https://bettercarenetwork.org/sites/default/files/Families%20Not%20Orphanages_0.pdf.

28. "Who Is NCLS Research?," NCLS Research, http://www.ncls.org.au/default.aspx?sitemapid=7086, accessed September 17, 2018.

29. "Cambodia Refugee Crisis: History," Columbia CNMTL Forced Migration, http://forcedmigration.ccnmtl.columbia.edu/book/export/html/26, accessed September 17, 2018.

30. "Cambodia Has 406 Orphanages with 16,579 Children: New Survey," *Global Times*, April 20, 2017, http://www.globaltimes.cn/content/1043360.shtml.

31. Christopher Knaus, "The Race to Rescue Cambodian Children from Orphanages Exploiting Them for Profit," *Guardian*, August 18, 2017, https://www.theguardian.com/world/2017/aug/19/the-race-to-rescue-cambodian-children-from-orphanages-exploiting-them-for-profit.

32. Sascha Kouvelis, "Evil People Are Exploiting Cambodia's Orphans," *VICE*, March 16, 2013, https://www.vice.com/sv/article/xd4bp4/cambodian-orphanages.

33. Prak Chan Thul, "Cambodia, U.N. Launch Plan to Tackle Fake Orphanages," Reuters, April 20, 2017, https://www.reuters.com/article/us-cambodia-orphanage/cambodia-u-n-launch-plan-to-tackle-fake-orphanages-idUSKBN17M0UD.

34. "Closing African Orphanages May Be Less Heartless Than It Seems," *Economist*, August 24, 2018, https://www.economist.com/middle-east-and-africa/2017/08/24/closing-african-orphanages-may-be-less-heartless-than-it-seems.

35. "CN Advisories," Charity Navigator, https://www.charitynavigator.org/index.cfm?bay=search.cnadvisories, accessed September 17, 2018.

36. Ubuntu Pathways: Pilot, Pivot, Progress for South African Children, Lipman Family Prize, Wharton School, University of Pennsylvania, posted April 19, 2018,

https://lipmanfamilyprize.wharton.upenn.edu/story/ubuntu-pathways-south-african
-education.

37. Jacob Lief, "What's the Impact of One Pink Dress?," Devex, November 15, 2012, https://www.devex.com/news/what-s-the-impact-of-one-pink-dress-79741, accessed October 22, 2018.

38. TNN, "Infant Mortality Rate Takes a Marginal Dip in Rajasthan," *Times of India*, September 30, 2018, https://timesofindia.indiatimes.com/city/jaipur/infant -mortality-rate-takes-a-marginal-dip-in-rajasthan/articleshow/60890541.cms.

39. Bradley Sawyer and Selena Gonzales, "How Does Infant Mortality in the U.S. Compare to Other Countries?," Peterson-Kaiser Health System Tracker, July, 7, 2017, https://www.healthsystemtracker.org/chart-collection/infant-mortality-u-s-compare -countries.

40. Dave Gilson, "Dr. Clooney, I Presume?," *Mother Jones*, March/April 2010, https://www.motherjones.com/politics/2010/04/africa-celebrities-madonna-oprah -brangelina-george-clooney.

41. "About Us," Raising Malawi, http://www.raisingmalawi.org/about-us/#about-us-2, accessed October 16, 2018.

42. Adam Nagourney, "Madonna's Charity Fails in Bid to Finance School," *New York Times*, March 24, 2011, https://www.nytimes.com/2011/03/25/us/25madonna.html.

43. Jeff Nelson, "How Madonna Is Raising Malawi: Inside Her Tireless Work Helping Children and Fighting Poverty in Africa," *People*, September 6, 2017, https:// people.com/music/madonna-raising-malawi-charity-helping-orphans-fight-poverty -africa.

44. "Raising Malawi Inc.," GuideStar, https://www.guidestar.org/profile/74-3248665, accessed September 17, 2018.

45. Szena Dayo, "Madonna Visits Malawi, Named Goodwill Ambassador for Child Welfare, Raising Malawi, December 24, 2014, http://www.raisingmalawi.org/latest -news-1/2016/6/23/madonna-visits-malawi-named-goodwill-ambassador-for-child -welfare, accessed October 22, 2018.

46. The Dodd-Frank Wall Street Reform and Consumer Protection Act was signed into law by President Barack Obama July 21, 2010.

47. Sudarsan Raghavan, "Obama's Conflict Minerals Law Has Destroyed Every- thing, Say Congo Miners," *Guardian*, December 2, 2014, https://www.theguardian .com/world/2014/dec/02/conflict-minerals-law-congo-poverty.

48. Mvemba Phezo Dizolele, "Dodd-Frank 1502 and the Congo Crisis," Center for Strategic & International Studies, August 22, 2017, https://www.csis.org/analysis /dodd-frank-1502-and-congo-crisis.

49. Helen Morgan, "Forest Whitaker: Work Together as a Unit to Resolve Global Problems," Devex, June 22, 2016, https://www.devex.com/news/forest-whitaker-work -together-as-a-unit-to-resolve-global-problems-88332.

50. David Hughes, "UK Ends £5.2m Taxpayer Support for Ethiopian Girl Band Project," *Independent*, January 6, 2017, https://www.independent.co.uk/news/priti-patel -yegna-girl-effect-52-million-uk-taxpayer-international-aid-ethiopia-a7513956.html.

51. Girl Effect Ethiopia, "Yegna Tribute Band," YouTube, October 2, 2015, https://www.youtube.com/watch?v=rVEpiVZLBNQ, accessed September 17, 2018.

52. *Daily Mail* front page, January 7, 2017, https://www.scoopnest.com/user /SkyNews/817486167172116480-daily-mail-front-page-aid-now-they-re-listening -skypapers.

53. Andrew Malone, "Question That Ended Daftest Foreign Aid Fiasco of Them All: Did Listening to a Girl Ban REALLY Stop 40,000 Young Ethiopian Girls Getting Married Too Early?," *Daily Mail*, January 11, 2017, https://www.dailymail.co.uk/news/article-4111498/Question-ended-daftest-foreign-aid-fiasco-Did-listening-girl-band-REALLY-stop-40-000-young-Ethiopian-girls-getting-married-early.html.

54. Girl Effect Team, "A Statement from Girl Effect About Yegna and Our Work with DFID," Girl Effect, January 6, 2017, https://www.girleffect.org/stories/statement-girl-effect-about-yegna-and-our-work-dfid.

55. Eliza Anyangwe, "Merlin, Save the Children and the Business of Not Merging," *Guardian*, July 17, 2013, https://www.theguardian.com/global-development-professionals-network/2013/jul/17/save-the-children-merlin-merger.

56. "Analysis: Merlin and Save the Children," Third Sector, July 30, 2013, https://www.thirdsector.co.uk/analysis-merlin-save-children/governance/article/1193125.

CHAPTER THREE: PEOPLE, NOT WIDGETS

1. Eline L. Korenromp et al., "Monitoring Mosquito Net Coverage for Malaria Control in Africa: Possession Vs. Use by Children Under 5 Years," *Tropical Medicine & International Health* 8, no. 8 (2003): 693–703, doi.org/10.1046/j.1365-3156.2003.01084.x.

2. Martin Abel, Shawn Cole, and Bilal Zia, "Debiasing on a Roll: Changing Gambling Behavior Through Experiential Learning," World Bank Group, Impact Evaluation Series Policy Research Working Paper No. WPS 7195, February 1, 2015, http://documents.worldbank.org/curated/en/496091468304853412/Debiasing-on-a-roll-changing-gambling-behavior-through-experiential-learning.

3. Karla Hoff, "Do Social Factors Determine 'Who We Are' as Well as the Choice Sets We Have?," *Let's Talk Development*, June 22, 2016, http://blogs.worldbank.org/developmenttalk/do-social-factors-determine-who-we-are-well-choice-sets-we-have.

4. David Segal, "Greed, Passion, Lust, Betrayal, and the Olympics in Between," *New York Times*, June 10, 2016, https://www.nytimes.com/2016/06/12/business/media/greed-passion-lust-betrayal-and-the-olympics-in-between.html.

5. Eliana La Ferrara et al., "Soap Operas and Fertility: Evidence from Brazil," *American Economic Journal: Applied Economics* 4, no. 4 (2012): 1–31, http://dx.doi.org/10.1257/app.4.4.1.

6. Ibid.

7. Vyjayanti T. Desai, Matthias Witt, Kamya Chandra, and Jonathan Marskell, "Counting the Uncounted: 1.1 Billion People Without IDs," *Information and Communications for Development (IC4D) Blog*, June 6, 2017, http://blogs.worldbank.org/ic4d/counting-uncounted-11-billion-people-without-ids.

8. "Internet Users in the World by Regions—December 31, 2017," Internet World Stats, https://www.internetworldstats.com/stats.htm, accessed September 17, 2018.

9. "Welcome to AADHAAR Dashboard," Unique Identification Authority of India, https://uidai.gov.in/aadhaar_dashboard, accessed September 17, 2018.

10. Lauren Etter, "What Happens When the Government Uses Facebook as a Weapon," *Bloomberg Businessweek*, December 7, 2017, https://www.bloomberg.com/news/features/2017-12-07/how-rodrigo-duterte-turned-facebook-into-a-weapon-with-a-little-help-from-facebook.

11. Jessi Hempel, "Inside Facebook's Ambitious Plan to Connect the Whole World," *Wired*, January 19, 2016, https://www.wired.com/2016/01/facebook-zuckerberg-internet-org.

12. Casey Newton, "Facebook Takes Flight," Verge, last modified November 21, 2016, https://www.theverge.com/a/mark-zuckerberg-future-of-facebook/aquila-drone-internet.

13. Devin Coldewey, "Facebook Permanently Grounds Its Aquila Solar-Powered Internet Plane," *TechCrunch*, July 2018, https://techcrunch.com/2018/06/26/facebook-permanently-grounds-its-aquila-solar-powered-internet-plane.

14. Catherine Cheney, "How to Achieve Internet for All: What We Learned in 2017," Devex, December 20, 2017, https://www.devex.com/news/how-to-achieve-internet-for-all-what-we-learned-in-2017-90718.

15. "How 4Afrika Is Improving Quality of Life," Microsoft, https://www.microsoft.com/africa/4afrika/default.aspx?aspxerrorpath=/africa/4afrika/tv-white-spaces.aspx, accessed September 17, 2018.

16. "Private Credit Bureau Coverage (% of Adults)," World Bank, https://data.worldbank.org/indicator/ic.crd.prvt.zs, accessed September 17, 2018.

17. Zeeshan Aleem, "Cellphones Have Lifted Hundreds of Thousands of Kenyans Out of Poverty," *Vox*, December 8, 2016, https://www.vox.com/world/2016/12/8/13875908/kenya-mobile-money-mpesa-poverty.

18. Daniel Runde, "M-Pesa and the Rise of the Global Mobile Money Market," *Forbes*, August 15, 2015, https://www.forbes.com/sites/danielrunde/2015/08/12/m-pesa-and-the-rise-of-the-global-mobile-money-market/#47db1a885aec.

19. "GSMA Announces Seven New Grant Recipients from the Mobile Money for the Unbanked Programme," Bill & Melinda Gates Foundation, https://gfov2.gatesfoundation.org/Media-Center/Press-Releases/2010/05/GSMA-Announces-Seven-New-Grant-Recipients-from-the-Mobile-Money-for-the-Unbanked-Programme.

20. Tom Groenfeldt, "Why the Gates Foundation Is Funding a MasterCard Lab," *Forbes*, December 9, 2014, https://www.forbes.com/sites/tomgroenfeldt/2014/12/09/why-the-gates-foundation-is-funding-a-mastercard-lab/#6129dfd5778f.

21. "The Grand Bargain–A Shared Commitment to Better Serve People in Need," ReliefWeb, May 23, 2016, 3, https://reliefweb.int/sites/reliefweb.int/files/resources/Grand_Bargain_final_22_May_FINAL-2.pdf.

22. Xavier Devictor and Quy-Toan Do, "How Many Years Do Refugees Stay in Exile?," *Development for Peace Solutions*, September 9, 2016, http://blogs.worldbank.org/dev4peace/how-many-years-do-refugees-stay-exile.

23. Jad Chaaban, "Should Lebanon Get More Funds for Hosting Refugees?," *Al Jazeera*, April 5, 2017, https://www.aljazeera.com/indepth/features/2017/04/lebanon-funds-hosting-refugees-170405082414586.html.

24. Catherine Cheney, "Q&A: How to Change Behavior Before Conservation Challenges Become Crises," Devex, August 23 2017, https://www.devex.com/news/q-a-how-to-change-behavior-before-conservation-challenges-become-crises-90860.

25. "Eliminate Open Defecation," UNICEF India, http://unicef.in/Whatwedo/11/Eliminate-Open-Defecation, accessed September 17, 2018.

26. Ibid.

27. Lelia Nathoo, "India's Trouble with Toilets: Government Sanitation Drives Fail to Sway Those Who Believe Going Outdoors Is More Wholesome," *Independent*, August 21, 2015, https://www.independent.co.uk/news/world/asia/india-rejects-the-toilet-how-government-sanitation-drives-have-failed-to-sway-those-who-believe-10466041.html.

28. "India GDP," Trading Economics, https://tradingeconomics.com/india/gdp, accessed September 17, 2018.

29. "Child Marriage Around the World: India," Girls Not Brides, https://www .girlsnotbrides.org/child-marriage/india/#stats-references, accessed September 17, 2018.

30. Roli Srivastava, "India Priests, Decorators in Child Marriage Crackdown: No Proof of Age? No Wedding," Reuters, March 21, 2017, https://www.reuters.com /article/us-india-childmarriage/india-priests-decorators-in-child-marriage-crackdown -no-proof-of-age-no-wedding-idUSKBN16S2HC.

31. Sajeda Amin, M. Niaz Asadullah, Sara Hossain, and Zaki Wahhaj, "Cash Transfers to End Child Marriage: The Indian Experience," Ideas for India for More Evidence-Based Policy, April 10, 2017, http://www.ideasforindia.in/topics/social -identity/cash-transfers-to-end-child-marriage-the-indian-experience.html.

32. Ibid.

33. Catherine Cheney, "What You Need to Know from F8: Connecting the Un-connected and Data for Good," Devex, May 3, 2018, https://www.devex.com/news /what-you-need-to-know-from-f8-connecting-the-unconnected-and-data-for-good -92663.

34. "All U-Report Members," U Report Voice Matters, https://ureport.in, ac-cessed September 17, 2018.

35. Scott Macmillan, "Glorious Failure: The Joy of Learning from Your Mistakes," *Guardian*, March 30, 2015, https://www.theguardian.com/global-development -professionals-network/2015/mar/30/glorious-failure-joy-learning-from-your-mistakes.

36. Ibid.

CHAPTER FOUR: THE "PURE" SOCIAL ENTERPRISE

1. Madhvi Sally, "Amul Turnover Grows 8% to Rs 29,085 Crore in 2017–18," *Economic Times*, April 2, 2018, https://economictimes.indiatimes.com/industry/cons -products/food/amul-turnover-grows-8-to-rs-29085-crore-in-2017–18/articleshow /63583079.cms.

2. "Milk Production Across Countries," National Dairy Development Board, last modified February 8, 2017, https://www.nddb.coop/information/stats/across.

3. "Water Buffaloes," Food and Agriculture Organization of the United Nations, http://www.fao.org/dairy-production-products/production/dairy-animals/water -buffaloes/en, accessed September 17, 2018.

4. "Cattle and Dairy Development," Department of Animal Husbandry, Dairying & Fisheries, Government of India, http://dahd.nic.in/about-us/divisions/cattle-and -dairy-development, accessed January 8, 2019.

5. The Journey of a Kiva Loan," Kiva, https://www.kiva.org/about/how, accessed September 17, 2018.

6. "Amul Dairy," CSSLight, https://www.csslight.com/website/19081/Amul-Dairy, accessed September 17, 2018.

7. Adel Peters, "This Startup Lets African Farmers Hire an On-Demand Tractor to Boost Their Harvests," *Fast Company*, August 29, 2018, https://www.fastcompany .com/90227534/hello-tractor-and-john-deere-bring-10000-tractors-to-africa.

8. "The Journey of a Kiva Loan," Kiva, https://www.kiva.org/about/how, accessed September 17, 2018.

9. "Impact," Kiva, https://www.kiva.org/about/impact, accessed September 17, 2018.

10. Annie Kelly, "Money 'Wasted' on Water Projects in Africa," *Guardian*, March 26, 2009, https://www.theguardian.com/society/katineblog/2009/mar/26/water-projects-wasted-money.

11. "WASH for School Children Provisional Draft," UNICEF, 2012, https://www.unicef.org/wash/schools/files/UNICEF_WASH_for_School_Children_South_Asia_Report.pdf, accessed September 17, 2018.

12. Michael J. Coren, "Tesla Has Emerged as America's Most Valuable Carmaker," *Quartz*, August 2, 2018, https://qz.com/1347031/tesla-is-americas-most-valuable-carmaker-again.

13. Adam Vaughan, "All Volvo Cars to Be Electric or Hybrid from 2019," *Guardian*, July 5, 2017, https://www.theguardian.com/business/2017/jul/05/volvo-cars-electric-hybrid-2019.

14. Paul Lienert, "Global Carmakers to Invest at Least $90 Billion in Electric Vehicles," Reuters, January 15, 2018, https://www.reuters.com/article/us-autoshow-detroit-electric/global-carmakers-to-invest-at-least-90-billion-in-electric-vehicles-idUSKBN1F42NW.

15. "Lessons Learned on Our Journey to Scaling Results for Children," UNICEF, June 29, 2018, http://unicefstories.org/2018/06/29/lessons-learned-on-our-journey-to-scaling-results-for-children.

16. "Social Business," Yunus Centre, http://www.muhammadyunus.org/index.php/social-business/social-business, accessed September 17, 2018.

17. Ibid.

18. "Impact Investing: Who Are We Serving?," Oxfam Discussion Papers, April 2017, 4, https://www.oxfamamerica.org/static/media/files/dp-impact-investing-030417-en.pdf.

CHAPTER FIVE: BIG BUSINESS FOR GOOD

1. Michael E. Porter and Mark R. Kramer, "Creating Shared Value," *Harvard Business Review*, January-February 2011, https://hbr.org/2011/01/the-big-idea-creating-shared-value.

2. Nick Paumgarten, "Patagonia's Philosopher-King," *New Yorker*, September 19, 2016, https://www.newyorker.com/magazine/2016/09/19/patagonias-philosopher-king.

3. "Home: 1% for the Planet," 1% for the Planet, https://www.onepercentfortheplanet.org/index.php, accessed September 17, 2018.

4. "Inclusive Economy 2018 Challenge," Certified B Corporation, https://bcorporation.net/for-b-corps/inclusive-economy-challenge, accessed September 17, 2018.

5. Anna Hensel, "What Patagonia Did When It Found Human Slaves in Its Supply Chain," *Inc.*, June 3, 2015, https://www.inc.com/anna-hensel/patagonia-pledges-to-implement-higher-standards-in-factories.htm.

6. Gillian B. White, "All Your Clothes Are Made with Exploited Labor," *Atlantic*, June 3, 2015, https://www.theatlantic.com/business/archive/2015/06/patagonia-labor-clothing-factory-exploitation/394658.

7. John H. Cushman Jr., "International Business; Nike Pledges to End Child Labor and Apply U.S. Rules Abroad," *New York Times*, May 13, 1998, https://www.nytimes.com/1998/05/13/business/international-business-nike-pledges-to-end-child-labor-and-apply-us-rules-abroad.html.

8. Matthew Townsend, "Nike's $50 Billion Bluster Looks Dead Just Two Years Later," *Bloomberg*, October 24, 2017, https://www.bloomberg.com/news/articles/2017 -10-24/nike-s-50-billion-bluster-looks-dead-just-two-years-later.

9. TOMS has been having financial struggles of late, but they are unrelated to the success of its shoes and buy-one-give-one model and instead have to do with a private equity firm piling a lot of debt on the company. Eliza Ronalds-Hannon and Kim Bhasin, "Even Wall Street Couldn't Protect Toms Shoes from Retail's Storm," *Bloomberg*, May 3, 2018, https://www.bloomberg.com/news/articles/2018-05-03/even-wall-street -couldn-t-protect-toms-shoes-from-retail-s-storm.

10. "Consumer-Goods' Brands That Demonstrate Commitment to Sustainability Outperform Those That Don't," Nielsen, October 12, 2015, https://www.nielsen.com /us/en/press-room/2015/consumer-goods-brands-that-demonstrate-commitment-to -sustainability-outperform.html.

11. "Flash Report: 85% of S&P 500 Index Companies Publish Sustainability Reports in 2017," Governance & Accountability Institute, https://www.ga-institute .com/press-releases/article/flash-report-85-of-sp-500-indexR-companies-publish -sustainability-reports-in-2017.html, accessed September 17, 2018.

12. "Nike Goes 100% Renewable in North America," Climate Action, January 23, 2018, http://www.climateactionprogramme.org/news/nike-goes-100-renewable-in -north-america.

13. "Unilever's Tea Beverages Market Share Worldwide from 2012 to 2021," Statista, https://www.statista.com/statistics/254626/unilevers-tea-beverages-market -share-worldwide, accessed September 17, 2018.

14. Melanie Warner, "You Want Any Fruit with That Big Mac?," *New York Times*, February 20, 2005, https://www.nytimes.com/2005/02/20/business/yourmoney/you -want-any-fruit-with-that-big-mac.html?mtrref=undefined.

15. "The MasterCard Foundation Financial Statements," MasterCard Foundation, December 31, 2016, https://mastercardfdn.org/wp-content/uploads/2018/06 /MASTERCARD-FOUNDATION-2016–12–31-FINAL-signed-e-version.pdf.

16. Stephanie Strom and Miguel Helft, "Google Finds It Hard to Reinvent Philanthropy," *New York Times*, January 29, 2011, https://www.nytimes.com/2011/01/30 /business/30charity.html?mtrref=undefined.

17. Ibid.

18. Ibid.

19. "Koch Industries," *Fortune*, http://fortune.com/most-important-private -companies/koch-industries-4, accessed September 17, 2018.

20. Alexandra Bruell, "Koch Brothers' Koch Industries Begins First National Ad Campaign," *Ad Age*, June 10, 2014, https://adage.com/article/agency-news/koch -industries-launches-national-campaign/293621.

21. Sam Levin, "Uber's Scandals, Blunders and PR Disasters: The Full List," *Guardian*, June 27, 2017, https://www.theguardian.com/technology/2017/jun/18/uber -travis-kalanick-scandal-pr-disaster-timeline.

22. Andrew J. Hawkins, "Lyft Is Growing at a Faster Rate Than Uber, but It Still Has a Long Way to Go," Verge, July 25, 2017, https://www.theverge.com/2017/7/25 /16026216/lyft-gross-booking-growth-faster-uber-2017.

23. Jon Sindreu and Sarah Kent, "Why It's So Hard to Be an 'Ethical' Investor," *Wall Street Journal*, September 1, 2018, https://www.wsj.com/articles/why-its-so-hard -to-be-an-ethical-investor-1535799601.

24. Eleanor Louise, "Oops: 'Socially Responsible' Funds Hold Big Stakes of BP," *Wall Street Journal*, July 17, 2010, https://www.wsj.com/articles/SB10001424052748 70468260457536928322057350 8.

25. Sindreu and Kent, "Why It's So Hard to Be an 'Ethical' Investor."

26. Ari I. Weinberg, "'Ethical' Investing's Smaller Niche: ETFs," *Wall Street Journal*, August 5, 2018, https://www.wsj.com/articles/ethical-investings-smaller-niche -etfs-1533520920.

27. "The Catholic Church Becomes an Impact Investor," *Economist*, August 19, 2017, https://www.economist.com/finance-and-economics/2017/08/19/the-catholic -church-becomes-an-impact-investor.

28. Ben Paynter, "The Ford Foundation Just Made a Billion Dollar Bet on Impact Investing," *Fast Company*, April 17, 2017, https://www.fastcompany.com/40405909/the -ford-foundation-just-made-a-billion-dollar-bet-on-impact-investing.

29. Paul Brest, "Investing for Impact with Program-Related Investments," Making Markets Work for the Poor, Summer 2016, https://pri.gatesfoundation.org/wp-content /uploads/2018/02/Chapter-7.pdf; "Sustainable Investing," Middlebury Endowment, http://www.middlebury.edu/offices/administration/vpfin/endowment/sustainable -investing, accessed September 17, 2018; "Tufts Launches Sustainability Fund," Tufts-Now, April 13, 2015, https://now.tufts.edu/articles/tufts-launches-sustainability-fund; "Global Health Grants and Investments: Bridging the Gap to Better Care," Pfizer, https://www.pfizer.com/purpose/responsibility/healthcare-access/global-health-grants, accessed September 17, 2018.

30. KPMG, *The Road Ahead: The KPMG Survey of Corporate Responsibility Reporting 2017* (2017), https://home.kpmg.com/content/dam/kpmg/campaigns/csr/pdf/CSR _Reporting_2017.pdf.

31. "SRI Basics," US SIF: The Forum for Sustainable and Responsible Investment, https://www.ussif.org/sribasics, accessed September 17, 2018.

32. Tami Luhby, "71% of the World's Population Lives on Less Than $10 a Day," CNN Money, July 8, 2015, https://money.cnn.com/2015/07/08/news/economy/global -low-income/index.html.

33. Vijay Mahajan, "How Unilever Reaches Rural Consumers in Emerging Markets," *Harvard Business Review*, December 14, 2016, https://hbr.org/2016/12/how -unilever-reaches-rural-consumers-in-emerging-markets.

34. Yue Wang, "More People Have Cell Phones Than Toilets, U.N. Study Shows," *Time*, March 25, 2013, http://newsfeed.time.com/2013/03/25/more-people -have-cell-phones-than-toilets-u-n-study-shows.

35. "Mobile Money Services Like M-PESA Key to Poverty Reduction in Africa," IPA, January 3, 2017, https://www.poverty-action.org/news/mobile-money-services -m-pesa-key-poverty-reduction-africa.

CHAPTER SIX: AID GOES RETAIL

1. Ben S. Bernanke, "What Tools Does the Fed Have Left? Part 3: Helicopter Money," *Brookings Blog*, April 11, 2016, https://www.brookings.edu/blog/ben-bernanke /2016/04/11/what-tools-does-the-fed-have-left-part-3-helicopter-money.

2. Catherine Cheney, "The Revolutionary Changing the Way You Do Development," Devex, June 6, 2016, https://www.devex.com/news/the-revolutionary-changing -the-way-you-do-development-88216.

3. "Penekas's Profile," GDLive Newsfeed, https://live.givedirectly.org/newsfeed
/1c58b53f-10e8-45ee-b2e5-d9f0686d995b/172572?context=search-penekas#payment
_2, accessed September 17, 2018.

4. "Lant Pritchett Talk: 'The Debate About RCTs in Development Is Over. We
Won. They Lost,'" NYU Africa House, February 21, 2018, http://www.nyuafricahouse
.org/?risen_event=dr-lant-pritchett-talk-the-debate-about-rcts-in-development-is-over
-we-won-they-lost.

5. "Our Work," New Story, https://newstorycharity.org/our-work, accessed September 17, 2018.

6. "About Us" GlobalGiving, https://www.globalgiving.org/aboutus, accessed
September 17, 2018.

7. "General Crowdfunding Statistics," *Fundly*, https://blog.fundly.com/crowdfunding
-statistics, accessed September 17, 2018.

8. Ibid.

9. Ibid.

10. Adva Saldinger, "Growfund Aims to 'Democratize' Donor-Advised Fund
Model of Philanthropy," Devex, March 16, 2016, devex.com/news/growfund-aims
-to-democratize-donor-advised-fund-model-of-philanthropy-87894.

11. "Meet the Founder," Charity: Water, https://www.charitywater.org/about
/scott-harrison-story, accessed October, 24, 2018.

12. Avery Hartmans, "Airbnb Now Has More Listings Worldwide Than the Top
Five Hotel Brands Combined," *Business Insider*, August 10, 2017, https://www
.businessinsider.com/airbnb-total-worldwide-listings-2017–8?r=UK&IR=T.

13. Matthew DeBord, "Uber's Biggest Potential Competitor Is Over 100 Years
Old," *Business Insider*, February 4, 2016, https://www.businessinsider.com/ubers-
biggest-potential-competitor-is-over-100-years-old-2016–2.

14. Patrick Shanley, "Why Aren't Video Games as Respected as Movies?," *Hollywood Reporter*, December 14, 2017, https://www.hollywoodreporter.com/heat-vision
/why-arent-video-games-as-respected-as-movies-1067314.

15. Michael Igoe, "Paul Farmer: 'We've Met the Enemy—and He Is Us,'" Devex,
December 15, 2014, https://www.devex.com/news/paul-farmer-we-ve-met-the-enemy
-and-he-is-us-85081.

16. "Stricter Rules for Microfinance After India Suicides," RNW Media, https://
www.rnw.org/archive/stricter-rules-microfinance-after-india-suicides, accessed September 17, 2018.

17. DM, "Tala: Using Machine Learning to Provide Access to Credit for the
World's Unbanked," Digital Initiative, April 9, 2018, https://digit.hbs.org/submission
/tala-using-machine-learning-to-provide-access-to-credit-for-the-worlds-unbanked.

18. "Building the Credit Bureau of the Future: Kiva Protocol," Kiva, https://www
.kiva.org/protocol, accessed October 22, 2018.

19. "Operating Model," GiveDirectly, https://givedirectly.org/operating-model,
accessed September 17, 2018.

20. Vince Chadwick, "EU 2018 Budget: Development Aid Cut as Humanitarian
Spending Rises," Devex, November 21, 2017, https://www.devex.com/news/eu-2018
-budget-development-aid-cut-as-humanitarian-spending-rises-91588.

21. "GiveDirectly Refugees," GiveDirectly, https://www.givedirectly.org/refugees,
accessed September 17, 2018.

CHAPTER SEVEN: OPEN SOURCE AID

1. Tom Murphy, "How PlayPumps Are an Example of Learning from Failure," Humanosphere, July 2, 2013, http://www.humanosphere.org/basics/2013/07/how -playpumps-are-an-example-of-learning-from-failure.

2. Laura Freschi, "Some NGOs CAN Adjust to Failure: The PlayPumps Story," Development Research Institute NYU, February 18, 2010, http://www.nyudri.org /aidwatcharchive/2010/02/some-ngos-can-adjust-to-failure-the-playpumps-story.

3. Ibid.

4. Ned Breslin, "Silicon Valley Won't Save the World, but . . . ," *Stanford Social Innovation Review*, July 3, 2013, https://ssir.org/articles/entry/silicon_valley_wont_save_the_world_but.

5. Michael Hobbes, "Stop Trying to Save the World," *New Republic*, November 17, 2014, https://newrepublic.com/article/120178/problem-international-development -and-plan-fix-it.

6. "HeroRATs Save Lives," APOPO, https://www.apopo.org/en/herorats/herorats -save-lives, accessed September 17, 2018.

7. "Development Innovation Ventures (DIV) 101: USAID's Tiered, Evidence-Based Innovation Fund Overview for Prospective Applicants," USAID US Global Development Lab, file:///Users/margaretrichardson/Downloads/DIV-101-Presentation -Dec-2016-for-website-%20(1).pdf, accessed September 17, 2018.

8. "Ukweli Test Strips for Urinary Tract Infections," Grand Challenges Canada, http://www.grandchallenges.ca/grantee-stars/1707-06595, accessed September 17, 2018.

9. "Investments: Talent Beyond Boundaries," Global Innovation Fund, https://global innovation.fund/investments/talent-beyond-boundaries, accessed September 17, 2018.

10. Katie Booth, "What I Learned About Disability and Infanticide from Peter Singer," AEON, January 10, 2018, https://aeon.co/ideas/what-i-learned-about -disability-and-infanticide-from-peter-singer.

11. Hauke Hillebrandt, "Effective Altruism, Continued: On Measuring Impact," *Boston Review*, July 31, 2015, http://bostonreview.net/blog/hauke-hillebrandt-giving -what-we-can-effective-altruism-impact.

12. Larissa MacFarquhar, "The Logic of Effective Altruism," *Boston Review*, July 1, 2015, http://bostonreview.net/forum/logic-effective-altruism/larissa-macfarquhar -response-effective-altruism.

13. Jennifer Rubenstein, "Forum Response: The Logic of Effective Altruism," *Boston Review*, July 1, 2015, http://bostonreview.net/forum/logic-effective-altruism/jennifer -rubenstein-response-effective-altruism.

14. Emily Clough, "Effective Altruism's Political Blind Spot," *Boston Review*, July 14, 2015, http://bostonreview.net/world/emily-clough-effective-altruism-ngos.

15. Rubenstein, "Forum Response: The Logic of Effective Altruism."

16. Ibid.

17. Samantha Custer, Brooke Russell, Matthew DiLorenzo, Mengfan Cheng, Siddhartha Ghose, Jacob Sims, Jennifer Turner, and Harsh Desai, *Ties That Bind: Quantifying China's Public Diplomacy and Its 'Good Neighbor' Effect*, Aiddata Policy Report, June 27, 2018, https://www.aiddata.org/publications/ties-that-bind.

18. "AD122: China's Growing Presence in Africa Wins Largely Positive Popular Reviews," AfroBarometer, 2016, http://www.afrobarometer.org/publications/ad122 -chinas-growing-presence-africa-wins-largely-positive-popular-reviews, accessed September 17, 2018.

19. Lisa Cornish, "China's New Aid Agency: What We Know," Devex, April 20, 2018, https://www.devex.com/news/china-s-new-aid-agency-what-we-know-92553.

CHAPTER EIGHT: SYSTEMS THINKING

1. Lex Rieffel, "Myanmar's Fast-Paced Mobile Phone Rollout," *Brookings TechTank*, October 19, 2016, https://www.brookings.edu/blog/techtank/2016/10/19/myanmars-fast-paced-mobile-phone-rollout.

2. Jason Motlagh, "When a SIM Card Goes from $2,000 to $1.50," *Bloomberg*, September 29, 2014, https://www.bloomberg.com/news/articles/2014-09-29/myanmar-opens-its-mobile-phone-market-cuing-carrier-frenzy.

3. Annie Gowen, "Cellphone Use Transforms Burmese Life After Government Opens Mobile Market," *Washington Post*, November 22, 2014, https://www.washingtonpost.com/world/asia_pacific/new-private-companies-spark-mobile-phone-revolution-in-once-isolated-burma/2014/11/21/eb4479c2-6c41-11e4-bafd-6598192a448d_story.html?utm_term=.e3eedoc54b78.

4. Jillian Keenan, "The Grim Reality Behind the Philippines' Economic Growth," *Atlantic*, May 7, 2013, https://www.theatlantic.com/international/archive/2013/05/the-grim-reality-behind-the-philippines-economic-growth/275597.

5. Robert J. Crawford, "Reinterpreting the Japanese Economic Miracle," *Harvard Business Review* (January–February 1998), https://hbr.org/1998/01/reinterpreting-the-japanese-economic-miracle.

6. "Philippines GDP Per Capita PPP," Trading Economics, https://tradingeconomics.com/philippines/gdp-per-capita-ppp, accessed September 17, 2018.

7. "Poverty & Equity Data Portal: Philippines," World Bank, http://povertydata.worldbank.org/poverty/country/PHL, accessed September 17, 2018.

8. Kelli Rogers, "In Rohingya Camps, Monsoon Threatens Hard-Won WASH Progress," Devex, May 15, 2018, https://www.devex.com/news/in-rohingya-camps-monsoon-threatens-hard-won-wash-progress-92751.

9. "Our Mission at PIH," Partners In Health, https://www.pih.org/pages/our-mission, accessed October 22, 2018.

10. "Rwanda: A Model for Building Health Systems," Partners In Health, https://www.pih.org/country/rwanda, accessed September 17, 2018.

11. Heather Perlberg, "TPG in Talks to Combine Abraaj's Health-Care Assets in Rise Fund," September 24, 2018, https://www.bloomberg.com/news/articles/2018-09-24/tpg-in-talks-to-combine-abraaj-s-health-care-assets-in-rise-fund.

12. "Philips Research Africa: Nairobi—Kenya," Philips Research, https://www.philips.com/a-w/research/locations/nairobi.html, accessed September 17, 2018.

13. Jenny Lei Ravelo, "Philips' Model Community Life Center in Kenya," Devex, November 16 2016, https://www.devex.com/news/philips-model-community-life-center-in-kenya-89081.

14. Landon Thomas Jr., "An Investor's Plan to Transplant Private Health Care in Africa," *New York Times*, October 8, 2016, https://www.nytimes.com/2016/10/09/business/dealbook/an-investors-plan-to-transplant-private-health-care-in-africa.html.

15. "Universal Health Coverage (UHC)," World Health Organization, December 31, 2017, http://www.who.int/en/news-room/fact-sheets/detail/universal-health-coverage-(uhc).

16. Amy Young, "What Internet of Medical Things (IoMT) Devices Mean for Healthcare Cybersecurity," HealthTech, April 18, 2018, https://healthtechmagazine

.net/article/2018/04/The-Internet-of-Medical-Things-Opens-Health-Organizations
-Up-to-More-Threats.

17. "Liberia Health Sector Scan," Africabio Enterprises, http://aeiglobal.com
/PDFs/Health_Sector_Scan_Building_Markets_v4.pdf, accessed September 17, 2018.

18. "Network Partners," Teach For All, https://teachforall.org/network-partners,
accessed September 17, 2018.

19. Peter Greene, "What Went Wrong with Teach for America," *Progressive*, February 17, 2016, https://progressive.org/public-school-shakedown/went-wrong
-teach-america.

20. Catrina Stewart, "Bridge International Academies: Scripted Schooling for $6 a
Month Is an Audacious Answer to Educating the Poorest Children Across Africa and
Asia," *Independent*, July 28, 2015, https://www.independent.co.uk/news/world/africa
/bridge-international-academies-scripted-schooling-for-6-a-month-is-an-audacious
-answer-to-educating-10420028.html.

21. "Who We Are," Bridge, https://www.bridgeinternationalacademies.com/who
-we-are, accessed September 17, 2018.

22. Winnie Hu and Elizabeth A. Harris, "A Shadow System Feeds Segregation in
New York City Schools," *New York Times*, June 17, 2018, https://www.nytimes.com
/2018/06/17/nyregion/public-schools-screening-admission.html.

23. Alphonso Toweh, "Liberia's Education System 'a Mess'—President Sirleaf,"
Reuters, August 29, 2013, https://www.reuters.com/article/us-liberia-education/liberias
-education-system-a-mess-president-sirleaf-idUSBRE97S0TO20130829.

24. Nigeria Bridge, "Government of Edo State in Nigeria Partners with Bridge
to Improve Public Schools," press release, October 10, 2018, https://www.bridge
internationalacademies.com/government-of-edo-state-in-nigeria-partners-with-bridge
-to-improve-public-schools.

25. William Parrett and Kathleen Budge, "How Does Poverty Influence Learning?," *Edutopia*, January 13, 2016, https://www.edutopia.org/blog/how-does-poverty
-influence-learning-william-parrett-kathleen-budge.

26. Sean F. Reardon, "The Widening Academic Achievement Gap Between the Rich
and the Poor: New Evidence and Possible Explanations," Stanford University, July 2011,
http://cepa.stanford.edu/sites/default/files/reardon%20whither%20opportunity%20
-%20chapter%205.pdf.

27. Janie Boschma and Ronald Brownstein, "The Concentration of Poverty in
American Schools," *Atlantic*, February 29, 2016, https://www.theatlantic.com/education
/archive/2016/02/concentration-poverty-american-schools/471414.

28. Kate Lamb, "Thousands Dead: The Philippine President, The Death Squad
Allegations and a Brutal Drugs War," *Guardian*, April 2, 2017, https://www.the
guardian.com/world/2017/apr/02/philippines-president-duterte-drugs-war-death
-squads.

29. Maxine Betteridge-Moes, "What Happened in Marawi?," *Al Jazeera*, October
29, 2017, https://www.aljazeera.com/indepth/features/2017/10/happened-marawi
-171029085314348.html.

30. Adva Saldinger, "A Look Inside the Educate Girls Development Impact Bond
and the First-Year Results," Devex, July 5, 2016, https://www.devex.com/news/a-look
-inside-the-educate-girls-development-impact-bond-and-the-first-year-results-88371.

31. "MCC Hammered," *Economist*, June 23, 2005, https://www.economist.com
/united-states/2005/06/23/mcc-hammered.

32. Curt Tarnoff, "Millennium Challenge Corporation," Congressional Research Service, April 18, 2018, https://fas.org/sgp/crs/row/RL32427.pdf.

33. Nancy Lee, "MCC and Vulnerable States," Center for Global Development, March 16, 2017, https://www.cgdev.org/blog/mcc-and-vulnerable-states.

34. Michael Igoe, "Can Tanzania Get Its MCC Suspension Lifted?," Devex, March 20, 2016, https://www.devex.com/news/can-tanzania-get-its-mcc-suspension -lifted-87956.

35. "World Bank Lending Annual Report 2016," World Bank Group, http:// pubdocs.worldbank.org/en/634801473443116208/WBAR16-FY16-Lending -Presentation.pdf, accessed September 17, 2018.

CHAPTER NINE: ENDING EXTREME POVERTY

1. "Europe Population," Worldometers, World Population Review, http://www .worldometers.info/world-population/europe-population, accessed September 17, 2018.

2. "Continent and Region Populations 2018," World Population Review, http:// worldpopulationreview.com/continents, accessed September 17, 2018.

3. "Measuring Poverty," World Bank, http://www.worldbank.org/en/topic /measuringpoverty, accessed September 17, 2018.

4. "Country Profiles India," UNICEF, https://data.unicef.org/country/ind, ac-cessed September 17, 2018.

5. Roser and Ortiz-Ospina, "Global Extreme Poverty."

6. Ian Bremmer, "5 World Leaders Riding Waves of Public Anger over Corruption," *Time*, October 1, 2018, http://time.com/5409932/world-leaders-corruption-anger.

7. Barry Bateman, "Stats SA Report Shows Increase in People Living in Extreme Poverty," Eyewitness News, September 2017, https://ewn.co.za/2017/08/22/stats-sa -report-shows-increase-in-people-living-in-extreme-poverty.

8. "India," World Bank Data, http://datatopics.worldbank.org/aspire/country /india, accessed September 17, 2018.

9. Roser and Ortiz-Ospina, "Global Extreme Poverty."

10. Ibid.

11. "Malaria Mortality Among Children Under Five Is Concentrated in Sub-Saharan Africa," UNICEF Data, June 2018, https://data.unicef.org/topic/child-health /malaria.

12. Roser and Ortiz-Ospina, "Global Extreme Poverty."

13. Laurence Chandy and Geoffrey Gertz, "The Changing State of Global Pov-erty," Brookings, August 26, 2011, https://www.brookings.edu/on-the-record/the -changing-state-of-global-poverty.

14. Duncan Green, "The Perils of Male Bias: Alice Evans Replies to Yesterday's 'Sausagefest,'" *From Poverty to Power*, Oxfam blog, January 11, 2018, https://oxfam blogs.org/fp2p/the-perils-of-male-bias-alice-evans-replies-to-yesterdays-sausagefest.

15. Duncan Green, "10 Top Thinkers on Development, Summarized in 700 Words by Stefan Dercon," *From Poverty to Power*, Oxfam blog, January 10, 2018, https://oxfamblogs.org/fp2p/10-top-thinkers-on-development-summarized-in-700 -words-by-stefan-dercon/.

16. "Amartya Sen," Wikipedia, https://en.wikipedia.org/wiki/Amartya_Sen, ac-cessed September 17, 2018.

17. Mark Thoma, "Sachs vs. Easterly vs. Collier," *Economist's View*, June 27, 2007, http://economistsview.typepad.com/economistsview/2007/06/sachs-vs-easter.html.

18. Daron Acemoglu and James A. Robinson, "Why Foreign Aid Fails—and How to Really Help Africa," *Spectator*, January 25, 2014, https://www.spectator.co.uk/2014/01/why-aid-fails.

19. Clifford Krauss, "Angolan Leader Ousts Predecessor's Daughter as Oil Chief," *New York Times*, November 15, 2017, https://www.nytimes.com/2017/11/15/business/energy-environment/angola-oil.html.

20. Stewart Rogers, "How Mobile Data Visualization Helped Reduce Malaria Cases by 93%—Zika Could Be Next," Venture Beast, August 31, 2016, https://venturebeat.com/2016/08/31/mobile-data-visualization-reduce-malaria-93-zika.

21. Richard Carter, Kamini N. Mendis, and Donald Roberts, "Spatial Targeting of Interventions Against Malaria," *Bulletin of the World Health Organization* 78, no. 12 (2000), http://www.who.int/bulletin/archives/78(12)1401.pdf.

22. "Unlock Human & Economic Potential," Broadreach, https://www.broadreachcorporation.com, accessed September 17, 2018.

23. Dany Bahar and Sebastián Strauss, "Neighbor Nations Can't Bear Costs of Venezuelan Refugee Crisis Alone," Brookings, March 7, 2018, https://www.brookings.edu/opinions/neighbor-nations-cant-bear-costs-of-venezuelan-refugee-crisis-alone.

24. Rosamond Hutt, "This is the State of LGBTI Rights Around the World in 2018," World Economic Forum, June 14, 2018, https://www.weforum.org/agenda/2018/06/lgbti-rights-around-the-world-in-2018.

25. "Somalia GDP Per Capita Ppp," Trading Economics, https://tradingeconomics.com/somalia/gdp-per-capita-ppp, accessed September 17, 2018.

26. "GDP per Capita, PPP Current International $," World Bank International Comparison Program, https://data.worldbank.org/indicator/NY.GDP.PCAP.PP.CD?locations=US, accessed September 17, 2018.

27. "Taking Stock of Aid to Least Developed Countries (LDCs)," OECD, July 2015, last modified February 2016, https://www.oecd.org/dac/financing-sustainable-development/Taking-stock-of-aid-to-least-developed-countries.pdf.

28. "Official Development Assistance 2017—Preliminary Data," OECD Compare Your Country, https://www2.compareyourcountry.org/oda?cr=oecd&lg=en, accessed November 14, 2018.

CHAPTER TEN: USHERING IN A NEW ERA

1. "2018 Factsheet," Peace Corps, https://files.peacecorps.gov/multimedia/pdf/about/pc_facts.pdf, accessed September 17, 2018; "March 1, 1961: Peace Corps Established," This Day in History, https://www.history.com/this-day-in-history/peace-corps-established, accessed September 17, 2018.

2. "VSO," weADAPT Organisations, https://www.weadapt.org/organisation/vso, accessed November 14, 2018.

3. "Download the Devex Jobs App," Devex, https://www.devex.com/jobs, accessed September 17, 2018.

4. Partner MDP Institutions, Global Association Master's in Development Practice, http://mdpglobal.org/global-mdp-association/partner-mdp-institutions, accessed November 9, 2018.

INDEX

ABOUT THE AUTHOR

RAJ KUMAR is the founding president and editor in chief of Devex, which the *Washington Post* compared to a "Bloomberg-style" media platform for the aid industry. A lifetime member of the Council on Foreign Relations, he is also a media leader for the World Economic Forum and chaired its humanitarian council, a trustee of Save the Children, an advisory board member for two Fortune 50 corporations, and a startup investor. He began his career as a political campaign strategist for elections in the US and around the world. Kumar has witnessed development efforts in over fifty countries. He lives in Washington, DC, with his family.